Applied economic forecasting techniques

Applied economic forecasting techniques

edited by

Stephen G. Hall
London Business School

HARVESTER
WHEATSHEAF

New York   London   Toronto   Sydney   Tokyo   Singapore

First published 1994 by
Harvester Wheatsheaf
Campus 400, Maylands Avenue
Hemel Hempstead
Hertfordshire, HP2 7EZ
A division of
Simon & Schuster International Group

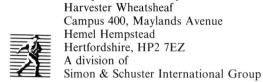

Typeset in 10/12 pt Times
by Vision Typesetting, Manchester.

Printed and bound in Great Britain at the
University Press, Cambridge

British Library Cataloguing in Publication Data

A catalogue record for this book is available from
the British Library

ISBN 0-7450-1392-9

---

1 2 3 4 5 98 97 96 95 94

Contents

Preface

Economic forecasting is an activity of enormous practical importance from a wide range of perspectives. Policy makers need to set economic policy in the light of a clearly articulated view about likely future events and practical business people will be only too aware of the profound effects of economic developments on potential profits. Yet economic forecasting is a far from exact science; there is a real gulf between the treatment of forecasting given in most statistics textbooks and the practices of real world forecasters. This book attempts to bridge this gap by bringing together the latest intellectual developments in statistics and econometrics with the practical constraints faced by forecasters. It argues that, while the technical aspects of forecasting are developing rapidly, there is still a need for the expert forecaster who blends a complex combination of real world institutional knowledge with formal academic modelling techniques to produce a credible view of the future.

Good forecasting is a complex blend of economics, statistics, econometrics and time series analysis. Few books attempt to describe all the components which go into the process. This book surveys some of the latest developments on the technical side of economic forecasting as well as describing the way these ideas are used and implemented in a practical setting.

Stephen G. Hall

Contributors

Chris Allen	Centre for Economic Forecasting, London Business School
Ray Barrell	National Institute of Economic and Social Research
Andrew Burrell	Centre for Economic Forecasting, London Business School
Guglielmo Maria Caporale	Centre for Economic Forecasting, London Business School
David Currie	Centre for Economic Forecasting, London Business School
Geoffrey Dicks	Centre for Economic Forecasting, London Business School, County Natwest
Anthony Garratt	Centre for Economic Forecasting, London Business School
Stephen Hall	Centre for Economic Forecasting, London Business School
Brian Henry	International Monetary Fund
Donald Robertson	Centre for Economic Forecasting, London Business School, Cambridge University
Ron Smith	Centre for Economic Forecasting, London Business School, Birkbeck College
John Whitley	Centre for Economic Forecasting, London Business School
Michael Wickens	Centre for Economic Forecasting, London Business School, York University

1 Economic forecasts

their relevance and use

David Currie

1.1 Introduction

This book is concerned with methods of forecasting economic time series, that is, the movement over time of variables such as output, inflation, unemployment, interest rates and exchange rates. The purpose of this introduction is to provide a context for the subsequent chapters. It starts by noting that forecasting in some form is an integral aspect of our ordinary lives. It goes on to examine the specific need for economic forecasts, and describes some aspects of those forecasts. It examines the fact of forecast error, and discusses some ways in which the resulting uncertainty can be handled. It then considers the major use by governments of forecasts and macro-econometric models for policy analysis. It concludes by examining the future research agenda for macromodelling. Many of the subsequent chapters of this book represent important contributions to that developing and exciting agenda.

1.2 Forecasting

In all aspects of our lives, we seek to anticipate or forecast events. When driving, we must anticipate the movements of other cars, with possibly fatal consequences if we fail. In social relations, we try to anticipate the behaviour and reactions of others, usually only imperfectly. In playing sport, we need to anticipate and pre-empt the actions of our opponents. In choosing what clothes to put on in the morning, we are anticipating the weather, helped perhaps by the formal forecasting activities of the Meteorological Office. In all these examples, we engage in a form of forecasting, however simple or intuitive. In economic and business life, forecasts are no less essential, and errors can be very costly.

Forecasting methods may be formal or intuitive, as the example of weather forecasting illustrates. But, as the future is unknown, all forecasting rests ultimately on learning from the past. Naïve methods extrapolate the past in a simple way, and are therefore prone to error when the world changes. More sophisticated methods seek to anticipate change, by understanding the source of past changes, and therefore build change into the forecast. Understanding past events is the only key that we have for unlocking the future.

In this book, we are concerned with formal, sometimes highly technical, methods of economic forecasting. This focus is deliberate: in our view, the use of best-practice statistical techniques is important if false inferences about the past are to be avoided and consequent forecasting errors avoided. We have adopted this focus also because of another unfortunate fact of life: intuition in forecasting may be helpful (the empirical record is unclear), but it is not easily communicable and learnt, except the hard way through much experience. Formal forecasting methods can be communicated, and offer a way of continually testing our views of how the world works against experience, thereby learning and improving. In contrast to pure intuition, such techniques offer a scientific way of testing our hypotheses against the evidence, and thereby advancing knowledge.

A good example of this process is provided by weather forecasting. The failure of the UK Meteorological Office to predict the 1987 UK hurricane led to a barrage of criticism about the failures of weather forecasting. The response was substantial investment in new super-computers and a much more frequent and comprehensive monitoring of climatic conditions at different points in the atmosphere. The result has been a very marked improvement in the accuracy of short-term weather forecasts.

It is important that the user of technical methods does not become too blinkered in their use: knowledge of past economic history and a sound grasp of economic principles (both outside the compass of this book) are important complements to the methods described in this book. But good technical methods are essential if the lessons of the past are not to be mis-read, and the future mis-predicted.

1.2.1 The need for and use of economic forecasts

Many people, organisations and companies are engaged in producing and using a whole range of different economic forecasts. These may be forecasts of developments in the aggregate economy: of growth in total demand in different markets around the world; of growth in total world trade; of inflation and interest rates; and of unemployment. They may be disaggregated forecasts relating to a specific sector (cars or steel, for example) or to a specific region. Forecasts may be even more specific, relating to demand for a single product line, or to the reactions of a key competitor.

The need for such forecasts arises because people are taking positions and entering into commitments about the future, and therefore need to form a view about the possible future consequences of these positions or commitments. The company investing in a new plant needs to be confident that the output of the plant will be in demand. The individual or company investing in skills and training wants to know that those skills will be relevant in a changing world. The government needs to know the likely take-up of a state benefit (e.g. unemployment benefit) in order to plan the likely cost. In considering whether to change the price of its products, a company needs to form a view about whether or not its competitors will match the change.

In all these instances, a view must be taken in order to reach a sensible judgement as to how to act, as to whether the forward commitment is likely to be advantageous. Only in a world without any forward commitments would forecasts be avoidable, but forward commitments (for example, in the form of investment) are essential for our economic prosperity. Forecasts are therefore inescapable: the only question is how to arrive at them.

In this book, we describe and illustrate a range of formal techniques for forecasting. We illustrate these in the context of macro-economic forecasting models, which are designed to forecast the main developments in the economy, either domestic or international or both, taken as a whole. Such models seek to explain the changes in key variables to be predicted (known as endogenous variables) in terms of past changes in endogenous variables and a set of exogenous variables determined outside the model (for example, policy instruments).

There is an important distinction here between models that are structural and those that are reduced form. Structural models aim to identify a set of behavioural relationships, often between endogenous variables, that together explain the overall workings of the economy (see Chapter 5). Reduced form models, by contrast, treat the economy as a black box, and aim only to identify the linkages between some key inputs and key outputs of interest (see Chapters 3 and 4). Either approach is legitimate for forecasting purposes, and both have their merits. The structural approach permits the use of economic theory to inform the construction of the model, whereas the reduced form approach can be much more atheoretic (although theory usually guides the choice of variables included in the study). With robust theories, the use of theory can be helpful; moreover, the estimation of the model can help to test, and possibly develop, economic theory. The atheoretic reduced form approach has the benefit that it will not be derailed by poor theories.

1.2.2 Forecast uncertainty

The standard output from macromodels is a central forecast; that is, a prediction of the most likely path for the variables of interest. This may be used by companies as their best estimate of variables of interest (demand, inflation, interest rates) relevant to forward planning decisions. But these central forecasts are subject to appreciable uncertainty (see Chapter 7), and this needs to be taken account of in using them. One way to do that is to associate with the central forecasts an estimate of their possible error (in the form of an estimated confidence interval). A wide confidence interval indicates that the central forecast is rather uncertain. Sensitivity analysis would then reveal whether this uncertainty is crucial for the decision for which the forecast is being used.

For example, a company might be carrying out an investment in a plant overseas, and may require forecasts of demand, interest rates and exchange rates to determine whether this investment is profitable and should therefore be undertaken. It may find that the investment is profitable for the central forecast, but that sensitivity analysis taking account of the uncertainty of the forecast shows that it is unprofitable for quite possible outcomes. This demonstrates the riskiness of the investment. The company might respond to this riskiness in several ways. It may decide that the risk is too high, and not proceed with the investment. It may seek further information (for example, market research), and possibly defer the decision until more information becomes available to narrow the range of uncertainty. It may seek to reduce the risk associated with exchange rates or interest rates by buying forward in financial markets (for example by forward purchases, swaps or options). Or it may decide that the risk is acceptable to the company, because its portfolio of investments provides sufficient diversification against the particular risks of the project. Similar considerations apply to government policy decisions, and the uncertainty associated with the forecasts on which such decisions are made.

For small, linear forecasting models, it may be possible to derive explicit estimates of forecast uncertainty and confidence intervals, but this is often not possible with large, non-linear models. An alternative approach that is often adopted is to undertake scenario analysis, developing several alternative views of the future, each of them coherent, and examining the consequences of these different possibilities. Models are an important tool in developing these different scenarios, and in ensuring their coherence. It is helpful in considering company or government policy to ask what is the appropriate response in each of these scenarios. There is advantage, if it is possible, in identifying actions that are robust, in the sense that they result in favourable outcomes in each possible scenario. Investments that pay off in all scenarios are clearly less risky than those that fail in some; policies that work in all scenarios are to be preferred, other things being equal, to those that do not. Some companies go further and consider the appropriate responses, at every level of the organisation, to these different scenarios. By anticipating such reactions in a hypothetical way, and learning from the exercise, it is hoped to benefit from a faster response when the company has to make such adjustments in reality.

1.2.3 Policy analysis

Governments are important users, and often producers, of macro-economic forecasts. This is because, in setting monetary, fiscal and exchange rate policy, governments must take account of the likely future course of the economy. Macro-economic models play an important role in the formulation of macro-economic policy. The formulation and analysis of macro-economic policy decisions requires the consistent framework provided by macro-economic models. For example, in deciding whether to raise or lower interest rates, and raise or lower taxes, governments need to take a view on likely growth and inflation prospects in the economy in the future. Forecasts are essential for this.

A good example of this is provided by the UK Government's recent target 1–4% range for inflation (measured in terms of the Retail Price Index excluding mortgage interest payments). Interest rates are the key instrument for attaining this target. But empirical evidence suggests that the lag between increases in interest rates and the resulting reduction in inflation may be as much as $1\frac{1}{2}$ to 2 years. Long lags of this kind pose a problem for the operation of the inflation target. Policy cannot operate by adjusting interest rates in response to current inflation, for then the policy response to a rise in inflation will come far too late. (Moreover, with lags of this kind, there is the danger of instability, called instrument instability, whereby policy changes themselves generate marked fluctuations in the system.)

Instead, policy must respond by anticipating what inflation is likely to be in $1\frac{1}{2}$ to 2 years time, and adjust interest rates accordingly. This may be done by means of forward indicators, using statistical techniques of the type outlined in Chapter 4. Alternatively it may be done by means of forecasts derived from a complete empirical macro-econometric model. The Bank of England currently uses a mixture of these methods. Thus the current operation of UK monetary policy places macro-economic forecasts at centre-stage.

Macro-econometric models also have a broader role to play in policy formulation. Thus, for example, key policy decisions, such as the rebalancing of the UK monetary/fiscal mix or the policy stance appropriate after the United Kingdom's departure from the Exchange Rate Mechanism, can be properly considered only in the context of a complete macro-economic model. Similarly, macro-economic models provide the means to carry out policy simulations, explore alternative scenarios, and to understand the past better by replaying history with alternative counter-factual assumptions.

In the United Kingdom, the government's use of macro-economic modelling leans rather heavily on the activities of the independent macro-economic modelling groups, which receive some public support. Innovations by the independent groups are a major source of new modelling ideas for the Treasury and Bank of England. The Treasury and Bank of England use GEM, the international model maintained and developed jointly by the National Institute of Economic and Social Research (NIESR) and London Business School. There is regular contact between economists in the Treasury and Bank of England and the staff of the macro-economic modelling groups. Without the strong independent macro-economic modelling groups, the public sector activity would be severely weakened.

There is also a broader public interest in maintaining independent macro-modelling groups that can comment independently and authoritatively on macro-economic developments, as both the London Business School and NIESR have done with distinction over several decades. Public funding has not gone into this activity directly: both organisations receive substantial private funding, including revenues from their publications, but public support for research into macro-economic modelling has been important in allowing these groups to speak with authority on the basis of a strong record of research, and has thereby been crucial in maintaining this consistent record. The UK macro-economic policy debate has, in consequence, been far more open and informed than in many other countries.

1.3 The future research agenda

The research agenda for the macro-economic modelling research community is to take theoretical innovations in macro-economics and to apply them in the economy-wide, system framework of a complete empirical macro-economic model. The pay-offs from this research are several and considerable. First, the system-wide consequences of innovations can only be understood in the context of a full system, thereby bringing out the full implications of the innovation. The alternative of using a reduced form macrosystem for this purpose has severe limitations. Second, the incorporation of an innovation into a complete macro-economic model allows its policy implications to be drawn out and analysed rigorously in a way that quickly enters and influences the public policy debate. The use of theoretical or very simple empirical models does not have the same impact on the policy debate, as it provides only a limited representation of the variables that concern policy-makers. Third, because macro-economic models are used regularly for forecasting and policy purposes, the incorporation of innovations into these models provides a framework in which these innovations are regularly tested against the data and ineffective ideas are sifted out.

The UK macro-economic modelling community has been very effective in this role, taking the newest ideas from diverse parts of macro-economics and combining and testing them in a policy-oriented setting. In the recent past, the macro-economic modelling teams have been at the forefront of developments in applied econometrics (most notably cointegration), applied game theory, supply side modelling and the modelling of expectations and learning. The results of these (sometimes) abstract ideas have been quickly and effectively transmitted into the policy forum. In turn, the effectiveness of these ideas has been assessed in a more comprehensive and practical way than would have been possible for any individual academic and the results fed back to the academic community. The rapid adoption of cointegration owes much to the practical success in application by the macro-economic modelling community, as did the earlier spread of dynamic modelling ideas. The simultaneous strength of UK macro-economic modelling and of UK econometrics is no coincidence but owes much to these research interactions. It is striking that the survey by Adrian Pagan, a world authority, at the World Econometric Society Conference in Boston, comparing the dynamic modelling approach of Hendry, the Bayesian approach of Leamer and the VAR approach of Sims gave decisive weight in favour of the Hendry approach not on conceptual grounds but rather in terms of its widespread adoption in applications of dynamic modelling.

An important element in the UK macromodelling industry has been the element of support for macromodelling research from public funds. This has led to an unusual degree of integration between the research and forecasting activities. In this respect, there is a marked contrast here with the United States, where macromodelling research and forecasting activities have been much more separated, to the detriment of both.

The future research agenda is not wholly predictable, as it will need to respond in a timely way to developments in theoretical macro-economics. But it is likely that an important part of this agenda will be that of economic convergence and structural change, as the world economy becomes increasingly integrated internationally. This is of particular significance in understanding trends in Eastern Europe as these newly emerging market economies integrate with the rest of the world; but it is also relevant to integration within the European Community and to analysis of developments in the Asian Pacific Rim and their impact on the rest of the world. Traditional economic theory and econometrics deals with stable economic structures, but it is clear that in analysing issues of integration the world must increasingly be thought of in terms of structural change. Issues of structural change are also relevant to domestic policy, such as the changing structure of the labour market, the supply side more generally, and the financial system. Indeed much of the explanation of the recent UK boom and slump lies in the behaviour of consumption, and the understanding of this lies in changing behaviour in response to financial deregulation.

Analysing these issues will require advances in econometrics and policy analysis. Econometric techniques will need to be developed to model structural change, aiding our understanding of the process of change and its management. Applied game theory, in the context of applied macro-economic models, will play an important role in understanding the policy-making process. The notion of fully informed rational agents becomes untenable in a system subject to structural change, and the developing literature on learning will need to be developed and extended (see Chapter 6).

These developments also place a greater premium on understanding long-run relationships. This has been helped by the new methods of cointegration, which for the first time take account of the fact that most economic time series are non-stationary. This can help to give better estimates of both the short- and long-term characteristics of models. The use of cointegration in macro-economic models tends to generate different dynamic characteristics, but has also been particularly helpful in giving a better understanding of the long term. The full impact of cointegration on macro-economic models has still to be felt, and our understanding of the cointegration methodology is still incomplete. In particular, the application of cointegration methods to full systems is an area of research that remains open. Understanding the full implications of cointegration, and the role of theory in helping to identify complete systems remains an important research task with considerable potential for advancing understanding.

A further important area of research is to implement the new endogenous growth theory in empirical macro-economic models. This is an area of current research activity, but it is likely to continue to flourish beyond 1995. An important aspect of this research is interdependency between countries, still in its infancy in terms of its theoretical aspects and almost totally unexplored in terms of empirical models. Research in this area would examine the role of trade, direct investment and migration in transferring skills and technologies between economies in order to help understand differences in growth performance between economies. Integrating such research into a complete international model will have very exciting research and policy pay-offs. It will also have important consequences for our more detailed, single economy models of the UK economy. Linked to this is the whole question of migration and labour mobility, particularly in a European context.

These research directions are new and exciting. In addition, there will continue to be the more routine, but important, research questions that the macro-economic modelling community will need to address: understanding developments in consumption and investment; understanding changes in financial markets, particularly in the light of the credit cycle (deregulation, credit boom and credit crunch); understanding the impact of the rise of the Asian Pacific Rim for international trade and capital flows, and for international competitiveness; understanding corporate behaviour; and analysing policy options, both domestically and internationally. Each of these could be expanded at length, and are of appreciable significance. Their systematic investigation and the consideration of the policy consequences require complete macro-economic models, and are therefore best undertaken as part of the macromodelling research agenda.

2 | Time series forecasting

Stephen Hall

2.1   Introduction

The primary purpose of this book is to discuss new developments in the general field of economic forecasting. By this we generally mean forecasting that is based on some articulated view of the underlying structure of the economy. In the case of the Centre for Economic Forecasting our view of the economy is formulated in our main econometric model. Other forecasters have their own models or formal frameworks which they use. Economic forecasting, in the sense in which we generally use the term, is then a mixture of statistics, institutional knowledge, economic theory and the intuition of the forecaster (this will be discussed more fully in Chapter 7).

This chapter is designed to survey pure time series forecasting techniques. These are a body of techniques that rely primarily on the statistical properties of the data, either in isolated single series or in groups of series, and do not exploit our understanding of the working of the economy at all. The objective is not to build models that are a good representation of the economy with all its complex interconnections, but rather to build simple models that capture the time series behaviour of the data and may be used to provide an adequate basis for forecasting alone. This chapter will concentrate on the types of models that have been used in time series forecasting; it will not discuss the detailed statistical issues of estimation and inference, which are well covered in many statistical textbooks and that could not be adequately treated here. A survey of up-to-date estimation techniques may be found in Cuthbertson *et al.* (1992) among other books.

It is important to emphasise just what can, and cannot, be done with a time series model. The primary purpose of a time series model is to forecast. It does not contain an explicit statement of how the economy works and so it is generally not possible to 'tell a story' about the forecast. A large part of a forecaster's job is to be able to explain why he sees a particular set of future events. This explanation and analysis is not easily carried out within the context of a time series model. Policy and scenario analysis is also not easily carried out within such a framework. It will not generally be possible to assess the effect of an increase in government expenditure on gross domestic product (GDP) from a univariate forecasting model, for example.

Time series models are used widely in a business context for forecasting, and they have proved to be a powerful aid to decision-making. In economic forecasting they play a number of subsidiary roles; we often need forecasts of exogenous variables in a large structural model and time series models form part of their selection procedure. The process of constructing a forecast often consists of reaching a compromise between a number of objectives, the forecaster's prior views, the econometric model, the general consensus and, as a major input, the recent behaviour of the data. This last point can be most easily represented as a simple univariate time series model.

This chapter will begin with an account of some of the basic concepts used later in the chapter – stationarity, non-stationarity and a statement of Wold's decomposition – which may be seen as the underlying justification of much univariate time series modelling. Section 2.3 will examine a number of *ad hoc* forecasting procedures that have been commonly used in business. Section 2.4 will discuss the Box–Jenkins forecasting procedure. Section 2.5 will show how the *ad hoc* forecasting procedures may be put within a more satisfactory framework – the structural time series model – and will relate this procedure to that of Box–Jenkins. Section 2.6 will consider multivariate time series models in the form of the vector autoregressive (VAR) model (although only briefly, as Chapter 3 will give a more complete discussion of this topic). Section 2.7 will outline some recent developments in non-linear modelling and Section 2.8 will conclude.

2.2 Some basic concepts

Two basic types of time series models exist, these are autoregressive and moving average models. The basic autoregressive model for a series X expresses that series as a function of past values of itself and an error component:

$$X_t = \theta(L)X_{t-1} + \varepsilon_t \tag{2.1}$$

where ε is a white noise error process and $\theta(L)X_{t-1} = \theta_1 X_{t-1} + \theta_2 X_{t-2} + \cdots + \theta_n X_{t-n}$.

This would be referred to as an nth order autoregressive process, or AR(n). The basic moving average model represents X as a function of current and lagged values of a white noise process:

$$X_t = \zeta(L)\omega_t \tag{2.2}$$

where ω is a white noise error process and $\zeta(L)\omega_t = \omega_t + \zeta_1\omega_{t-1} + \cdots + \zeta_q\omega_{t-q}$.

This would be referred to as a qth order moving average process, or MA(q). A mixture of these two types of model would be referred to as an autoregressive moving average model (ARMA)n, q, where n is the order of the autoregressive part and q is the order of the moving average term.

2.2.1 Wold's decomposition

An important theorem, which reconciles these two types of model, is that of Wold, whose theorem states that for any series (x), which is a covariance stationary (see page 13 for a definition) stochastic process with $E(x) = 0$, the process generating x may be written as:

$$x_t = \sum_{j=0}^{\infty} \alpha_j \varepsilon_{t-j} + d_t \qquad (2.3)$$

where:

$$\alpha_0 = 1$$

$$\sum_{j=0}^{\infty} \alpha_j < \infty$$

$$E(\varepsilon_t) = 0$$

$$E(\varepsilon_t^2) = \sigma^2$$

$$E(\varepsilon_t \varepsilon_s) = 0 \text{ for } t \neq s$$

where d_t is a process that can be predicted arbitrarily well by a linear function of only past values of x, that is to say it is a linear deterministic function. This means that any stationary autoregressive model of the form of eqn 2.1 may be given a moving average representation of the form of eqn 2.2 as long as the deterministic component is allowed for. d_t is termed the linearly deterministic part of x, while

$$\sum_{j=0}^{\infty} \alpha_j \varepsilon_{t-j}$$

is termed the linearly indeterministic part. It is common to assume that x is either purely indeterministic or that the deterministic part can be removed by a simple trend extraction process. In this case we can then move directly from the AR representation to the MA representation. Unfortunately, it is not true that all linearly indeterministic covariance stationary processes have an autoregressive representation. So Wold's theorem does not work in reverse. But this is true for a very wide class of models and it is common to assume that we can move freely between the AR representation of x and the MA representation.

As a general rule, a low order AR process will give rise to a high order MA process, and a low order MA process will give rise to a high order AR process. This may be seen by considering the simple AR(1) case:

$$x_t = \lambda x_{t-1} + \varepsilon_t \qquad \lambda < 1 \qquad (2.4)$$

By successively lagging this equation and substituting out the lagged value of x we may rewrite this as:

$$x_t = \sum_{j=1}^{\infty} \lambda^j \varepsilon_{t-j} \quad \text{where} \quad \lim_{J \to \infty} \lambda^J \varepsilon_{t-J} = 0 \tag{2.5}$$

So the first order AR process has been recast as an infinite order MA one. Of course a finite MA process can approximate the true MA representation as closely as desired as the high order terms will have less and less importance. The correct specification of an ARMA model rests essentially on finding a mix of AR and MA terms that allows the data to be described well by a minimum number of parameters (parsimoniously), this will be discussed further below under the Box–Jenkins section.

2.2.2 The correlogram and partial autocorrelation function

This chapter will not dwell on econometric details of estimation and inference but it is worth defining two descriptive statistical tools that will be important in some of the analytical procedures defined below. These are the autocorrelation function, often referred to as the correlogram when we are dealing with only an estimate, and the partial autocorrelation function. The correlogram shows the correlation between a variable X_t and a number of past values. The correlogram thus comprises a number of values, one for each order of the lag length examined, which measure the correlation between that lag and the current observation. The partial autocorrelation function is similar to the correlogram except that it looks at the correlation between a particular lag and the current value after the effects of the other lags have been partialled out. The formula for the correlogram is given by:

$$C_i = \frac{\dfrac{1}{T} \sum_{t=1}^{T-k} (X_{t+k} - X^*)(X_t - X^*)}{\dfrac{1}{T} \sum_{t=1}^{T} (X_t - X^*)^2} \tag{2.6}$$

where

$$X^* = \frac{1}{T} \sum_{t=1}^{T} X_t$$

The partial autocorrelation function is given as the coefficients from a simple autoregression of the form:

$$X_t = A_0 + \sum_{i=1}^{n} P_i X_{t-i} + u_t \tag{2.7}$$

where P_i is the estimate of the partial autocorrelation function. The importance of these two descriptive measures will be discussed below.

2.2.3 Stationarity

Much of the analysis described within this chapter has been developed within a framework that takes stationarity of the data as one of its key assumptions. As shown later, the appropriateness of this assumption can be a key ingredient in choosing a good forecasting model. We are primarily concerned with weak, or covariance, stationarity, such a series has a constant mean and constant, finite, variance. This may at first sight seem to be a fairly innocuous assumption but in fact it implies that a series will constantly return to a given value and that no matter where we start from in the long run we expect it to attain that value. Such a series is clearly easy to forecast, at least in the long run, but it is not representative of most of the series we deal with in economics. In particular, a series that exhibits a stochastic trend, or even simply wanders around at random, will not be stationary and does not fall within much of the strict theory outlined below. An important theoretical distinction can be drawn between a series that exhibits a deterministic trend and one that exhibits a stochastic trend. The simplest form of stochastic trend is given by the following, random walk with drift, model:

$$X_t = \alpha + X_{t-1} + \varepsilon \tag{2.8}$$

where, if $X_0 = 0$ we can express this as:

$$X_t = \alpha t + \sum_{i=1}^{t} \varepsilon_{t-i} \tag{2.9}$$

This equation has a stochastic trend, given by the term in the summation of errors, and a deterministic trend given by the term involving t. The basic property of such a series is that over time it can wander anywhere, as the stochastic trend will come to dominate, and we can not forecast it far in the future. If, however, eqn 2.9 was modified in the following way:

$$X_t = \alpha t + \sum_{i=1}^{t} \lambda^i \varepsilon_{t-i} \tag{2.10}$$

where $\lambda < 1$, then the moving average error term would no longer cumulate indefinitely and the series would be stationary around the deterministic trend. The forecasting properties of this model are quite different to eqn 2.9: in the long run it will always return to its deterministic trend line and it will have a finite variance around this trend, it is therefore relatively easy to forecast in the long run.

The term 'persistence' is sometimes used to characterise the difference between these two models, a shock that hits eqn 2.9 will persist for ever, while the effects of a shock that hit eqn 2.10 will eventually disappear. This distinction is also sometimes referred to as that between a long memory process and a short memory one.

The difference in our ability to forecast deterministic trend stationary models and stochastic trend models into the distant future means that the distinction between the two classes of process is important. Unfortunately at present there exists no powerful way of testing for the distinction, although a number of statistical tests do exist. The problem is that eqn 2.9 will look exactly like a trend stationary process as the variance of the error term approaches zero. So over a finite sample a stochastic trend process with sufficiently small variance will always be indistinguishable from a trend stationary one.

2.2.4 Integration

An important class of non-stationary series that has received considerable attention is that of integrated series. An integrated series is one that may be rendered stationary by differencing, so if X_t is non-stationary:

$$Y_t = \Delta X_t = X_t - X_{t-1} \tag{2.11}$$

and Y_t is stationary, then X is an integrated process. Further if, as above, X only requires differencing once to produce a stationary series it is defined to be integrated of order 1, often denoted as $I(1)$. A series might be $I(2)$, which means that it must be differenced twice before it becomes stationary, or even a higher order, although orders above two are not often encountered in real data. Once a series is made stationary it is then possible to build an ARMA model of the stationary series and this is then termed an autoregressive, integrated moving average (ARIMA) model n, d, q, where the d refers to the order of differencing.

It is important to remember that, at least in principle, not all series are integrated. Consider the model:

$$X_t = 1.5X_{t-1} \tag{2.12}$$

If we transform this so that the dependent variable is a first difference:

$$\Delta X_t = X_t - X_{t-1} = 0.5X_{t-1} \tag{2.13}$$

then we are still left with the level of X on the right-hand side of the equation, further differencing will not remove this level effect so the dependent variable will never become stationary. In the case of eqn 2.12 it is possible to transform the model first by taking logs to generate an integrated process, thus:

$$Y_t = \log(X_t) = \log(\alpha) + \log(X_{t-1}) \tag{2.14}$$

and hence Y_t may then be differenced to produce a stationary series. This is one of the reasons for often working with the logarithm of series that exhibit growth trends.

2.3 Ad hoc forecasting procedures

By *ad hoc* forecasting procedures I mean a set of procedures that have the general advantage that they seem to be a broadly sensible approach to forecasting in many situations, but that are not the result of a particular economic or statistical view about the way the data was generated. It is not generally possible, therefore, to assess formally when they will, or will not, work well, as there is no attempt to define the class of data generation processes for which they will work well.

The main building block of these forecasting techniques is the exponentially weighted moving average (EWMA) model. The basic idea of this model is to mimic the type of process any of us perform when faced with a graph of some univariate process. That is to say, we look for a trend line and then we consider whether this trend has been changing. In other words, we construct a set of local trend estimates and then weight them together to get some idea of the 'underlying' trend in the data (although it can become incredibly difficult from this viewpoint to define the term 'underlying'). The main process is to focus on a given point of time, on which we wish to base our estimate, and then to try and use the information in the surrounding data points to form an estimate of the underlying trend process. If we have a sample X_t, $t = 1 \ldots T$, and we wish to form an estimate of X at time k, then we can do this in one of two ways:

$$X_k = \sum_{j=1}^{k-1} w_j X_{t-j} \tag{2.15}$$

or

$$X_k = \sum_{j=1}^{k-1} w_j^* X_{t-j} + \sum_{j=1}^{T-k} w_j' X_{t+j} \tag{2.16}$$

where the w in eqns 2.15 and 2.16 sums to unity and represents the weight we give to the various data points. In the true EWMA model these weights would decline at an exponential rate as we move further from period k. Thus for the case when only past data is used, we might specify the weights as:

$$w_j = \lambda(1 - \lambda)^{t-j} \tag{2.17}$$

for $0 < \lambda < 1$. This will automatically produce weights that sum to unity for sufficiently large T, but in some cases we might choose to scale all the weights by a parameter to ensure a total weight of unity. Equation 2.15 is clearly more useful in a forecasting context and this is the usual form of the model. Equation 2.16 is often useful in retrospective analysis of data; it is referred to as a centred moving average and may be thought of as giving the 'best' measure of X at period k conditional on the whole sample information. The EWMA model may be used to forecast in a straightforward way if we assume that the smoothing weights (w) are known. These may either be fixed *a priori* or they may be estimated by forming an error function and minimising the squared error in the usual way.

Note that eqn 2.15 is not capable of forecasting a continuing trend. It will essentially forecast any series as a constant path, and we might think of it as forecasting an estimate of the mean of the series into the future. This can be seen as a sensible strategy for stationary series, which are inherently mean-reverting, but it is clearly not effective as a way of forecasting most non-stationary series. The basic EWMA model was adapted in Holt (1957) and Winters (1960) so as to allow the model to capture a variable trend term. If we define f_t to be the forecast of X_t using only past information, then the Holt procedure uses the following formulae to forecast X_{t+1}:

$$f_{t+1} = m_t + g_t \qquad (2.18)$$

where g is the expected increase in the series at each point of time and m is our best estimate of the underlying value of the series. We can then develop a recursion to produce a set of estimates for g and m through time:

$$m_{t+1} = \lambda_0 X_{t+1} + (1 - \lambda_0)(m_t + g_t) \qquad (2.19)$$

Our estimate of m_t is produced as a weighted average of the observed value of x and the forecast for x made last period. The estimate of the expected growth rate may also be updated in a similar way, thus:

$$g_{t+1} = \lambda_1(m_{t+1} - m_t) + (1 - \lambda_1)g_t \qquad (2.20)$$

Equations 2.19 and 2.20 together form the set of recursion formulae that makes up the Holt extension of the EWMA model. Once again we can either perform the recursion conditional on prior values of the two smoothing parameters, or we may use the sequence of forecasts to form a set of forecast errors and then choose the parameters so as to minimise the sum of the squares of the forecast errors.

An alternative, although closely related, approach has developed from the work of Brown (1963) on discounted least squares estimation. The basic idea here is that standard ordinary least squares (OLS) will derive an estimate of the mean value of a series by simply regressing that series on a constant. If we split the sample into a number of subsamples we can achieve estimates of the mean at a number of points in time. What we would like is to derive a constantly changing estimate of the mean, and one answer might be to have a set window and move it recursively through the period. Some people have used this approach but the choice of window length is essentially arbitrary. Brown's answer to the problem was to use all the data up to period t but to weight the errors in the sum of squared error functions so that more distant observations carried increasingly less weight. Consider the following function:

$$E = \sum_{i=1}^{t-1} w^i (X_{t-i} - m)^2 \qquad w < 1 \qquad (2.21)$$

where w is a scalar weighting factor. Clearly, when $w = 1$ this will simply be the standard OLS objective function for estimating m; when $w < 1$, greater weight will be given to the observations closest to t. The value of m that minimises this function will be an estimate of the underlying level of x at time t. It will, however, have the same basic defects as the standard EWMA model in that it will not forecast a trend effectively and its long-run forecast will always be at a constant level. We can however make an adjustment to the model, analogous to the one made by Holt, by respecifying eqn 2.21 as:

$$E = \sum_{i=1}^{t-1} w^i (X_{t-i} - m + bi)^2 \qquad w < 1 \qquad (2.22)$$

where b is the expected change in the series; this function may then be minimised with respect to m and b to give estimates of both the slope and the level of x at time t. A sequence of such minimisation for varying t will then lead to a sequence of estimates for m and b. The local trend observed at the last observation may then be extrapolated into the future to produce a forecast for x.

Both the EWMA model and the discounted least squares approach may be adapted to include seasonal effects; this will not be discussed here, a thorough treatment is provided in Harvey (1981).

2.4   The Box—Jenkins approach

Box and Jenkins' (1976) modelling strategy for pure time series forecasting has received considerable attention over recent years. In contrast to the *ad hoc* procedures discussed above, which essentially imposed a fairly arbitrary model and forecasting structure on the data, this procedure gives great weight to finding a valid statistical representation of the data. The Box–Jenkins procedure may be seen as one of the early attempts to confront the problem of non-stationary data. Although many researchers would now view the Box–Jenkins approach as having been superseded by cointegration and multivariate non-stationary analysis, it should still be regarded as a useful element in the overall armoury of econometric techniques, with a particularly important role in univariate modelling.

The Box–Jenkins modelling procedure consists of three stages: (1) identification; (2) estimation; and (3) diagnostic checking. At the identification stage a set of tools is provided to help identify a possible ARIMA model, which may be an adequate description of the data. Estimation is simply the process of estimating this model and diagnostic checking is the process of checking the adequacy of this model against a range of criteria and possibly returning to the identification stage to respecify the model.

The distinguishing stage of this methodology is identification. Because the aim is to produce an adequate but parsimonious (not too many parameters) model, this approach tries to identify an appropriate ARIMA specification. It is not generally possible to specify a high order ARIMA model and then proceed to simplify it as such a model will not be identified and so can not be estimated. This is illustrated in eqns 2.4 and 2.5, above, where it is shown that a simple AR(1) process may be represented either as a low order AR process or as a high order MA process. If this is the true model and we try to estimate a model with both high order MA and AR processes, the estimation procedure will simply be unable to choose between the different ways of representing the data and very poor parameter estimates will result. This problem generalises, so that data which was generated by an ARMA(2, 2) process should not be used in the estimation of an ARMA(3, 3) (or higher order) model as the model will not be identified.

The first stage of the identification process is to determine the order of differencing that is needed to produce a stationary data series. That is, what order of integration is the series? In general there are two elements to this. We often work with the logarithm of the data rather than the pure level as many series exhibit constant growth rates, such as eqn 2.12, and are not integrated series. Taking logarithms transforms the series into an integrated one, thus the log of eqn 2.12 is:

$$\ln(X_t) = \ln(1.5) + \ln X_{t-1} \tag{2.23}$$

The unstable co-efficient 1.5 in the levels equation is turned into the constant in the logged equation and the series can now be reduced to stationarity by first differencing. The second element is differencing and testing the series for stationarity until a stationary version of the data is found. In the original Box–Jenkins approach, stationarity was detected simply by examining the correlogram of the series to see if it 'looked' stationary. More recent work on testing stationarity has produced a range of more formal tests such as the Dickey–Fuller test or the tests due to Phillips. We will not discuss these testing procedures here, they are discussed in Cuthbertson *et al.* (1992). The important point is that they are simply a more rigorous way of detecting the appropriate degree of differencing needed to produce stationarity in the series.

Once the appropriate degree of integration has been determined, the next stage of the identification process is to assess the appropriate ARMA specification of the stationary series. This is done by examining both the correlogram and the partial autocorrelation function and relying on the fact that AR and MA processes have quite different theoretical properties. For a pure autoregressive process of lag p, the partial autocorrelation functions up to lag p will be the autoregressive coefficients while beyond that lag we expect them all to be zero. So in general there will be a 'cut-off' at lag p in the partial autocorrelation function. The correlogram, on the other hand, will decline asymptotically towards zero and not exhibit any discreet cut-off point. An MA process of order q, on the other hand, will exhibit the reverse property. The partial autocorrelation function will die away slowly towards zero with no clear cut-off, while the correlogram will exhibit a discreet cut-off at the qth point.

If neither the correlogram nor the partial autocorrelation function show a discreet cut-off point then the indication is that we are dealing with a mixed ARMA process. The identification of such processes can, in practice, be quite hard, but in principle we may think of the correlogram and partial autocorrelation function of the separate AR and MA parts of the model as being superimposed on each other. If both the correlogram and the autocorrelation function seem to decline smoothly with no sign of a sudden drop then an ARMA(1, 1) model is suggested. If the partial autocorrelation function shows a sudden drop after the second point and then slowly tapers off while the correlogram seems to decline steadily, then an ARMA(2, 1) model is suggested. Other cases may be easily constructed from the pure MA and AR case although in practice, given that the estimation of both the correlogram and partial autocorrelation function is inexact high order mixed cases can be very hard to identify.

The next two stages in the Box–Jenkins procedure (estimation and diagnostic checking) are essentially straightforward and may be performed in many modern pieces of software; we will not discuss these details here. Once a satisfactory ARIMA model is estimated it may easily be used for forecasting as far into the future as is desired. Note that the MA part of the equation will only have a direct effect on the forecast for q periods ahead, as future errors will be given their expected value of zero. Perhaps the main disadvantage of the univariate Box–Jenkins model is that it is very hard to give an interpretation to either the co-efficient of the model or to the model as a whole. We might like to ask what the underlying trend in the data is? Or can we remove the measurement error from the series? These (and other) questions can not be easily answered from this framework simply because the Box–Jenkins model is a purely statistical artifact, which is not built up from a structural view of how the data was generated. In the next section a model is described which combines the intuitive appeal of the *ad hoc* procedures with the greater statistical rigour of the Box–Jenkins approach.

2.5   The 'structural time series' forecasting model

The history of the 'structural time series' model goes back to the early work of Harrison and Stephens (1971, 1976) among others, but the main proponent of its use in economics and econometrics is Harvey (see, among many other references, 1981, 1989). This model may be thought of as a generalisation of the local trend models of Holt, Winters and Brown, discussed above. It has a more clearly articulated statistical framework than the earlier models and the notion of an underlying trend can be more easily made precise within this framework. The basic structure of the model is a state space statement of the stochastic trend model and it is estimated by using the Kalman filter (the estimation strategy will not be discussed here, this may be found in Cuthbertson *et al.* (1992) or Harvey (1989)). The underlying notion here is that a time series can be decomposed into a basic underlying trend component and an irregular component, which may be thought of as measurement error or 'noise' that is obscuring the true picture. The underlying trend can evolve over time both in terms of its level and in its growth rate. The basic state space formulation of the model is as follows:

$$x_t = m_t + \varepsilon_{1t}$$
$$m_t = m_{t-1} + b + \varepsilon_{2t}$$
$$b_t = b_{t-1} + \varepsilon_{t3}$$
$$\varepsilon_1 \sim N(0, \sigma_1^2)\varepsilon_2 \sim N(0, \sigma_2^2)\varepsilon_3 \sim N(0, \sigma_3^2) \qquad (2.24)$$

The relationship between this model and a simple deterministic trend model may be easily seen; if the error terms in the second and third equations are both set to zero then these equations will simply act to produce a series m_t, which increases by b at every period. This will simply be a linear deterministic trend. When these error terms are non-zero then either the slope of the trend (b) may change in a stochastic way or the local level of the trend (m) will change. The statistical view underlying this model is that the data is generated by a stochastic trend of this type but that it is further obscured by measurement error. The objective of this model is one of signal extraction, to get an estimate of the underlying trend which is purged of this noise.

Using this framework to derive estimates of b and m requires estimates of the variances of the three error terms in the model, which may either be fixed *a priori* as is the case with the weighting factor in the discounted least squares approach, or estimated through maximum likelihood procedures as a part of the Kalman filter. The Kalman filter works by taking the forecast error and allocating it between the three error terms of the model in accordance with the estimated variances of each equation. For the pure deterministic model, therefore, the variance on the second and third equations would be set to zero so that all errors are seen as occurring in the first equation and are interpreted as measurement errors or noise. The other extreme assumption would be where all the errors were allocated to the stochastic trend and it was assumed that there was no measurement error. This is achieved by setting the variance of the first equation to zero, forcing all the errors in each period to be allocated to the level and trend component of the model.

The *ad hoc* models discussed above can be seen as special cases of this scheme where the errors in the structural model are allocated in one particular way. For example if we define v_t to be the one-step-ahead forecasting error made by a particular model then the Holt–Winters estimation procedure may be expressed as:

$$m_t = m_{t-1} + b_t + \lambda_0 v_t$$
$$b_t = b_{t-1} + \lambda_0 \lambda_1 v_t \tag{2.25}$$

and similarly the discounted least squares model may be expressed as:

$$m_t = m_{t-1} + b_t + (1 - w^2) v_t$$
$$b_t = b_{t-1} + (1 - w)^2 v_t \tag{2.26}$$

The structural time series model may then be seen to encompass both of these formulations for particular values of the variances of the three error terms.

In general, any state space model, such as the structural time series model, may also be represented as an ARIMA model and so there is a general correspondence between these types of models and the Box–Jenkins models discussed above. By direct substitution the structural time series model may be expressed as:

$$x_t = 2x_{t-1} - x_{t-2} + v_{1t} - 2v_{1t-1} + v_{1t-2} + v_{2t} - v_{2t-1} + v_{3t}$$
$$\Rightarrow \Delta\Delta x_t = \theta_1 \eta_t + \theta_2 \eta_{t-1} + \theta_3 \eta_{t-2} \tag{2.27}$$

which is a particular ARIMA$(0, 2, 2)$ model with restrictions placed on the coefficients of the moving average error process. In one sense, the structural time series model may be seen as less general than the fully unrestricted ARIMA model. The great advantage of the structural time series model, however, is that it is much easier to interpret in a simple way. The interpretation given here of the underlying trend is not generally possible in an ARIMA model and so it is not possible to extract particular components from the ARIMA model easily, such as the trend. One view would argue that the structural time series model allows sensible restrictions to be incorporated into the ARIMA model, which allows us to make a purely statistical artefact interpretable in an economic or intuitive way.

2.6 Multivariate time series forecasting

A univariate model, by its very nature makes no use of any information except that contained in the variables' own lags. The advantage of this is that spurious correlations between variables will not give a misleading forecast and it provides a very simple and robust approach to forecasting. The disadvantage is that a considerable deterioration in the forecasting ability of the model may result. Suppose, for example, that there was a very strong causal link from money to prices with a lag of, say, two periods. Then a univariate model of prices that ignores the information in past money will be ignoring some very useful forecasting information. For this reason many time series forecasters have moved to a multivariate setting for their models. An example of this is the leading indicator work undertaken in the United States and the United Kingdom, discussed more fully in Chapter 4 below.

The basic work-horse of the multivariate time series analysis is the vector autoregressive model (VAR), this is a direct generalisation of the AR model discussed above to a system of variables. So a VAR(p) model would have the following general form; let X be a vector of N variables, then the VAR for X would be:

$$X_t = \Lambda(L)X_{t-1} + \varepsilon_t \tag{2.28}$$

where ε is a vector of white noise error processes and $\Lambda(L)X_{t-1} = \Lambda_1 X_{t-1} + \cdots + \Lambda_p X_{t-p}$ where Λ_i are $N \times N$ parameter matrices.

This model may be viewed as an unrestricted reduced form of a structural model. It combines some of the features of a standard time series model with those of a structural model. Its advantage from the time series perspective is that it does not impose any strong identifying restrictions on the model, which are a necessary part of a structural economic model. If these restrictions are invalid the model may be rendered invalid. It does, however, retain all the information that is in the whole vector of variables so that it does not make the efficiency losses of the univariate model. It is also possible to use the model for policy exercises to a limited extent, although this will not be discussed here.

Note that from a forecasting viewpoint we need the complete system to forecast further than one period ahead. If money affects prices next period then to forecast money two periods ahead we need to know money next period. This is not a problem, however, as the whole VAR can be used to forecast one period ahead and then these forecast values used to forecast the second period, and so on.

In estimation the VAR can be estimated on a single equation basis, one equation at a time. Some researchers would simplify each equation and choose the overall lag length in an *ad hoc* way, choosing different values for each equation. Often, however, a decision is made not to impose these rather arbitrary restrictions and so the only choice variable becomes the overall lag length of the VAR, that is to say, p. A number of criteria have been proposed for helping with this choice, perhaps the best known are the AIC (Akaike's information criterion) and SC (Schwartz criterion). These criteria essentially look at the goodness of fit of the VAR after a correction for degrees of freedom has been made.

A more detailed discussion of the VAR model is given in Chapter 3.

2.7 Non-linearities and forecasting

Most of the discussion in this chapter has been predicated on the assumption that the underlying process generating the data is, in fact, linear. When this assumption is false many of the basic results still hold. The Wold representation theorem, for example, still holds. We can also think of the *ad hoc* local trend models as being local approximations to the true process. So the preceding analysis is not without value even in the general non-linear case. If the true data-generating process is non-linear, however, any linear forecasting technique will be dominated by the appropriate non-linear model and further, the non-linearity may well be the cause for an unexpectedly poor out-of-estimation sample forecasting performance. For this reason in recent years there has been a growing interest in the issues of non-linearity. This has taken two main directions: (1) a theoretical interest has arisen in non-linear systems and the possibility that the non-linearity may give rise to fundamentally different dynamic behaviour. This is the literature on chaos and our understanding and ability to test for the presence of chaotic systems has been developing rapidly over the last few years; (2) a number of techniques have been developed for estimating an unknown non-linear system. Nearest neighbour estimation is one example, and we will consider the use of neural networks in this section as an example of an approach that is finding an increasing number of applications, especially in the field of finance.

2.7.1 Chaos

Many of the popular accounts of chaos theory give a grossly misleading account of its nature and implications. A chaotic system is simply a non-linear dynamic system where, either for all parameter values or for a range of parameter values, the dynamic behaviour of the system is qualitatively different from a linear system. The difference lies primarily in the way a change in the initial conditions of the system affects the dynamic development of the system. A deterministic linear dynamic system will generally be completely predictable; a change in initial conditions will have an obvious and easily calculated effect and doubling that change will produce twice the effect. A chaotic system develops a dynamic path, which is highly sensitive to its initial conditions. Any change in the initial conditions will produce a new path that diverges from the old one in an exponentially increasing way. An infinitely small change in the initial conditions will, therefore, ultimately bring about a dynamic path that is completely unrelated in any way to the original path. A property of such systems is that even if the true chaotic system is completely deterministic with no measurement error, if we try to model it with standard linear techniques then we will appear to find a linear but stochastic process. This has raised the fundamental question of whether we are really dealing with a non-linear but deterministic world, rather than the traditional assumption of a linear stochastic one. A number of tests have been developed to try to distinguish between deterministic chaotic systems and linear stochastic ones. Of course the real problem is that, almost certainly, the world is stochastic and chaotic. Good introductions to the subject may be found in Scheinkman (1990), Frank and Stengos (1988) and a collection of recent work in Pesaran and Potter (1993).

There are a number of good examples of simple dynamic systems that may give rise to chaotic behaviour. The tent map is one example; this is a simple mapping from the unit interval $[0, 1]$ onto itself, it takes the form:

$$x_t = 2x_{t-1} \quad \text{for } 0 < x < 0.5$$
$$x_t = 2(1 - x_{t-1}) \quad \text{for } 0.5 < x < 1 \tag{2.29}$$

This is a fairly simple dynamic equation, for $x = \frac{2}{3}$ it will give rise to a constant value of $\frac{2}{3}$. For any other value of x, however, it will give rise to a complex dynamic path which will not exhibit any obvious simple linear relationship. It is possible to demonstrate that for almost all values of x the tent map will generate autocorrelation function values at lag k ($k > 0$), which will be zero in sufficiently large samples. In other words the series will appear to be a white noise stochastic process from the viewpoint of linear modelling techniques.

Another simple system, which is even more typical of the general models that give rise to chaotic behaviour, is the logistic map. This is given by the following simple non-linear equation:

$$x_t = ax_{t-1}(1 - x_{t-1}) \tag{2.30}$$

This has two fixed points (constant solutions), $x = 0$ and $x = 1 - 1/a$; more than one fixed point solution is a common property of systems that will give rise to chaotic behaviour. Another common property is that the behaviour of the system changes its basic nature for various values of the parameters, in this case a. For values of a between zero and unity the system will tend to move towards a solution of $x = 0$ for any starting value within the interval $0 - 1$. For values of a between 1 and 3 the solution at zero becomes an unstable one and the x will tend towards $1 - 1/a$. For values of a greater than 3 both fixed points become unstable and the system will not settle down to any long-run solution. As a increases above 2, the solution path begins to cycle with an increasingly rapid cycle until, as a reaches 3.57, the frequency of the cycles becomes infinite, regularity disappears from the behaviour of x and the system becomes chaotic.

An important tool in chaos theory is the Lyapunov exponent. This may be thought of as a generalisation of the standard idea of an eigenvalue to the case of a non-linear system. If we define a mapping as:

$$x_{t+1} = f(x_t) \tag{2.31}$$

then we may think of the effect on the solution path for x of a small change in the initial conditions, x_0. We may then define:

$$\lim_{T \to \infty} (\delta x_T) = \delta x_0 e^{\lambda^i T} \tag{2.32}$$

where λ^i is the Lyapunov exponent.

If the system was a stable linear one then the Lyapunov exponent would be negative, as this implies that, ultimately, any initial shock dies out. If the system was an unstable one, then the Lyapunov exponent would be infinite, implying that any initial shock would lead to an ever-increasing departure of the new path from the original one. If the system was a pure unit root one (such as the random walk model), then the Lyapunov exponent would be zero, implying that the initial shock persists indefinitely but does not grow. Chaotic systems (of, say, N variables) will generally have at least one positive Lyapunov exponent, which is finite. This implies that the two paths will tend to diverge at an exponential rate but that their divergence does not become unbounded. The tent map for example gives rise to a dynamic path for x, which is always bounded between 0 and 1, so the two paths can not diverge to an infinite extent. But a positive Lyapunov exponent would suggest that, for this function, a perfect knowledge of the solution path starting from x_0 can tell us nothing about the long-run solution path starting from x_0 plus a very small amount. Figure 2.1 illustrates this property of chaotic processes. It shows two dynamic simulations of the logistic map where $a = 3.8$, in the chaotic region of the parameter space. They differ only in the starting values, one simulation starts with an initial value of 0.5 and the other starts from 0.5001.

The simulations are reported for 60 periods, and two important features need to be noted: (1) for the first 30 periods the two solution paths are virtually identical, so it is

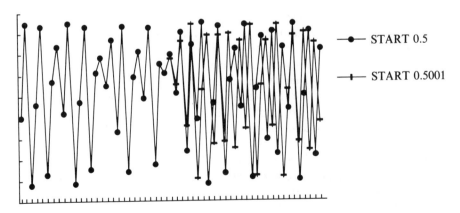

START 0.5

START 0.5001

Figure 2.1 An example of chaos

quite wrong to suggest that the series are unforecastable simply because they are chaotic. For a considerable period the difference in initial conditions makes no appreciable difference to the solution path; (2) once the two paths do diverge they become completely different and, by the end of the period, there appears to be no correlation between them. The divergence between the two paths grows at an exponential rate governed by the Lyapunov exponent. Starting from a small initial value it takes some time to build up to a significant amount but once it shows itself the divergence between the two paths quickly becomes complete.

The possibility of chaos in economic time series has intrigued researchers for some time and a number of formal test procedures have been proposed, including a residual-based test of Brock (1986), Scheinkman and LeBarron's (1986) shuffle diagnostic, the formal tests of Brock *et al.* (1987) and the more general and well known tests for non-linearity, such as the RESET test (see Ramsey (1969) or Cuthbertson *et al.* (1992)); these will not be discussed here. All the tests of chaos are, however, tests of a deterministic chaotic system against the alternative of a stochastic linear one. It is generally believed that their power to discriminate between stochastic chaotic processes and linear ones is not good.

The fact that very simple non-linear systems can give rise to such complex dynamic behaviour is striking, as is the fact that a number of theoretical economic models are now known to give rise to chaotic behaviour (two examples from macro-economics are Day and Shafer (1985) and Van der Ploeg (1986)). The presence of chaos does not simply mean that, in the long run, we cannot forecast a series, it also means that in the medium term we might be able to dramatically improve our forecasting ability over that provided by a linear forecasting rule if we knew the correct form of non-linearity. In the physical sciences, theory, or experimentation, often provides a good guide as to the appropriate non-linear form to choose. In economics, this is seldom the case so we need some way to model non-linear systems without first knowing the true structure of the underlying data-generation process. This is the problem we turn to in the next section on neural networks.

2.7.2 Neural networks

Over the last decade a number of techniques have been developed that allow the estimation of general non-linear models without specifying an exact functional form. One of the most popular of these is neural networks, so called for the suggested parallel between this computer model and the way a biological brain works. A neural network has many close parallels with a conventional econometric model, although it is often described in very different language and this often acts to obscure the similarities rather than highlight them. White (1989a) has done considerable work recently emphasising the relationship between traditional classical statistics and neural network theory.

A neural network maps a set of inputs (X_t) into a set of outputs (Y_t), where for ease of exposition we will think of just one output rather than a vector and, of course, the inputs could be simply lagged values of Y. The characteristic feature of a neural network is the way this mapping is constructed. We begin by setting up a number of sets of unobserved variables, called hidden layers. These layers are then connected to each other, and the inputs, through a set of simple functions. The effect of all the interconnections, however, is to create complex combinations of the simple interconnecting functions and it is this extreme complexity that allows the neural network to achieve its ability to mimic a wide range of functional forms. A convenient way to think of a neural net is as an approximation tool for an unspecified non-linear functional form.

The usual way of describing a neural network is shown in Figure 2.2; the input layer consists of four variables, in this case there is only one hidden layer. Each input is connected to each element of the hidden layer and then the hidden layers in turn feed a modified signal into the single output. The input into each element of the hidden layer may be expressed as:

$$H_i = \sum_{j=1}^{n} \gamma_j X_j \tag{2.33}$$

where there are n inputs and i denotes the element in the hidden layer. The final output can then be expressed as:

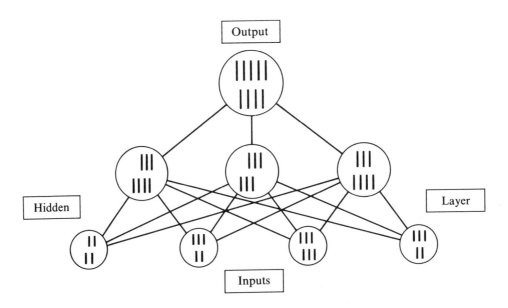

Figure 2.2 Neural network architecture

$$Y = \sum_{i=1}^{k} \alpha_i f(H_i)$$

$$= \sum_{i=1}^{k} \alpha_i f\left(\sum_{j=1}^{n} \gamma_j X_j \right) \tag{2.34}$$

where f represents the way the hidden layer modifies the input that passes through it. Note that if f were simply a linear function the neural network would simply be a reparameterisation of a linear equation between Y and X. Typically, however, it is specified as a simple non-linear function, such as a sigmoid function, and then the neural network architecture acts to produce complex combinations of these simple non-linearities, the outcome of which can be an extremely complex non-linear function. From an economic forecasting point of view, the main interest in neural networks lies in this universal approximation property, although much of the actual neural network literature is concerned with the 'estimation' of the parameters of the network. Hornik *et al.* (1989) have demonstrated that, with a sufficient number of hidden layers, a neural network can approximate any given functional form to any desired accuracy level.

Much of the neural network literature is concerned with the problem of selecting the parameters, which is often confusingly termed 'learning'. It is usually done using a variant on a technique known as 'back propagation', which amounts to picking an arbitrary set of values for the parameters of the network and then passing through the data, forecasting with the network and changing the parameters so as to improve the forecasting ability of the network. This is clearly related to standard least squares estimation and indeed White (1989b) has shown that the two are closely related, although back propagation does not make efficient use of the data.

There are, however, a number of problems with the use of neural networks, which come essentially from their power as a universal approximator. In general, a sufficiently complex (in terms of numbers of hidden layers) network will be able to fit any data set perfectly. If the data really does have a stochastic element this will mean that the network is achieving a spuriously good fit; it is over-fitting the data and is in many ways similar to a highly over-parameterised model. There is then an art in choosing how well the network should fit. When the back propagation techniques are used, the data is passed through a number of times and each time the network will improve its explanatory power. The stopping point in the training exercise can be very important in terms of achieving a sufficiently good fit without over-fitting. One danger of neural networks, then, is that they can appear to offer extraordinarily good explanatory power within their training sample but they may well break down completely out of the sample. A further problem arising from the extreme generality of the functional form is that, typically, large data sets are required for the estimation exercise. Engineering and natural science applications of neural networks often make use of many thousand data points. Economics is often limited to less than 100 observations and sometimes, in the case of annual data, say, to less than 30 observations. The usefulness of applying such a powerful modelling tool to such a limited data set may well be doubted.

The traditional neural network literature has offered little firm guidance in the way the specification choice can be made. Recent work by White (1989a) has emphasised that traditional statistical tools can be brought to bear to ask about the significance of extra hidden layers or parameters and so reduce the risk of spurious over-fitting. The combination of the extremely rich functional forms of the neural network and the tools of statistical inference offers a potentially promising and exciting new avenue of research to the forecaster, although much remains to be done to prove the practical usefulness of these techniques, especially for small-sample applications.

2.8 Conclusions

This chapter has given a brief overview of the techniques used in time series forecasting. This non-structural approach to forecasting plays a number of roles. It is often used when a simple, quick forecast for a single series is needed. In a full economic forecast setting, it is a useful tool for setting exogenous variables and as a bench mark against which to judge the structural forecast. And, finally, time series models play an important role in formalising our intuition about what is likely to happen.

Time series techniques are, however, by no means a unified body of theory. The early *ad hoc* procedures were derived in a largely intuitive way and, while they will often work well, they are not suitable for all circumstances. The Box–Jenkins and structural time series models both have a firmer statistical base and are likely to be more satisfactory. They are, however, still limited by their underlying assumption of linearity. Recent work has tried to go beyond this limit by testing for non-linearities and chaos and by using more flexible modelling techniques, such as neural networks. In principle the potential of these approaches is enormous, but there are still severe limitations to them, particularly when they are applied to macro-economic data. The most striking limitation is their need for large sample sizes in contrast to the available economic data. In practice estimation is often a difficult process involving a compromise between consistency and efficiency. We achieve efficiency by building prior information into the estimation procedure in the form of functional forms, error distributions, conditioning assumptions, etc. But if these assumptions are wrong then we lose consistency and may achieve very misleading results. Given the limited data sizes available in macro-economics, it may therefore be unwise to go beyond the confines of linear techniques without firm evidence for the presence of non-linearities and some guidance as to their forms. The potential power of non-linear techniques is, however, enormous and they may well be the main area of development in forecasting in coming decades.

3 | VAR modelling

Donald Robertson and *Michael Wickens*

3.1 Introduction – why VAR modelling?

Throughout this book the emphasis is on obtaining statistically robust estimates from a tightly specified theoretical model. The use of economic theory provides a large number of exclusion and cross-equation restrictions. In this chapter we describe a different approach, which attempts to be much more sceptical about what prior theory can deliver in terms of the nature of such restrictions, and uses vector autoregression (VAR) models as a means to describe the dynamic interactions of the data. This use of VAR models to describe the data and in particular to analyse the impulse response functions of macro-economic variables was first proposed by Sims (1980). His motivation is precisely the argument that conventional structural models involve incredible identifying restrictions, which are untested and provide a spurious number of degrees of freedom. The alternative use of VAR models can be seen as an implementation of a multivariate version of Wold's decomposition theorem (Wold, 1938), in which covariance stationary stochastic processes have an orthogonal decomposition into a linearly deterministic component and a linearly indeterministic component (see Chapter 2). If we assume for the moment that any linearly deterministic part has been removed (e.g. by removing constants or deterministic seasonal components, etc.) then let the vector of time series be $\mathbf{x}'_t = (x_{1t}, x_{2t}, \ldots, x_{mt})$ where the individual series are jointly covariance stationary. The vector of variables $\mathbf{x}_t$ can be represented as

$$\mathbf{x}_t = c(L)\boldsymbol{\varepsilon}_t \tag{3.1}$$

where $c(L)$ is a matrix in the lag operator L and $\boldsymbol{\varepsilon}_t$ is a vector white noise. If the matrix $c(L)$ can be expressed as the product of two matrices $a^{-1}(L)$ and $b(L)$ (note there may be a multiplicity of such decompositions) then eqn 3.1 can be rewritten as:

$$a(L)\mathbf{x}_t = b(L)\boldsymbol{\varepsilon}_t \tag{3.2}$$

which represents the series $\mathbf{x}_t$ as a multivariate ARMA process. If the decomposition of the matrix $c(L)$ yields $b(L) = B = \text{constant}$, then the expression (eqn 3.2) reduces to:

$$a(L)\mathbf{x}_t = B\varepsilon_t \tag{3.3}$$

or:

$$\mathbf{x}_t = (a_0)^{-1}(a_1\mathbf{x}_{t-1} + a_2\mathbf{x}_{t-2} + a_3\mathbf{x}_{t-3} + \cdots + B\varepsilon_t) \tag{3.4}$$

which is the pure vector autoregression representation of $\mathbf{x}_t$.

The Wold decomposition theorem asserts the existence of this linear representation (eqn 3.1). Better non-linear representations of the data may exist, but if we confine ourselves to a linear world then this model will provide a reasonable approximation to the data, and could in theory be identified and estimated given sufficient data. Thus the multivariate Wold decomposition theorem gives one justification for the use of unrestricted VAR models. In a macro-economic modelling framework we may also think of the VAR model as arising from the unrestricted reduced form of some assumed structural model. The macro-economic modeller need select only which variables (and any appropriate transformations) should enter the VAR. Statistical procedures can then be applied to determine the optimal lag length in eqn 3.4. VAR modelling thus provides an atheoretic framework in which to analyse macro-economic variables where only the minimal number of restrictions on the covariance matrix sufficient to identify the shocks are imposed, thus providing an alternative to the conventional modelling strategy that escapes Sims' criticism. In the next section we develop the outline above for VAR modelling in the case of stationary variables. Section 3.3 discusses the problems that arise when the variables under consideration are non-stationary, and there is the possibility of cointegration among the set of variables. Section 3.4 discusses briefly the imposition of Bayesian priors in a VAR framework. Section 3.5 gives some examples in forecasting and applications. More comprehensive treatments of some of the topics discussed below can be found in Canova (1992), Lutkepohl (1991) and Granger and Newbold (1986).

3.2 VAR modelling with stationary variables

Suppose $\mathbf{x}_t$ is a vector of m stochastic variables, no distinction being made between endogenous and exogenous variables, and $\mathbf{d}_t$ is a vector of deterministic variables. We suppose the structural model can be defined as

$$a(L)\mathbf{x}_t = F\mathbf{d}_t + B\varepsilon_t \tag{3.5}$$

where ε_t is serially independent, $E(\varepsilon_t\varepsilon_t') = I$ and the roots of $a(L) = \Sigma_i a_i L^i$ lie outside the unit circle.[1] The solved reduced form of eqn 3.5 can be written in VAR form as indicated in eqn 3.4 above. Write this more fully as:

$$\Gamma(L)\mathbf{x}_t = G\mathbf{d}_t + \mathbf{e}_t \tag{3.6}$$

where $\Gamma(L) = \Sigma_i \Gamma_i L^i = a_0^{-1}a(L)$, $\Gamma_0 = I$, $G = a_0^{-1}F$ and $a_0\mathbf{e}_t = B\varepsilon_t$.

Equation (3.6) is a VAR if all identifying restrictions arising from the structural form are ignored. As the VAR is an unrestricted reduced form it can be estimated consistently by single equation least squares, the estimates being efficient if the disturbances are normally distributed. A moving average representation of eqn 3.6 is obtained as:

$$\mathbf{x}_t = h(L)\mathbf{d}_t + c(L)\mathbf{e}_t \tag{3.7}$$

where $c(L) = \Sigma_i c_i L^i = \Gamma(L)^{-1}$, $c_0 = I$, $h(L) = \Gamma(L)^{-1}G$. If $\mathbf{d}_t$ consists of polynomials in t or trigonometric variables then $h(L)$ will not depend on L. Estimation of eqn 3.6 requires the econometrician to specify the set of (stationary) variables to be included in the VAR, the nature of any deterministic components, and the lag length of the autoregression. The set of variables chosen and the nature of the deterministic functions are generally motivated by economic theory or prior experience. In choosing the lag length one must trade off a better approximation to the underlying specification of the model against the rapid rise in the number of parameters to be estimated as the lag length increases. Formal statistical criteria exist for determining the optimal lag length (see, for example, Akaike's (1974) criterion, Parzen (1976), Hannan and Quinn (1979)). In general the lag length chosen will increase with the data available. As an alternative approach some authors (e.g. Lutkepohl, 1991) suggest linking the number of parameters to be estimated directly to the sample size (in Lutkepohl's case the cube root of the sample size). The econometrician having selected the included variables (plus any transformations of the same), the type of deterministic components and the lag length, estimates of eqn 3.6 are easily derived.

The problem of concern can now be defined. It is to find the response of $\mathbf{x}_{t+s}$ to changes in the structural shocks ε_t from unrestricted estimates of eqn 3.6, i.e. $\partial\mathbf{x}_{t+s}/\partial\varepsilon_t$. To identify the structural shocks ε_t from the shocks $\mathbf{e}_t$ in eqn 3.6 requires identifying restrictions on $R = a_0^{-1}B$, enabling one to move from the estimated reduced form (eqn 3.6) to the structural model (eqn 3.5). As R is an $n \times n$ matrix, the complete identification of R requires n^2 restrictions. The constraint $E(\mathbf{e}_t\mathbf{e}_t') = \Omega = E(R\varepsilon_t\varepsilon_t'R') = RR'$, where Ω is the estimated variance covariance matrix of the VAR (eqn 3.6) provides $n(n + 1)/2$ of these restrictions, leaving $n(n - 1)/2$ restrictions to be found. Two proposals for obtaining these are Sims' triangular orthogonalisation (recursive ordering) and Blanchard's method of structural vector autoregression.

3.2.1 Triangular orthogonalisation

This method is based on Wold's (1938) causal chain analysis. It involves restricting R to be a lower triangular matrix, having first ordered the variables in $\mathbf{x}_t$. As the number of zero elements in R that this entails is $n(n - 1)/2$ this provides the additional restrictions that are needed. This identification scheme has the disadvantage of assuming that there is a structural model that has a contemporaneously recursive form, i.e. the chains of causality in the structural model take a particular recursive form. This may be objected to both on the grounds that: (1) economic theory rarely delivers such a recursive structure; and (2) there are a multiplicity of such lower triangular decompositions and the selection of a particular one nominates the causal ordering of the economic variables. There are $n!$ such possible orderings and if prior economic theory fails to specify a causal ordering then any particular choice will be arbitrary.

3.2.2 The structural VAR approach

The basic idea here is to identify R by introducing restrictions directly on a_0 and B. A simple way of doing this is to make both B and a_0 lower triangular. This makes R lower triangular once again. As it involves $n(n-1)$ restrictions, there are $n(n-1)/2$ over-identifying restrictions. If $\hat{e}_t$ is the estimated VAR disturbance, a_0 and B can be estimated using recursive least squares on:

$$a_0 \hat{e}_t = B \hat{\varepsilon}_t \qquad (3.8)$$

Blanchard (1989) uses a modified version of this to take account of the assumption that a_0 and B both have a single unknown element above the diagonal.[2] Provided restrictions are introduced on some of the elements of a_0 and B below the diagonal, this can be accomplished by prespecifying the elements above the diagonal and then choosing optimal values for them using a grid search. Blanchard also specifies $E(\varepsilon_t \varepsilon_t')$ to be diagonal and not an identity matrix as in eqn 3.5, but as he also restricts the elements of the leading diagonal of B to be unity the two approaches are equivalent in this respect.[3] The advantage of Blanchard's method over the triangular orthogonalisation approach is that it allows identifying information to be brought to bear from the structural equations. The use of structural identifying information was, of course, exactly what Sims was trying to avoid in moving to VAR modelling. However, as Blanchard's method does not aim to use all of the structural over-identifying information, it may be seen as taking an intermediate position between full structural and unrestricted VAR modelling.

3.3 VAR modelling with non-stationary variables

When it was first introduced, VAR analysis was formulated in the terms of the levels of variables. Subsequently it was realised that this was only valid if all of the variables are stationary. The response was to difference all non-stationary variables until they become stationary. It is now recognised that this solution is inappropriate if the non-stationary variables are co-integrated, because the VAR model omits the cointegrating residuals. This misspecification is remedied by the use of a vector error correction model (VECM).

permanent effects

3.3.1 VAR modelling with non-stationary variables without cointegration

identifying restriction.

In our previous discussion it was assumed that all of the variables in the VAR were stationary. In general, however, the VAR may contain both stationary and non-stationary variables. This creates new problems for model specification and the interpretation identification and estimation of shocks.

The most common way of dealing with non-stationary $I(1)$ variables is to form the VAR from first differences of the $I(1)$ variables and from the levels of the stationary $I(0)$ variables. This is the procedure suggested in Lutkepohl (1991) and adopted for example in Blanchard (1989), Blanchard and Quah (1989), Bayoumi and Eichengreen (1991) and Cecchetti and Karras (1991). It provides the correct method of estimation provided there is no cointegration between the variables, as we have assumed in this section. The methods of identifying the shocks proposed for stationary variables can then be used again. The interpretation of the shocks is, however, different and depends on whether the variables are $I(1)$ or $I(0)$. For variables that are stationary in levels a shock can have only a temporary effect, whereas for the first differenced variables a shock has a temporary effect on the change, but a permanent effect on the level. Thus zero identifying restrictions on R imply only that the levels of various stationary variables, and the change in certain of the $I(1)$ variables, are contemporaneously unaffected by the shock. Subsequently there may be temporary effects and, in the case of the levels of the $I(1)$ variables, permanent long-run effects.

The presence of the $I(1)$ variables also allows a different type of identifying restriction to be employed in moving from the estimated to the structural form. Constraints on the long-run impact of a shock can be imposed (see Blanchard and Quah (1989), Bayoumi and Eichengreen (1991) and Cecchetti and Karras (1991)). To illustrate, let $\mathbf{x}_t' = \{\Delta\mathbf{y}_t', \mathbf{w}_t\}$ with $\mathbf{y}_t$ a p-vector of $I(1)$ variables and $\mathbf{w}_t$ a q-vector of $I(0)$ variables with $q = n - p \geqslant 0$. Rewrite eqn 3.7 as:

$$\mathbf{x}_t = h(L)\mathbf{d}_t + c(1)\mathbf{e}_t + c^*(L)\Delta\mathbf{e}_t \tag{3.9}$$

where $c(L) = c(1) + c^*(L)(1 - L)$. If $\xi_t = Q^{-1}\mathbf{e}_t$ are the shocks that are of interest then eqn 3.9 can be rewritten as:

$$\mathbf{x}_t = h(L)\mathbf{d}_t + d(1)\xi_t + d^*(L)\Delta\xi_t \tag{3.10}$$

where $d(L) = c(L)Q$ and $d(L) = d(1) + d^*(L)(1 - L)$. Imposing constraints on the permanent effect on $\mathbf{x}_t$ of a shock implies restricting the elements of $d(1)$. For example, a zero long-run impact implies a corresponding zero element in the first p rows of $d(1)$. In general these long-run restrictions satisfy

$$d(1) = c(1)q \tag{3.11}$$

As before, complete identification of the structural form requires n^2 restrictions in all. $n(n + 1)/2$ of these are given by using the constraint that $E(\xi_t\xi_t') = I$, implying $\Omega = QQ'$. If the additional long-run restrictions (eqn 3.11) are insufficient to provide the remaining $n(n - 1)/2$ restrictions then additional constraints can be imposed on $d(1)$, possibly including some on the last q rows, which are associated with the stationary variables. An example would make Q triangular, as above.

3.3.2 VAR modelling with non-stationary variables and cointegration

When the $I(1)$ variables are cointegrated, the approach of formulating the VAR model in first differences is inappropriate. Unrestricted vector autoregressions will be misspecified if estimated in differences due to the omission of the cointegrating residual, and will have omitted important constraints if estimated in levels, as cross-equation restrictions associated with the co-integration will not be imposed. Whilst these constraints will be satisfied asymptotically there will be a loss of efficiency in finite sample estimation if they are not imposed. The correct model is a cointegrated VAR in levels or a vector error correction model (VECM), i.e. a VAR in first differences together with the vector of co-integrating residuals, which is also $I(0)$, as an additional set of right-hand-side variables. In the following we restrict attention to the case where all the variables are $I(1)$. This problem is also discussed in King *et al.* (1991) who adopt a different, less general, solution method from that proposed here.

The VECM is obtained from rewriting the reduced form (eqn 3.6) as:

$$a(L)\Delta \mathbf{x}_t = A\mathbf{x}_{t-1} + G\mathbf{d}_t + \mathbf{e}_t \tag{3.12}$$

where $\Gamma(L) = a(L)(1 - L) - AL$, $a_0 = I$ and $A = -\Gamma(1)$. If there are r cointegrating vectors among the $\mathbf{x}_t$ variables then the results of Engle and Granger (1987) imply that rank $(A) = r$ and we may write $A = \alpha\beta'$, where β is an $n \times r$ matrix of r cointegrating vectors, and α is an $n \times r$ matrix of factor loadings. If we write $\mathbf{z}_t = \beta'\mathbf{x}_t$ as the vector of r cointegrating residuals we may then express eqn 3.12 solely in terms of $I(0)$ variables as:

$$a(L)\Delta \mathbf{x}_t = \alpha\mathbf{z}_{t-1} + G\mathbf{d}_t + \mathbf{e}_t \tag{3.13}$$

When all the variables are $I(1)$ and there is no cointegration then the n variables of the vector $\mathbf{x}_t$ are subject to n independent permanent shocks. If there are r cointegrating vectors then there are only $n - r$ independent permanent shocks, called the common stochastic trends (CST) (see Stock and Watson, 1988b). This is important for identification, as any restrictions must be imposed on the CSTs, and not on the VECM formulation disturbances, $\mathbf{e}_t$.

In order to find the CSTs, the VECM must be inverted to give a moving average representation. The VAR representation (eqn 3.6) of the reduced form cannot immediately be inverted because cointegration of the variables implies that the coefficient matrix $\Gamma(1)$ of the VAR representation will be singular. The solution is to operate on the VECM directly. Engle and Granger (1987) and Engle and Yoo (1991) have shown that eqn 3.12 can be rewritten as a vector moving average (VMA) process in $\Delta \mathbf{x}_t$:

$$\Delta \mathbf{x}_t = h(L)\mathbf{d}_t + c(L)\mathbf{e}_t \tag{3.14}$$

$$= h(L)\mathbf{d}_t + c(1)\mathbf{e}_t + c^*(L)\Delta \mathbf{e}_t \tag{3.15}$$

where $c(1) = \gamma \theta'$, $c(1)\gamma = 0$, $\theta'c(1) = 0$ and γ and θ are $n \times (n - r)$ matrices. The $n - r$ CSTs can be defined as τ_t, where $\Delta \tau_t = \theta' \mathbf{e}_t$. Note that τ_t is then by definition a vector of $(n - r)$ difference stationary variables. Thus:

$$\Delta \mathbf{x}_t = h(L)\mathbf{d}_t + \gamma \Delta \tau_t + c^*(L)\Delta \mathbf{e}_t \tag{3.16}$$

The level of $\mathbf{x}_t$ is then obtained by integrating eqn 3.16:

$$\mathbf{x}_t = x_0 + j(L)\mathbf{d}_t + \gamma \tau_t + c^*(L)\mathbf{e}_t \tag{3.17}$$

Thus the $I(1)$ components of $\mathbf{x}_t$ are due to various linear combinations, given by the rows of γ, of the $n - r$ stochastic trends τ_t, hence the terminology common stochastic trends. The term in $\mathbf{e}_t$ is stationary and so defines only a stationary component, the remaining terms define a non-stochastic trend. The long-run behaviour of the series is governed by the common stochastic trends and the non-stochastic trends alone.

As before, identification can be enabled by imposing restrictions on the long-run impact of shocks. In applying such long-run restrictions the aim is to construct appropriate shocks η_t that are a linear transformation of $\Delta \tau_t$ that have the desired long-run effect on $\mathbf{x}_t$. These shocks can be obtained from eqn 3.16 in an analogous way to that in which eqn 3.10 was derived from eqn 3.9.

Thus if we define η_t and P to satisfy $\eta_t = P^{-1}\Delta \tau_t = P^{-1}\theta' \mathbf{e}_t$ then the required model is:

$$\Delta \mathbf{x}_t = h(L)\mathbf{d}_t + F\eta_t + c^*(L)\Delta \mathbf{e}_t \tag{3.18}$$

where the long-run restrictions are:

$$F = \gamma P \tag{3.19}$$

As F is an $n \times (n - r)$ matrix, complete identification requires $n(n - r)$ restrictions. $(n - r)(n - r + 1)/2$ of these restrictions can be obtained by choosing P to satisfy $E(\Delta \tau_t \Delta \tau_t') = \theta' \Omega \theta = PP'$ so that the constructed shocks η_t satisfy $E(\eta_t \eta_t') = E(P^{-1}\Delta \tau_t \Delta \tau_t' P^{-1'}) = I$ (that is, they are assumed to be orthogonal). If P is also chosen to be lower triangular this would provide another $(n - r)(n - r - 1)/2$ constraints, thereby leaving a further $r(n - r)$ to be found. These can be obtained by constraining the elements of β or γ.[4]

In order to obtain the impact and interim multipliers of the shocks η_t it is necessary to express eqn 3.18 differently. Noting that η_t is an $(n - r)$-vector, whereas the reduced form shocks $\mathbf{e}_t$ are an n-vector, we define $\omega_t' = (\eta_t', \mathbf{e}_{2t}')$ where $\mathbf{e}_{2t}$ contains the last r elements of $\mathbf{e}_t$, that is $\mathbf{e}_{2t} = J\mathbf{e}_t$ where $J = [0, I_r]$. Using $\eta_t = P^{-1}\Delta \tau_t = P^{-1}\theta' \mathbf{e}_t$, we then have $\omega_t = W\mathbf{e}_t$ with:

$$W = \begin{bmatrix} P^{-1}\theta' \\ 0 \quad I_r \end{bmatrix}$$

wherein $P^{-1}\theta'$ is an $(n - r) \times n$ submatrix, and $[0, I_r] = J$ provides the other r rows.[5]
Rewrite (3.18) as:

$$\Delta \mathbf{x}_t = h(L)\mathbf{d}_t + f(1)\boldsymbol{\omega}_t + f^*(L)\Delta\boldsymbol{\omega}_t \qquad (3.20)$$

where we have defined $f(L) = c(L)W^{-1} = f(1) + f^*(L)(1 - L)$ where $c(L)$ is as in eqn 3.14.[6]

Although the multipliers are then defined by $f(L)$, in practice there is no need to calculate $f(L)$ explicitly. It is sufficient to calculate W and simulate the VECM – eqn 3.13 – using the fact that the disturbances in eqn 3.13 are $\mathbf{e}_t = W^{-1}\boldsymbol{\omega}_t$ and the cointegrating residuals $\mathbf{z}_t = \beta'\mathbf{x}_t$. In other words simulate:

$$[a(L)(1 - L) - \alpha\beta'L]\mathbf{x}_t = G\mathbf{d}_t + W^{-1}\boldsymbol{\omega}_t \qquad (3.21)$$

for unit shocks $\boldsymbol{\omega}_t$. Note that eqn 3.21 is simply a rearrangement of eqn 3.13 using the fact that $A = \alpha\beta'$. Thus if we define $K = [I_{n-r}, 0]$, an $(n - r) \times n$ matrix, the long-run multiplier for a one standard deviation shock is $\partial\mathbf{x}/\partial\boldsymbol{\eta} = (\partial\mathbf{x}/\partial\boldsymbol{\omega})K' = F = \gamma P$. The impact multiplier is $\partial\mathbf{x}_t/\partial\boldsymbol{\eta}_t = W^{-1}K'$.

The remaining problem is to calculate W. This requires estimates of γ, θ and P. The latter is obtained from Ω, the estimated covariance matrix of the VECM disturbances $\mathbf{e}_t$ in eqn 3.13, and θ. θ itself can be estimated from eqn 3.12 using the Smith–McMillan–Yoo form, a generalised inversion formula, to invert the autoregressive representation and obtain the moving average representation (see Yoo (1986) and Engle and Yoo (1991)). The general result provides the following relation between the AR form (eqn 3.12) and the MA form (eqn 3.14): rewrite eqn 3.12 as $\bar{a}(L)\mathbf{x}_t = G\mathbf{d}_t + \mathbf{e}_t$, where $\bar{a}(L) = a(L)(1 - L) - AL$, then there exists a decomposition of $\bar{a}(L)$ such that $\bar{a}(L) = v(L)\bar{m}(L)u(L)$ and $c(L)$ of eqn (3.14) then satisfies $c(L) = u(L)^{-1}m(L)v(L)^{-1}$, where all the roots of $\det[u(L)] = 0$ and $\det[v(L)] = 0$ lie outside the unit circle and:

$$m(L) = \begin{bmatrix} I_r(1 - L) & 0 \\ 0 & I_{n-r} \end{bmatrix} \quad \text{and} \quad \bar{m}(L) = \begin{bmatrix} I_r & 0 \\ 0 & I_{n-r}(1 - L) \end{bmatrix}.$$

This can be used to calculate $c(1)$ from knowledge of $A = -\bar{a}(1)$ by setting $L = 1$. Thus:

$$m(1) = \begin{bmatrix} 0 & 0 \\ 0 & I_{n-r} \end{bmatrix} \quad \text{and} \quad \bar{m}(1) = \begin{bmatrix} I_r & 0 \\ 0 & 0 \end{bmatrix}.$$

If $u(1) = \{u_{ij}\}$, $v(1) = \{v_{ij}\}$, $u(1)^{-1} = \{u^{ij}\}$, $v(1)^{-1} = \{v^{ij}\}$ for $\{i, j = 1, 2\}$ where we partition the matrices $u(1)$ and $v(1)$ conformably with $m(1)$ and $\bar{m}(1)$ (i.e. into r and $n - r$ blocks), then:

$$a(1) = -A = \begin{bmatrix} v_{11} \\ v_{21} \end{bmatrix}[u_{11} \quad u_{12}] = -\alpha\beta' \qquad (3.22)$$

and:

$$c(1) = \begin{bmatrix} u^{12} \\ u^{22} \end{bmatrix} [v^{21} \quad v^{22}] = \gamma\theta' \tag{3.23}$$

by direct calculation. Now eqns 3.22 and 3.23 do not determine α, β, γ and θ uniquely. In general $\alpha' = A'[v'_{11} \quad v'_{21}]$, $\beta' = A^{-1}[u_{11} \quad u_{12}]$, $\gamma' = B'[u^{12'} \quad u^{22'}]$ and $\theta' = B^{-1}[v^{21} \quad v^{22}]$ where A and B are arbitrary non-singular matrices.[7] γ and θ can be derived from α and β, again non-uniquely, by writing A as:

$$A = - \begin{bmatrix} v_{11} & 0 \\ v_{21} & F \end{bmatrix} \begin{bmatrix} I_r & 0 \\ 0 & 0 \end{bmatrix} \begin{bmatrix} u_{11} & u_{12} \\ 0 & I_{n-r} \end{bmatrix}$$

when:

$$c(1) = \begin{bmatrix} u_{11}^{-1} & -u_{11}^{-1}u_{12} \\ 0 & I_{n-r} \end{bmatrix} \begin{bmatrix} 0 & 0 \\ 0 & I_{n-r} \end{bmatrix} \begin{bmatrix} v_{11}^{-1} & 0 \\ -F^{-1}v_{21}v_{11}^{-1} & F^{-1} \end{bmatrix}$$

$$= \begin{bmatrix} -u_{11}^{-1}u_{12} \\ I_{n-r} \end{bmatrix} F^{-1}[-v_{21}v_{11}^{-1} \quad I_{n-r}] \tag{3.24}$$

The presence of the non-singular matrix F in eqn 3.24 implies that $c(1)$ is not uniquely defined with respect to $a(1)$ and that γ and θ are not uniquely defined. From eqns 3.23 and 3.24 it follows that:

$$\gamma' = G[-u'_{12}u_{11}^{-1'} \quad I_{n-r}] \tag{3.25}$$

and

$$\theta' = H[-v_{21}v_{11}^{-1} \quad I_{n-r}] \tag{3.26}$$

where G and H are arbitrary full rank matrices satisfying $G'H = F^{-1}$. As F can be chosen arbitrarily, γ' is an arbitrary linear transformation of $[-u'_{12}u_{11}^{-1'} \quad I_{n-r}]$ and θ' is an arbitrary linear transformation of $[-v_{21}v_{11}^{-1} \quad I_{n-r}]$. Both can be calculated from the estimates of α and β. Now that θ has been formed, the matrix W can be calculated, and since θ is non-unique, so is W.

The lack of identifiability in the above procedure is difficult to remove without imposing arbitrary restrictions that would include an ordering for the variables. One way of doing this would be to restrict the elements of β and θ such that any linear combination of the columns of β and θ would still satisfy these restrictions. This would be equivalent to introducing into these long-run matrices the sort of identifiability conditions familiar in simultaneous equation models. An example would be to restrict certain elements of β and θ to zero in such a way that there exists no linear combination of the columns in which these elements are still zero. Such zero restrictions on β are equivalent to imposing zero restrictions on certain variables in forming the co-integrating vector.[8] For θ they are equivalent to excluding particular stochastic errors in forming the stochastic trends.[9]

To recap, when the variables under consideration are $I(1)$ and there is co-integration:

1. Estimate the VECM (eqn 3.12) determining r, the number of cointegrating vectors and α and β using the method of Johansen (1988).
2. Construct γ and θ from eqns 3.25 and 3.26 using suitable values of H and G, such as the identity matrix I_{n-r}.
3. Calculate P using $\theta'\Omega\theta = PP'$ and the long-run identifying restrictions (eqn 3.19).
4. Form W from θ and P.
5. Simulate eqn 3.21 to obtain the impulse response function for a one standard deviation shock to $\boldsymbol{\omega}_t$.
6. The corresponding impulse response function for a shock to $\boldsymbol{\eta}_t$ (which is the $n - r$ independent shocks in eqn 3.21) is then the first $n - r$ rows.

This completes the description of estimation and inference in the classical VAR framework, both for stationary variables and for non-stationary variables, including the case of cointegration. To summarise, first one obtains a dynamic specification that performs well in terms of lag length, functional forms of the included variables, the choice of those variables themselves, the presence of deterministic components such as seasonal dummies and the statistical properties (serial correlation, uncorrelatedness, normality) of the residuals. Identification of the structural form from the estimated system then takes place through the imposition of a sufficient number of restrictions, motivated by economic theory, such as causal orderings, or the zero long-run impact of a particular shock on a variable. The system can then be transformed to a moving average representation, either directly or via the Smith–McMillan–Yoo form, giving the impulse response functions of the included variables to the (structural) shocks. Note that this sequential procedure leaves open the possibility that if inference is suspect at any stage of the estimation (for instance in determining the optimal lag length, the order of integration of variables, or possible cointegration between them), then inference at subsequent stages can only be conditional upon the acceptance of any earlier hypotheses, and may thus have much reduced power relative to the classical implementation of a test. The entire procedure can be extremely sensitive to the acceptance or rejection of hypotheses at any stage, and the overall results may not be robust to these sorts of problems.

3.4 Bayesian VARs

A different approach to the specification of VAR models associated with the work of Litterman (1980, 1986) is to allow a Bayesian perspective on the parameters of a VAR model. This permits a large number of parameters, as arises naturally in high order unrestricted VARs because of the number of variables in each equation, to be expressed more parsimoniously in terms of a small number of parameters governing probability distributions. The hope is that the poor estimation properties of high order VARs (in terms of the standard errors of estimated coefficients) can be 'sharpened up' by the use of appropriate priors. This should then enhance forecast performance whilst avoiding the usual trade-off between over parameterising the VAR and the arbitrariness associated with restricting lag lengths or excluding variables.

Briefly the Bayesian approach assumes some non-sample or prior information is available in terms of a prior density function $g(\xi)$ for the vector of parameters of interest ξ. Additionally it is assumed that the information in the observed sample, conditional on the value of this vector ξ, is given by some density function, $f(\mathbf{y} \mid \xi)$, say. Bayes' theorem can then be applied to give:

$$g(\xi \mid \mathbf{y}) = f(\mathbf{y} \mid \xi) g(\xi) / f(\mathbf{y})$$

where $f(\mathbf{y})$ is the unconditional sample density. This expresses the posterior distribution for ξ as a function of the conditional distribution of the sample information and the prior distribution of the vector ξ. Note that for any particular sample the unconditional density $f(\mathbf{y})$ will just appear as a constant. The posterior distribution $g(\xi \mid \mathbf{y})$ is then available as a basis for inference on the vector ξ.

In the case of a VAR model the above framework is implemented by specifying two equations, one consisting of the autoregressive specification, and the other describing the evolution of the coefficients:

$$\mathbf{x}_t = a_t(L)\mathbf{x}_{t-1} + f_t(L)\mathbf{d}_t + \boldsymbol{\varepsilon}_t \tag{3.27}$$

$$\boldsymbol{\psi}_t = G\boldsymbol{\psi}_{t-1} + F\bar{\boldsymbol{\psi}} + \mathbf{u}_t \tag{3.28}$$

where $\boldsymbol{\psi}$ is $\mathrm{vec}(a_t(L), f_t(L))$, assumed to have unconditional mean $\bar{\boldsymbol{\psi}}$, G and F are matrices of appropriate dimension, and $\mathbf{u}_t$ is a white noise process with covariance matrix Ω_t. The specification (eqn 3.28) allows for quite general behaviour in the evolution of the coefficients of the VAR (eqn 3.27): in particular if $G = I$, $F = 0$ and $\Omega_t = 0$ then the VAR coefficients are constants; $G = 0$, $F = I$ implies the coefficients are randomly distributed about their mean levels; $F = 0$ and $G = I$ gives random walk coefficients. The conditional distribution of the vector of parameters is then governed by an assumption about the distribution of the $\mathbf{u}_t$ (e.g. normality). Of course the formulation (eqn 3.27–eqn 3.28) so far involves an increase in the number of parameters. The reduction in the number of parameters to be estimated is then achieved by assuming that the prior or non-sample information is such that the unknowns in eqns 3.25 and 3.26 (that is the matrices $G, F, \Omega_0, \bar{\boldsymbol{\psi}}$, and the law of motion relating Ω_t to Ω_{t-1}) depend upon a smaller vector of parameters ξ. The advantage of this approach over imposing restrictions directly on the structural form parameters is that the probabilistic structure of the Bayesian framework allows an evolution of the parameters, governed by some underlying hyperparameters, so that the initial restrictions can be 'looser' relative to, say, zero restrictions on the structural form.

One specification could be $G = \xi_0 I$, $F = I - G$, so that the coefficients revert to the mean (at a rate governed by ξ_0), the mean $\bar{\boldsymbol{\psi}}$ is given by specifying the known first lag coefficients in $a(L)$ as 1 and all others as 0. The matrices Ω_0 and the relation between Ω_t and Ω_0 are also to be specified in terms of further ξ_i parameters. This specification is then determined by the low dimensional vector ξ. There is still great freedom for the parameters of the VAR to evolve as the data requires. The zero reversion prior forces parameters that are not strongly drawn away from zero to 'shrink' back to zero, so that the Bayesian formulation then incorporates the usual technique of excluding variables from the equations of an econometric model whenever the coefficients are deemed to be statistically insignificant. This exclusion procedure is often felt to improve estimation and forecasting performance of models, and the prior set out above attempts to mimic this process in a Bayesian framework.

The unknown parameters of the model are the vector ξ with a given posterior distribution function. This can then be interpreted as a likelihood function and optimised over the parameters ξ using, for example, Kalman filter techniques. Note that the Bayesian technique is not affected by the presence of non-stationary variables. Inference is via the likelihood function, which with the assumption of normality of the error processes is then conditional only on the sample and priors. No asymptotic distributional problems arise. However the presence of integrated or cointegrated variables may have a strong influence on the types of prior that are admissible, and problems may easily arise if the priors are misspecified. There may be little overall improvement in performance if good priors are not available.

3.5 An empirical example

In this section we give an example of estimating a small VAR macromodel for the UK economy. This highlights both the application of the techniques discussed above and the pitfalls. The primary aim of building such a model is for forecasting purposes, rather than finding the impulse response functions, and this is the area on which we shall concentrate. Despite the aims of VAR modelling in providing an atheoretical framework in which to address such issues, it is clear that the judgement of the econometrician/modeller becomes involved at the outset in the choice of variables to be included and the transformations (if any) of these variables that are thought to be appropriate for forecasting. In the context of a macromodel this is a particularly sensitive decision because the issue of cointegration will obviously be to the fore, and choosing to include, say, real variables has implicitly imposed a $(1, -1)$ cointegrating vector with the price deflator. Restrictions of this sort may be felt to be required in a sensible model of the economy, but note that we are already straying from the pure atheoretical approach. Even if we do not wish to impose such transformations on the data it is difficult for the econometrician's judgement not to become intertwined in the modelling process. The constraints of computing technology means that we must restrict the dimensions of any VAR that we estimate. This will usually mean the inclusion of at most those variables felt to be important for the modelling purpose. The availability of a sufficient time series of data will also constrain the possible length of the VAR to be estimated.

For the purpose of illustration we investigate a VAR on quarterly data from 1965q3 to 1992q1 including the log of gross domestic product (GDP), the log of consumption, the log of investment, the log of the GDP deflator, the log of sterling M4, the unemployment rate and the real short interest rates (defined as the short interest rate minus the quarterly inflation rate), all expressed at annual rates, and, finally, the spread (i.e. difference) between short and long nominal interest rates. We separate the analysis into several stages for expositional ease. In principle some of the steps can be combined and the number of estimations performed reduced. Stationarity tests indicate that GDP, consumption, investment and the unemployment rate can be treated as $I(1)$ variables, although note that these are not unambiguous results. The GDP deflator and M4 qualify as $I(2)$ – they were transformed to $I(1)$ variables by differencing and forming the ratio (log) of real M4. Cointegration analysis was then carried out on these seven $I(1)$ variables, including quarterly dummies, the short real interest rate, the spread between short and long interest rates and a dummy for the post-1979 period as additional $I(0)$ variables. The dummy allows for a change in the operation of macro-economic policy after 1979, reflecting the emergence of monetary aggregate targeting. This analysis essentially estimates a VAR such as eqn 3.12 and looks at the rank of the estimated matrix A in eqn 3.12, which, as noted there, has rank r if there are r cointegrating vectors. We restrict the lag length of the VAR to 1. Although statistical criteria may favour the use of additional lags, the computational and expositional burdens associated with the longer lag structure favour parsimony. Table 3.1 reports Johansen maximum likelihood statistics for the null of $\leqslant r$ cointegrating vectors against the alternative of precisely r cointegrating vectors using the maximal eigenvalue method, or the alternative of $\geqslant r$ cointegrating vectors for the test based on the trace. Table 3.1(a) reports the tests based on the maximal eigenvalue, and Table 3.1(b) reports statistics based on the trace (see Pesaran and Pesaran (1992) for details of the calculations involved). For the maximal eigenvalue test we accept $r = 4$ at the 95% level. For tests based on the trace we accept $r \leqslant 4$ and reject $r \leqslant 3$ at the 95% level. In both cases we can reject $r \geqslant 5$ and accept all values of r less than 4 at 95% levels. The conclusion is obviously to accept $r = 4$, although the statistical tests for the number of cointegrating vectors, and the cointegrating vectors themselves, are quite sensitive to the specification, the presence or absence of dummies (and because we are working with seasonally adjusted data the presence of quarterly dummies is not inevitable *a priori*). As all subsequent hypothesis testing is strictly only conditional on this assessment, the unconditional power and size of future tests may be distorted. Note also that the inclusion of such variables as the short–long interest rate spread embodies the assumption of cointegration of short and long interest rates if these are deemed to be $I(1)$ variables. The estimated normalised cointegrating vectors for $r = 4$ are reported in Table 3.2. In general, these cointegrating vectors do not have direct structural interpretations, being arbitrary linear combinations of the underlying structural equilibrium relationships. However vector 1 clearly links inflation and the rate of growth of sterling M4, and links between GDP and consumption and GDP and

Table 3.1 Cointegration tests

Null	Alternative	Statistic	95% critical value	90% critical value
Results based on the maximal eigenvalue of the stochastic matrix				
$r = 0$	$r = 1$	–	45.2770	42.3170
$r \leqslant 1$	$r = 2$	101.3612	39.3720	36.7620
$r \leqslant 2$	$r = 3$	44.5181	33.4610	30.9000
$r \leqslant 3$	$r = 4$	34.0684	27.0670	24.7340
$r \leqslant 4$	$r = 5$	11.0227	20.9670	18.5980
$r \leqslant 5$	$r = 6$	6.0304	14.0690	12.0710
$r \leqslant 6$	$r = 7$	0.0636	3.7620	2.6870
Results based on trace of the stochastic matrix				
$r = 0$	$r \geqslant 1$	–	124.2430	118.5000
$r \leqslant 1$	$r \geqslant 2$	197.0644	94.1550	89.4830
$r \leqslant 2$	$r \geqslant 3$	95.7032	68.5240	64.8430
$r \leqslant 3$	$r \geqslant 4$	51.1852	47.2100	43.9490
$r \leqslant 4$	$r \geqslant 5$	17.1167	29.6800	26.7850
$r \leqslant 5$	$r \geqslant 6$	6.0940	15.4100	13.3250
$r \leqslant 6$	$r = 7$	0.0636	3.7620	2.6870

Variables included: log(GDP), log(consumption), log(investment), Δ log(GDP deflator), Δ log(M4), log(M4/GDP deflator), unemployment rate.
Additional $I(0)$ variables: quarterly dummies, real short interest rates, post-1979 dummy, short–long interest rate spread.
Number of lags in VAR: 1.
Sample period: 1965q4–1992q1.

investment with unit coefficients are apparent in vectors 2, 3 and 4.

The VAR is then re-estimated, including the (lagged) cointegrating vectors as additional right-hand-side variables, so that the entire structure now consists of $I(0)$ variables with the cointegrating vectors embodying the long-run relationships between the non-stationary variables.

The estimated VAR together with the cointegrating vectors now forms a system that can be used to forecast the variables. We do not report the full VAR estimation to economise on space. The forecasts of the model are reported in Table 3.3, which gives first the quarterly profiles for the growth rates of the $I(1)$ variables, GDP, consumption, investment, the levels of the $I(1)$ variables Δ log(GDP deflator) and Δ log(M4) (expressed at annual rates), the level of the $I(1)$ variable unemployment, the levels of the $I(0)$ variables real short interest rates and the short–long spread, and the $I(0)$ variable growth in real M4. These are chosen as the variables of most interest. Table 3.4 reports annual averages for the same set of variables. The tables also report the ratio of consumption to GDP and investment to GDP; note that in the forecasts these sum to more than one, implying budget/trade deficits.

Table 3.2 Estimated cointegrating vectors (normalised) (results based on the Johansen likelihood procedure)

	Vector 1	Vector 2	Vector 3	Vector 4
log(GDP)	0.0000	−1.0000	−1.0000	−1.0000
log(consumption)	0.0000	0.4572	1.3017	0.9001
log(investment)	0.0000	1.0255	0.0466	0.1410
Δlog(PGDP[1])	−7.6994	2.5781	−1.8044	3.1742
Δlog(M4)	7.6994	−1.0535	−0.8217	0.0608
log(M4/PGDP)	0.0000	−0.3224	−0.2839	−0.1371
Unemployment rate	0.0000	0.0164	0.0124	0.0002

[1] PGDP = GDP deflator.
Variables included: log(GDP), log(consumption), log(investment), Δlog(GDP deflator), Δlog(M4), log(M4/GDP deflator), unemployment rate.
Additional $I(0)$ variables: quarterly dummies, real short interest rates, post-1979 dummy, short–long interest rate spread.
Number of lags in VAR: 1.
Sample period: 1965q4–1992q1.

Table 3.3 VAR forecasts (data to 92:1, forecasts thereafter)

Year:quarter	Δlog(GDP)	Δlog(cons)	Δlog(inv)	Δlog(PGDP)	Δlog(M4)
1990:1	3.09067	−0.85678	22.55402	8.86669	14.72664
1990:2	2.04735	3.40958	−0.07744	11.09276	13.81569
1990:3	−4.44603	−2.54135	−20.44106	9.52988	9.14497
1990:4	−3.10936	−2.86407	−28.89442	4.79755	7.91092
1991:1	−3.48015	−1.55525	−17.59987	4.85554	7.12700
1991:2	−3.16086	−3.90015	−8.20236	7.93571	6.34117
1991:3	0.35400	−0.13161	−3.10783	3.78399	4.80766
1991:4	−1.41335	−0.18539	−3.06129	3.49979	4.51126
1992:1	−1.77002	−2.84843	21.55838	5.84755	3.63922
1992:2	3.21882	2.97402	0.85306	3.14179	6.08347
1992:3	−0.05095	1.66463	1.01294	4.53630	7.90604
1992:4	1.61601	3.32822	2.53063	3.27581	10.32772
1993:1	3.24767	4.05947	4.99371	2.16466	10.71437
1993:2	4.48021	4.71535	11.92922	0.67517	11.44178
1993:3	3.12622	4.87754	12.74900	1.54887	12.07620
1993:4	3.48135	4.70098	8.42505	1.49109	13.56848
1994:1	4.59935	4.96927	7.85195	1.10456	13.06267
1994:2	5.04142	5.12021	11.84610	0.57661	13.08441
1994:3	3.08227	4.93553	10.42403	2.19789	13.16680
1994:4	2.93923	4.47043	4.34892	2.74985	14.20619
1995:1	3.70498	4.50162	2.79647	2.75804	13.35344

Table 3.3 continued

Year:quarter	Δ log(GDP)	Δ log(cons)	Δ log(inv)	Δ log(PGDP)	Δ log(M4)
1995:2	3.94105	4.47447	6.44944	2.44488	13.09716
1995:3	1.89536	4.16205	5.20797	4.11500	12.97032
1995:4	1.76572	3.62232	−0.32640	4.59010	13.85350
1996:1	2.61608	3.62655	−1.11459	4.42818	12.89380
1996:2	2.98499	3.61599	3.40495	3.88621	12.57216
1996:3	1.09912	3.35603	3.04065	5.29643	12.41654
1996:4	1.13958	2.89658	−1.67269	5.50369	13.30142

Year:quarter	Real short	Real M4 growth	Spread	Unemployment
1990:1	6.27331	5.86014	−3.84000	5.65740
1990:2	3.75724	2.72293	−4.20000	5.65050
1990:3	5.23012	−0.38490	−3.56000	5.80760
1990:4	8.70245	3.11317	−3.06000	6.24050
1991:1	7.04446	2.27165	−1.88000	7.02100
1991:2	3.10429	−1.59454	−0.78000	7.88950
1991:3	6.15601	1.02348	−0.28000	8.54330
1991:4	6.95021	1.01166	−0.69000	8.93730
1992:1	4.63245	−2.20833	−0.53000	9.34360
1992:2	6.64217	2.94169	0.01231	9.77785
1992:3	4.66213	3.36973	−0.24143	10.06552
1992:4	5.90489	7.05189	−0.52395	10.27485
1993:1	6.23031	8.54972	−0.21439	10.38303
1993:2	7.69689	10.76662	−0.08997	10.48182
1993:3	7.14222	10.52731	−0.69468	10.44903
1993:4	7.76867	12.07738	−1.25377	10.35400
1994:1	7.84466	11.95813	−1.16893	10.18237
1994:2	8.66105	12.50781	−1.14658	10.05264
1994:3	7.55109	10.96889	−1.76324	9.84919
1994:4	7.64661	11.45634	−2.25162	9.64694
1995:1	7.32111	10.59542	−2.03845	9.42703
1995:2	7.84964	10.65229	−1.85187	9.30181
1995:3	6.57261	8.85530	−2.28835	9.14580
1995:4	6.59862	9.26340	−2.59728	9.02352
1996:1	6.28376	8.46564	−2.21760	8.90538
1996:2	6.88027	8.68595	−1.88584	8.89397
1996:3	5.71013	7.12009	−2.20317	8.85526
1996:4	5.86528	7.79772	−2.42081	8.84681

Table 3.3 continued

Year:quarter	con/GDP[1]	inv/GDP[1]
1990:1	75.97209	23.13331
1990:2	76.23126	23.01075
1990:3	76.59512	22.10876
1990:4	76.64210	20.72853
1991:1	77.01181	20.00960
1991:2	76.86961	19.75898
1991:3	76.77634	19.58871
1991:4	77.01240	19.50818
1992:1	76.80505	20.67974
1992:2	76.75804	20.55779
1992:3	77.08801	20.61256
1992:4	77.41866	20.65974
1993:1	77.57594	20.75011
1993:2	77.62152	21.14015
1993:3	77.96219	21.65489
1993:4	78.20026	21.92418
1994:1	78.27263	22.10320
1994:2	78.28801	22.48242
1994:3	78.65155	22.89888
1994:4	78.95321	22.97972
1995:1	79.11066	22.92760
1995:2	79.21620	23.07184
1995:3	79.66637	23.26368
1995:4	80.03701	23.14231
1996:1	80.23939	22.92749
1996:2	80.36605	22.95155
1996:3	80.82083	23.06323
1996:4	81.17663	22.90168

[1] con/GDP and inv/GDP are consumption as a percentage of GDP and investment as a percentage of GDP, respectively.

Table 3.4   Annual averages, data to 92:1, forecasts thereafter

Year	$\Delta\log(\text{GDP})$	$\Delta\log(\text{cons})$	$\Delta\log(\text{inv})$	$\Delta\log(\text{PGDP})$	$\Delta\log(\text{M4})$
1990	−0.60434	−0.71316	−6.71473	8.57172	11.39956
1991	−1.92509	−1.44310	−7.99284	5.01876	5.69677
1992	0.75346	1.27961	6.48875	4.20036	6.98911
1993	3.58386	4.58834	9.52424	1.46995	11.95021
1994	3.91557	4.87386	8.61775	1.65723	13.38002
1995	2.82678	4.19012	3.53187	3.47700	13.31861
1996	1.95994	3.37379	0.91458	4.77863	12.79598

Year	Real short	Real M4 growth	Spread	Unemployment
1990	5.99078	2.82784	−3.66500	5.83900
1991	5.81374	0.67806	−0.90750	8.09777
1992	5.46041	2.78875	−0.32077	9.86545
1993	7.20952	10.48026	−0.56320	10.41697
1994	7.92585	11.72279	−1.58259	9.93278
1995	7.08549	9.84160	−2.19399	9.22454
1996	6.18486	8.01735	−2.18186	8.87535

Year	con/GDP[1]	inv/GDP[1]
1990	76.36014	22.24534
1991	76.91754	19.71637
1992	77.01744	20.62746
1993	77.83997	21.36733
1994	78.54135	22.61605
1995	79.50756	23.10136
1996	80.65073	22.96099

[1] con/GDP and inv/CDP are consumption as a percentage of GDP and investment as a percentage of GDP, respectively.

Notes

1. This has the implication that all of the variables are stationary. If there were $I(1)$ variables then $a(L)$ would have roots on the unit circle. We deal with this case in Section 3.3.
2. In the present discussion we are assuming that all of the $\mathbf{x}_t$ variables are stationary. In Blanchard's model, however, some of the variables are non-stationary. Before carrying out the analysis described here, therefore, he makes them stationary by taking first differences.
3. It may be noted that in general the triangular orthogonalisation (or orthonormalisation) case of making $E(\varepsilon_t\varepsilon_t')$ diagonal and restricting R to have unit elements on the leading diagonal, is equivalent to setting $E(\varepsilon_t\varepsilon_t') = I$ and leaving the leading diagonal of R unrestricted.

4. In effect King *et al.* obtain these additional restrictions by constraining γ. In practice they obtain γ from co-integrating regressions estimates that embody *a priori* restrictions. The method proposed here is based on unrestricted estimates of the cointegrating vectors.

5. This particular choice of J is purely for convenience. Any linear transformation of the $\mathbf{e}_t$ of rank r for which rank $(W) = n$ will suffice.

6. It may be noted that $f(1) = [F, 0] = [\gamma P, 0] = c(1)W^{-1}$, so that $f(1)W = \gamma \theta'$.

7. It is shown in Wickens (1993) that as a result of the non-uniqueness (or lack of identifiability) of α and β they cannot in general be given an economic interpretation. There are certain circumstances when they can and this in effect involves choosing A appropriately. See Wickens (1993) for further discussion.

8. It is shown in Wickens (1993) that as a result of the non-uniqueness (or lack of identifiability) of α and β they cannot in general be given an economic interpretation. There are, however, certain circumstances when they can and this can be done by restricting the loading matrix. In effect, this is equivalent to choosing A appropriately.

9. If one were to start with a structural model instead of a VAR none of these identification problems would arise. This, of course, assumes away the very problem that VAR analysis seeks to overcome, namely that the identifying restrictions are thought to be 'incredible'.

4 | Measuring and forecasting underlying economic activity

Anthony Garratt, Stephen Hall and *Brian Henry*

4.1   Introduction

The measurement of underlying economic activity is an issue with a long history. The original work was carried out by Mitchell and Burns in 1938 (Mitchell and Burns, 1938; Burns and Mitchell, 1946) at the National Bureau of Economic Research (NBER) where lists of leading, coincident and lagging indicators were developed. This work was, much later (in 1975), replicated in the United Kingdom where the Central Statistical Office (CSO) produces and publishes a set of lagged, coincident and leading economic indicators. Despite the importance attached to coincident and other leading indicators in both the United States and the United Kingdom, the methodology of constructing such series has remained unchanged since the early 1970s. In this chapter, we adopt a new methodology of constructing coincident and leading economic indicators suggested by Stock and Watson (1988a,b, 1991) and provide an empirical application to the United Kingdom. The application modifies Stock and Watson (1988a, 1991) by allowing for cointegration between a set of variables. Stock and Watson use a state space form and the Kalman filter as a framework in which an optimal estimate of an unobserved component may be derived from a set of observed indicator variables. The unobserved component forms the measure of underlying economic activity or coincident indicator.

The method adopted by the CSO in the United Kingdom, for example, is a rather mechanical approach, the econometric foundations for which are unclear. The first step taken is to de-trend each series in the group using a 5-year moving average process. Each de-trended series is then re-scaled so that all series in the group have the same average amplitude. The component series, thus adjusted, are averaged in a composite series with a weight of 3 on GDP and 1 for the other four variables (Table 4.A1 in the Appendix (page 67) lists the component series of CSO indicator variables). It should also be noted that the underlying series are each seasonally adjusted before the adjustments noted above are applied. Where the series is not already adjusted, this adjustment is done using the US Bureau of Census X-11 procedure (Lomax, 1983).

These indicators have had a major influence on the timing and conduct of macro-economic policy in both the United States and the United Kingdom. The most influential of the indicators is the coincident indicator, which measures current economic activity. The intuition of such a measure is that while we have many macro-economic series to measure the level of economic activity, they are all subject to distortion and measurement error, and no single measure summarises the whole economy adequately. Hence, the coincident indicator combines a range of economic series together to give, in some sense, a better measure of overall economic activity. Leading economic indicators, as constructed by the CSO, are similar in that the component variables are thought to contain information on the future level of economic activity.

In Section 4.2 we describe the Stock and Watson framework and, in Section 4.3, we provide a modification that allows for cointegration between the variables used to derive the unobserved component. Section 4.4 applies the modified Stock and Watson technique to the problem of forming an indicator of underlying economic activity using the same variables as the CSO for the United Kingdom. Section 4.5 forecasts two versions of the constructed variables, using the CSO longer leading indicator variables plus finance spread variables proposed by Stock and Watson, constructing an alternative leading economic indicator to that of the CSO. Section 4.6 concludes.

4.2 The Stock and Watson approach

Stock and Watson (1988b, 1991) view the problem of identifying a concurrent economic indicator as one of extracting a common component from a set of series. Let $\mathbf{X}_t$ denote an $n \times 1$ vector of economic series that are assumed to contain some information about the underlying performance of the economy, S_t. Define a set of measurement equations of the form:

$$\mathbf{X}_t = \beta + \gamma S_t + v_t \tag{4.1}$$

where the same S variable affects each of the observed variables with different weights and the final term v is an idiosyncratic term, which captures all movements in $\mathbf{X}$ not associated with S. The model is then completed by specifying the following two state equations:

$$\zeta(L)S_t = \delta + \varepsilon_t \tag{4.2}$$

and[1]

$$\xi(L)v_t = \omega_t \tag{4.3}$$

The term δ represents a growth term in the state equation and will accommodate any deterministic trend.[2]

The above model will filter any common information from the X variables into S and all remaining variation in X will be relegated to the idiosyncratic effect. This model is in fact the generic one that Stock and Watson outline. However, the model they implement states the measurement equations in first differences and, therefore, the state variables are implicitly estimated as changes in the underlying series. Stock and Watson's argument for using first differences is that all their X series are integrated ($I(1)$) series with no cointegrating vector between them. Under these conditions, we would expect to find n independent stochastic trends underlying the data, and a reformulation into first differences is appropriate. The complete model is then estimated in this form and the S variable is recovered.

Using first differences, however, leaves certain questions unanswered. How should the model be specified when some of the variables are, in fact, cointegrated or when some of the variables are stationary? If none of the variables are cointegrated, to what extent can we be confident that there really is an underlying series that is driving them all? In particular, if the n series are driven by n separate stochastic trends and thus have no long-run movement in common, the association of any emerging state variable with underlying economic activity may be tenuous.

In the next section we discuss briefly the relationship between cointegration and the moving average representation that identifies common stochastic trends. Then it is shown how the general moving average representation may be put into state space form and conclude that this is a generalisation of the framework used by Stock and Watson.

4.3 Stochastic trends and cointegration

4.3.1 Error correction and moving average representations

There is an important duality between cointegration within a set of variables (X) and the number of stochastic trends that underlie them. If we state the reduced form error correction model as:

$$B(L)\Delta X_t = \alpha\beta' X_{t-k} + \varepsilon_t \tag{4.4}$$

where the dimensions of α and β are $n \times r$, where n is the number of variables in X and r is the number of cointegrating vectors (Johansen, 1988), providing $B(L)$ has no roots within the unit circle, this model may also be expressed as:

$$\Delta X_t = C(L)\varepsilon_t \tag{4.5}$$

a moving average representation (see Engle and Granger (1987) or Engle and Yoo (1991)). We may then decompose $C(L)$ into:

$$C(L) = C(1) + C^*(L) \tag{4.6}$$

so that $C(1)$ contains the components that have a permanent effect on the level of X while $C^*(L)$ contains the transient components and:

$$C(1) = \gamma\theta', \quad C(1)\gamma = 0, \quad \theta'C(1) = 0 \tag{4.7}$$

where γ, θ are $n \times (n - r)$ and so eqn 4.5 may be restated as:

$$\Delta x_t = C(1)\varepsilon_t + C^*(L)\Delta\varepsilon_t \tag{4.8}$$

According to eqn 4.8, given r co-integrating vectors, this implies $n - r$ common stochastic trends. Identifying the long run shocks requires imposing restrictions on the $C(1)$ matrix and imposing the correct number of stochastic trends is a crucial part of this procedure (see Robertson and Wickens (1992) for a complete description of the identification problem). When specifying either the vector error correction form (eqn 4.4) or the moving average form (eqn 4.5) it is important to impose the correct number of cointegrating vectors or stochastic trends. If the estimated error correction form is unrestricted, the estimation will be consistent but not fully efficient while, if the levels terms are omitted or inappropriately restricted, the model will be misspecified and the estimates themselves will no longer be consistent. In the moving average form, if the model allows for the inclusion of n unrestricted stochastic trends, then identification will be difficult. However, if more than $n - r$ stochastic trends are suppressed, the model will be misspecified.

4.3.2   A state space formation

An alternative to either eqn 4.4 or eqn 4.5 is to formulate the model in state space. It should be emphasised that this is simply another representation and, hence, has no general priority, but in some cases it is possible to impose sensible prior restrictions more easily when the model is formulated this way. In particular, when dealing with a set of integrated variables that include cointegrating relationships, it is often simpler to see how such restrictions may be imposed.

An exact state space representation of eqn 4.5 may then be given as follows, where the measurement equation is given by:

$$\mathbf{X}_t = AS_t^1 + BS_t^2 + \mathbf{U}_t \tag{4.9}$$

where $\mathbf{X}_t$ is the vector of n observed variables, both S^1 and S^2 are sets of state variables and $\mathbf{U}_t$ is the vector of error terms normally distributed, $N \sim (0, W)$, where the covariance matrix W is usually assumed to be diagonal. In eqn 4.9 the A matrix will be $n \times (n - r)$ and S^1 will be an $(n - r) \times 1$ matrix (r being the number of co-integrating vectors) and will have the following form:

$$S_{it}^1 = S_{it-1}^1 + \delta_i + \varepsilon_i \quad i = 1, n - r \tag{4.10}$$

The S^2 state variables in turn consist of n sets of equations of the following form:

$$S_{j1t}^2 = \omega_{jt} \quad j = 1, \ldots, n$$
$$S_{jk,t}^2 = S_{jk-1,t-1} \quad k = 2, \ldots, p \tag{4.11}$$

where p is the lag depth associated with C^* in eqn 4.5. The error terms in eqns 4.10 and 4.11 have a covariance matrix Q, which is usually assumed to be diagonal. Here the S^1

variables give the long-run effect on X and they represent the common stochastic trends; hence, there are $n - r$ of them, and a deterministic trend component is allowed for. The S^2 variables are the transitory effects and are equivalent to the C^* matrix in eqn 4.5. There are suitable dimensioned covariance matrices for the error terms in eqns 4.7 and 4.8.

In this formulation the specification of the A matrix allows us to impose prior restrictions on the way the stochastic trends affect the X variables. Consider the case of n stochastic trends. If A is a completely unrestricted $n \times n$ matrix, it will not generally be possible to identify the common trends. At the very least, A must be triangular so that the trends are uniquely determined. However, the form of the triangularisation will affect the estimates of the trends and hence the way we interpret them. For example, if A is lower triangular, then S_1^1 will be associated with X_1, while X_2 will be represented by a combination of S_1^1 and S_2^2 and so on. If the A matrix is diagonal, then one variable is uniquely associated with each trend and there are no interactions between the variables. The advantage of the state space form is that we are clearly able to specify the A matrix (as well as the other matrices) in order to bring out particular aspects of the underlying stochastic trend processes.

As an explicit example of the form of the A matrix, we take the case for $n = 5$. The general case is where there is no cointegration between the series and they are all $I(1)$, the form of the A matrix will then be:

$$
\begin{pmatrix}
1 & 0 & 0 & 0 & 0 \\
a_{21} & 1 & 0 & 0 & 0 \\
a_{31} & a_{32} & 1 & 0 & 0 \\
a_{41} & a_{42} & a_{43} & 1 & 0 \\
a_{51} & a_{52} & a_{53} & a_{54} & 1
\end{pmatrix}
\tag{4.12}
$$

The unit leading diagonal is simply a normalisation restriction. It will cause S_i to be scaled conformably with X_i. Because the full lower triangle of the matrix is non-zero, there are no restrictions on the form of interrelationships between the stochastic trends. However, the choice of the order of the X variables will affect the numerical estimates of the trends, given the diagonal nature of A.

The other extreme case is where there are four co-integrating vectors, hence there is only one stochastic trend. The A matrix would then have the following form:

$$
\begin{pmatrix}
1 \\
a_{21} \\
a_{31} \\
a_{41} \\
a_{51}
\end{pmatrix}
\tag{4.13}
$$

As before, we have the arbitrary normalisation that S^1 will be scaled conformably with X_1 and the one stochastic trend now drives all of the X variables. An intermediate case, where X_1 cointegrates with X_2 can be stated as follows:

$$\begin{pmatrix} 1 & 0 & 0 & 0 \\ a_{21} & 0 & 0 & 0 \\ a_{31} & 1 & 0 & 0 \\ a_{41} & a_{42} & 1 & 0 \\ a_{51} & a_{52} & a_{53} & 1 \end{pmatrix} \tag{4.14}$$

There are basically two ways to reduce the number of stochastic trends within the state space form. The first is, as above, to reduce the number of variables in the S^1 set. The other way is to keep the number of state variables constant but to impose a zero error on one of the state equations in eqn 4.10. This is done by imposing a zero variance on the appropriate error term in eqn 4.10. The state variable then ceases to be a random walk and becomes a constant.

Having set up the general state space form, we can illustrate the special case that gives rise to the general Stock and Watson model and which will be our point of departure in the next section. In the Stock and Watson model given in eqns 4.1 to 4.3, there is only one stochastic trend, and so the A matrix equivalent to this case is given by eqn 4.13. In their application, Stock and Watson express eqns 4.1 and 4.2 in first differences; this is equivalent to specifying the following A matrix:

$$\begin{pmatrix} 1 & 0 & 0 & 0 & 0 \\ a_{21} & 1 & 0 & 0 & 0 \\ a_{31} & 0 & 1 & 0 & 0 \\ a_{41} & 0 & 0 & 1 & 0 \\ a_{51} & 0 & 0 & 0 & 1 \end{pmatrix} \tag{4.15}$$

The above matrix implies that there are n stochastic trends in the model, one of which has some connection with all the series but the others each operate in isolation. In effect, we are interested in an estimate of the common stochastic trend, the first state variable in the S^1 vector, but we have to include the others because there is potentially no cointegration between the variables. Equations 4.1 to 4.3, if specified in levels, imply that there are $n - 1$ cointegrating vectors, while if specified in first differences the implication is that there are n stochastic trends and no cointegrating vectors. The advantage of the specification in eqn 4.15 is that it allows the intermediate cases to be investigated by placing restrictions on the A matrix, or more easily by restricting the covariance matrix of eqn 4.10, matrix Q.

The model outlined in eqns 4.9 to 4.10 with the restricted A matrix given in eqn 4.15 provides us with a starting point for our specification search in the next section when we apply the model to UK data.

4.4 Construction of a new coincident index

The objective of this empirical application is to construct an alternative composite coincident index to that of the CSO using the adapted technique of Stock and Watson (1988a,b, 1991) described in the previous section.

4.4.1 Time series properties of the CSO variables

For a direct comparison, the vector of indicator variables used is the same as those used by the CSO and comprises the following: GDP average income at factor cost 1985 = 100 (GDP); output of the production industries 1985 = 100 (IP); Confederation of British Industry (CBI) quarterly survey of below capacity utilisation in percentage terms (CBICU); the volume of Retail Sales 1985 = 100 (RES); CBI quarterly survey of expected change in stocks of raw materials in percentage balance terms (CBIRM).

The five variables used by the CSO fall broadly into two categories (see Figures 4.1 to 4.3). First, a trended, non-stationary group GDP, IP and RES (in all that follows natural logs are used for these variables). Second, the CBI variables CBICU and CBIRM, which have no obvious trend and are possibly a stationary process with large variance. Table 4.1 reports DF, ADF(4) and the likelihood ratio test from the Johansen procedure when applied to each variable in turn. The first group of variables is $I(1)$ where the critical values on the ADF(4) is -2.89 and for the Johansen statistic is 3.76. The second group is confirmed as $I(0)$ but have large variances.

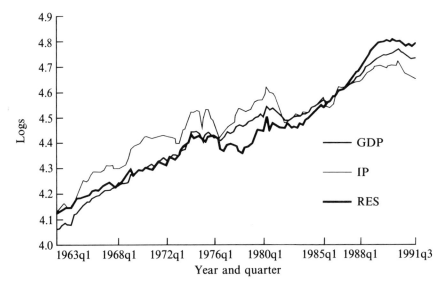

Figure 4.1 CSO trended component variables

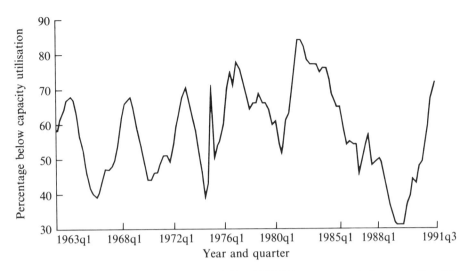

Figure 4.2   CSO stationary component variables (CBICU, percentage below capacity utilisation)

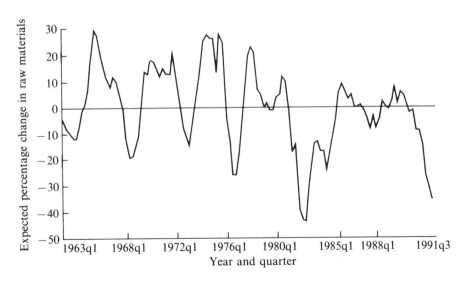

Figure 4.3   CSO stationary component variable (CBIRM, expected percentage change in raw materials)

Table 4.1 Orders of integration for coincident variables

	Levels			First difference		
	DF	ADF(4)	John	DF	ADF(4)	John
GDP	-2.07	-1.27	2.03	-10.77	-4.72	26.99
IP	-2.25	-1.61	2.58	-10.84	-5.32	35.08
RES	-0.51	-0.18	0.09	-15.08	-4.35	20.05
CBICU	-2.63	-3.56	12.05	-9.39	-4.64	22.80
CBIRM	-2.38	-3.69	22.32	-7.45	-7.19	39.24

Sample period 1963q1 to 1991q3.
Dickey–Fuller (DF), Augmented Dickey–Fuller (ADF) and Johansen (John) statistics.

The three $I(1)$ variables – GDP, IP and RES – may be combined in one cointegrating vector (likelihood ratio test of 51.31, versus critical value of 34.91) or two when a restricted constant is included (likelihood ratio tests of 51.36 and 21.86, second critical value of 19.96). The presence of two cointegration vectors implies that in fact there is one common stochastic trend between the three $I(1)$ variables. As highlighted, the procedure adopted is able to accommodate a variety of relationships between the variables of interest by allowing a separate stochastic process for each variable (via the transition equation) or, as in this case a common trend between the variables.

4.5 Constructing different measures of economic activity

Adopting the procedure outlined in the previous section, we start from an unrestricted version (combined with various identifying assumptions) where all five variables are included and proceed to a number of restricted forms. This highlights the effects on the resulting measure of economic activity of taking account of the differing orders of integration of the component variables and the relationships between them. Two different measures of economic activity are derived. The first from the unrestricted form where all five variables are used (case 1 in Table 4.2), which is highly cyclical; the second, where only trended variables are used (case 6 in Table 4.2) resulting in a very strongly trended series.

In what follows in cases 1 to 6, we use a restricted version of the state space form described in eqns 4.9, 4.10 and 4.11. The B matrix in eqn 4.9 is implicitly set to zero such that no dynamics are included in the measurement equation.[3] The restrictions imposed on the system are implemented via the A and Q matrix, where the Q matrix describes the covariance matrix of the error terms ε_i from eqn 4.10. The dimensions of S^1 are in this case (5×1), as we chose (in the first instance) not to impose the cointegrating

Table 4.2 Results of the Kalman filter procedure

	Unrestricted to restricted					
	Case 1	Case 2	Case 3	Case 4	Case 5	Case 6
g	0.001	0.001	0.001	0.001	0.001	0.001
GDP a_{11}	1.00	1.00	1.00	1.00	1.00	1.00
IP a_{21}	0.33	0.22	0.18	0.17	0.23	1.00
	(1.25)	(2.49)	(5.49)	(6.21)	(3.74)	
RES a_{31}	0.23	0.18	0.16	0.16	0.18	1.00
	(1.42)	(2.15)	(7.28)	(8.06)	(4.33)	
CBICU a_{41}	0.001	0.000	0.007	0.000	0.000	0.000
	E-03		(0.002)			
CBIRM a_{51}	2.82	4.30	3.61	3.63	0.00	0.00
	(2.93)	(13.57)	(0.86)	(1.76)		

t-statistics in parenthesis. Sample period 1963q1–1991q3. g is the constant term from the first state equation representing the basic growth of the economy.

relationship identified above but allow the various stochastic trends to be estimated in their most unrestricted form. The A matrix used is given in eqn 4.15 where the diagonal of ones represents a normalisation (in the case of the first element of the A matrix diagonal this corresponds to the measurement for GDP) of the parameters attached to the stochastic trends for each of the variables. With the exception of GDP, each variable via the measurement equations has a common trend component with varying weights (a_{21} through to a_{51}), which represents the measure of underlying economic activity, plus a separate stochastic trend, which becomes a deterministic constant if the variance attached to the error term of the process is set to or is estimated to be zero. In addition, we set the first element in the covariance matrix of the error term U_t in eqn 4.9 equal to 1, which has the effect of concentrating the likelihood function. Finally, we allow for an estimated growth term in the measurement equation for GDP, denoted by g in Table 4.2.

Table 4.2 describes the results starting from the unrestricted form in case 1 and proceeding to the most restricted form in case 6. The interim results (cases 2 to 5) either follow from the estimation, in that the parameters that are insignificantly different from zero are imposed as such, or the variance terms of the errors from the state equations (diagonal of the Q matrix) are set to zero imposing a deterministic constant rather than a stochastic trend.

In case 1, which forms the basis of the first of our measures of economic activity, the coefficients on the common trend indicate a relatively low weight attached to industrial production and retail sales ($a_{21} = 0.326$ and $a_{31} = 0.227$) whilst the coefficient on the CBIRM term appears to be large ($a_{51} = 2.815$) and significant compared with the coefficient on the CBICU variable, which is insignificantly different from zero. The variance of the error terms from the state equations is low for the three trended series whose profiles are relatively smooth, but high for the more cyclical CBI terms. As a result of the estimation, the Kalman filter has constructed the unobserved component (the common trend) therefore producing our measure of underlying economic activity, which we refer to as C1. This corresponds to the first state vector of the system. Figure 4.4 plots a scaled up version (absolute terms are not directly comparable so we multiply by 20) of the new measure and compares it with the concurrent coincident index produced by the CSO. This illustrates that we can, in fact, produce a similar although not identical index to that of the CSO, where the movements appear to approximate those of the CSO index, with the exception of 1977 and the downturn in 1990–1, which happens sooner according to the new index. Figure 4.5 plots the new coincident index along with the log of GDP. The graph highlights that, although very volatile, there is an upward trend in the new index. In case 2, the coefficient on the common trend in the CBICU equation is restricted to be zero and the result is to induce greater volatility into the series measuring economic activity. The weight on the common trend in the CBIRM equation in case 2 increases from 2.8 to 4.3.

In cases 3 through to 6 the crucial difference is the restriction to zero of the variance of the error terms in the stochastic components associated with the industrial production and retail sales. This amounts to imposing the cointegrating restriction identified above and results in a strongly trended measure of underlying economic activity. In case 6, we also impose unit coefficients for the weights on the common trend for the variables GDP, IP and RES, and zero coefficients on the CBI terms. The measure of economic activity derived from case 6 (C6) forms the second of the variables forecast in the next section. Figure 4.6 plots the levels terms of the three trended

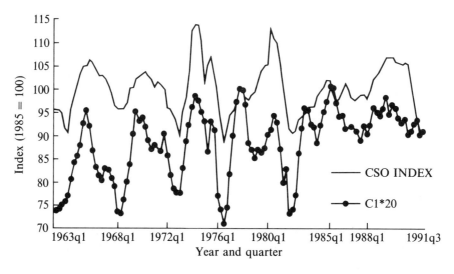

Figure 4.4 Coincident indicator: CSO versus Kalman filter

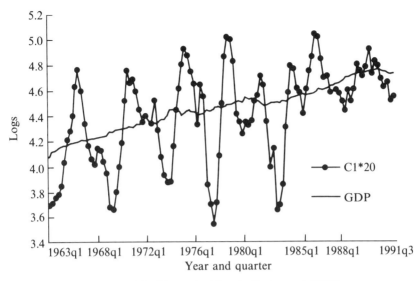

Figure 4.5   New coincident indicator and GDP

components – GDP, IP and RES – plus the resulting measure of economic activity C6. The measure is now clearly a trended variable similar to its component variables with contemporaneous movements. The percentage change in the same four series is plotted in Figure 4.7, where the volatility of the C6 measure is more pronounced than GDP but is less volatile than industrial production, although the movements are approximately contemporaneous. This is broadly what one might expect when adopting such a technique using the movements of the trended components of the CSO indicator.

The two different measures of economic activity highlight the point that it is important to consider both the time series properties and the relationship between the variables used to construct the coincident index. Stationary and non-stationary variables may be combined together to produce an index close to that of the CSO but taking account of the cointegrating relationships between the variables can alter the profile of the measure of economic activity considerably. The flexibility of the framework used here is that all possibilities can be accounted for and the relationship between variables is an empirical matter.

When assessing the measure of economic activity derived, it is important that it should not be judged in terms of how well it mimics GDP. Like the CSO indicator it is considered to be (composites of) economic and financial series (this is more relevant to the leading economic indicator to be constructed in the next section), which have a consistent timing relationship with turning points in activity. The more relevant comparison is with the CSO coincident index and the forecasting record of the leading economic indicator, which may be derived by forecasting the C1 and C6 variables.

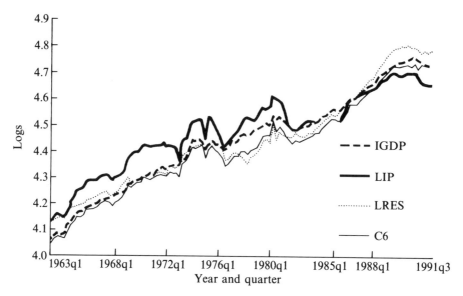

Figure 4.6   C6 and trended component variables

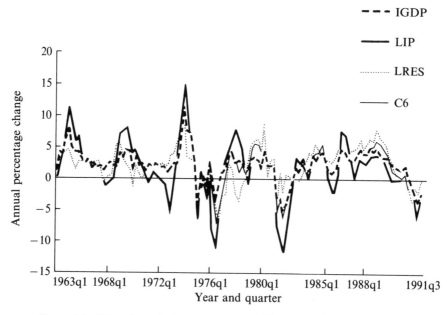

Figure 4.7   C6 and trended component variables: annual percentage change

4.5.1 Constructing a leading economic indicator

As in Stock and Watson (1988a,b, 1991), we construct a leading economic indicator (LEI) by forecasting the coincident index. We take two of the measures of economic activity from the previous section, the first being the unrestricted form (C1) in case 1 and the second the fully restricted form (C6) in case 6.

The LEI is constructed by modelling a leading set of variables (Y_t) in combination with our measures of underlying economic activity. Stock and Watson (1988a,b, 1991) undertake this using a VAR (Vector autoregression) where the order of the lag polynomials is determined empirically. We adopt a similar approach in this chapter, but an important difference is the use of an error correction term defining a long-run cointegrating relationship.[4] We introduce a preliminary stage into the process where we test a set of variables for inclusion in the cointegrating vectors. The error correction or long-run terms are then embedded in a system VAR.

4.5.2 Testing for the appropriate cointegrating vector

As a guide to the initial vector of leading variables Y_t we take the variables used by the CSO to construct their longer leading economic indicator plus two financial variables which were shown to contain useful additional information in the work of Stock and Watson (1988a,b, 1991). This choice of variables is clearly restrictive and involves priors, but is thought necessary for comparative reasons and for parsimony. The seven variables that we test in combination with the two measures of economic activity are the following: (1) financial deficit/surplus of the industrial and commercial companies divided by the GDP deflator (FINSD); (2) CBI quarterly survey changes in optimism (percentage balance, CBICO); (3) *Financial Times* actuaries 500 share index (FT500, natural logs used); (4) rate of interest, 3-month prime bank bills (R3); (5) total dwellings started in the United Kingdom (TDW, natural logs used); (6) a yield curve variable, which we define as the difference between the 20-year bond rate and the 3-month interest rate (YCUR); and (7) a variable intended to measure the quality of credit constructed as the difference between the corporate bond rate and the 20-year bond rate (CREDQ). Table 4.3 reports the DF, ADF(4) and likelihood ratio tests from the Johansen procedure when applied to each variable in turn.

The results in Table 4.3 indicate a range of orders of integration of the variables to be used. The first three variables – FINSD, FT500 and TDW – and the measure of economic activity C6 all appear to be $I(1)$, the other variables are mostly borderline $I(0)/I(1)$ with the exception of the CBICO and C1 variables, which are closer to being $I(0)$. The measure of economic activity C1 being $I(0)$ is somewhat problematic but we think this result highlights the ambiguity of the critical values as, by construction, C1 is a trended variable. In the procedure that follows, both the initial regression to test whether variables should be in the cointegrating vector and the Johansen procedure

Table 4.3 Orders of integration of leading variables

	Levels			First differences		
	DF	ADF	John	DF	ADF	John
FINSD	−2.77	−2.23	4.59	−13.34	−3.67	18.40
FT500	0.31	0.07	0.09	−6.74	−4.29	32.30
TDW	−1.94	−1.76	1.76	−9.76	−3.92	18.69
R3	−2.23	−2.85	10.48	−6.98	−4.52	22.74
CBICO	−3.15	−3.54	13.78	−10.55	−4.79	21.81
YCUR	−2.04	−2.64	5.79	−7.89	−4.09	18.15
CREDQ	−2.02	−2.33	6.42	−9.02	−4.09	19.51
C1	−2.77	−3.65	21.25	−6.75	−6.62	32.35
C6	−0.12	−0.05	0.12	−9.96	−4.12	17.38

Sample period 1969q2–1991q2.
Dickey–Fuller (DF), Augmented Dickey–Fuller (ADF) and Johansen (John) statistics.

used to calculate the vectors remain valid when applied to combinations of $I(0)$ and $I(1)$ variables.

Here we adopt the procedure proposed by Stock and Watson (1989b) to determine which variables make up the cointegrating vectors. Then we apply Johansen (1988) to estimate the vectors themselves. Using the first of our applications as an example the type of equation to be estimated may be written as:

$$CI_t = \gamma Y_t + U_{1t} \tag{4.16}$$

$$\Delta Y_t = U_{2t} \tag{4.17}$$

where U_{1t} and U_{2t} are stationary and the constant term is omitted for simplicity. As Y_t is endogenous, it is likely that $\mathrm{Cov}(Y_t, U_{1t})$ is not equal to zero. In this case, γ will be biased (although consistent) in any finite sample. Therefore, any test statistic on γ must take account of this bias. Rewriting eqns 4.16 and 4.17:

$$CI_t = \gamma_0 + \gamma Y_t + \beta(L)\Delta Y_t + U_{1t} \tag{4.18}$$

where $\beta(L)$ is a polynomial in the lag operator, L, and where its general form would be the following: $\beta(L) = (L^n + L^{n-1} + \cdots + L + 1 + L^{-1} + \cdots + L^{-n+1} + L^{-n})$, with unknown coefficients attached to the leads and lags. The idea of rewriting eqn 4.16 in this form is to include as many leads and lags of ΔY on the right-hand side of the equation to make U_{1t} independent of Y. The estimated forms, for C1 and C6, are reported in Table 4.4. We exclude the estimated β where the polynomial included one lead term, current and two lagged variables.

The results in Table 4.4 show that, in the case of C6, all the variables with the exception of the CREDQ are significant and should, on this basis, be included in the

Table 4.4 Stock and Watson regressions for co-integrating vectors

	C1		C6	
Constant	4.570	(2.20)	2.630	(1.95)
FINSD	0.00009	(2.58)	−0.000005	(1.95)
FT500	0.230	(2.05)	0.200	(23.49)
TDW	−0.130	(0.42)	0.120	(4.75)
R3	−0.110	(3.08)	0.014	(5.15)
CBICO	−0.015	(3.87)	−0.002	(6.48)
YCUR	−0.010	(0.42)	0.017	(8.06)
CREDQ	−0.190	(1.76)	−0.011	(1.12)
DW	0.819		0.850	
R^2	0.689		0.981	

t-statistics in parenthesis. Sample period 1969q2–1991q2.

Johansen vector. In the case of C1, all variables are significant with the exception of TDW, YCUR and CREDQ. However, for consistency and comparative purposes we adopt, for both C1 and C6, the cointegrating vector that includes all the above variables with the exception of the CREDQ term, as the variable CREDQ was insignificant in both instances. In addition to the above regressions, a version where the polynomial used only three lagged terms was estimated and CREDQ was insignificant for both C1 and C6. Table 4.5 reports the cointegrating vectors.

Two cointegrating vectors are identified between the six leading variables and each of the two measures of economic activity, C1 and C6. The second vector in both cases falls below the critical values but was thought to be sufficiently close to warrant inclusion nevertheless. The interpretation of the vectors is not immediately clear as causation between variables may go in a variety of directions. The important factor in this instance is that these are allowed to appear in the general VAR structure where each of the seven (in each of the two cases) variables has an equation and the system as a whole determines forecasts for future economic activity.

4.5.3 Forecasting underlying economic activity

The basic structure adopted is that of a system VAR, where the error correction terms in the form of E1C1 and E2C1 for the C1 case and E1C6 and E2C6 for C6 are included. All variables are in first differences, with no contemporaneous effects included in any equation. In total, 14 equations are estimated (seven equations each for cases C1 and C6), where we start from a reasonably general specification of four lags in each variable and proceed to test down to a specific form. For brevity, we report in Table 4.6 the two

Table 4.5 Johansen cointegrating vectors to be included in VAR systems

	Co-integrating vector including C1		Co-integrating vector including C6	
	E1C1	E2C1	E1C6	E2C6
C1	2.321	2.339		
C6			27.12	−31.37
FINSD	−0.0003	−0.0002	0.00001	−0.00027
FT500	−1.373	−1.255	−6.311	6.208
R3	0.464	−0.267	−0.179	0.810
TDW	0.229	−3.096	−3.30	6.935
CBICO	0.073	−0.009	0.0892	−0.038
YCUR	−0.175	−0.101	−0.672	0.312
Likelihood	where $r = 0$	144.8	where $r = 0$	139.1
ratio test	$r = 1$	90.48	$r = 1$	91.99
Eigenvalue	0.451	0.344	0.411	0.287

t-statistics in parenthesis.
Where r, the maximum number of cointegrating vector and critical values for 0 and 1, is 124.2 and 94.15, respectively.
Sample period 1969q3–1991q3.

Table 4.6 Forecasting equations for two measures of economic activity

Dependent variable $\Delta C1$		Dependent variable $\Delta C6$	
Constant	−2.320 (8.13)	Constant	
$\Delta FT500_{t-2}$	0.433 (2.45)	$\Delta FT500_{t-1}$	0.0316 (1.75)
$\Delta FT500_{t-3}$	−0.378 (2.14)	$\Delta FT500_{t-2}$	−0.0330 (2.07)
$\Delta R3_{t-1}$	−0.066 (4.52)	$\Delta FT500_{t-3}$	−0.0580 (3.33)
$\Delta R3_{t-2}$	−0.047 (3.23)	$\Delta R3_{t-1}$	−0.0038 (2.01)
ΔTDW_{t-1}	−0.618 (4.10)	$\Delta R3_{t-3}$	0.0062 (3.29)
ΔTDW_{t-4}	−0.293 (2.03)	ΔTDW_{t-1}	−0.0220 (1.64)
$\Delta CBICO_{t-1}$	−0.007 (6.79)	ΔTDW_{t-2}	0.0260 (1.99)
$\Delta CBICO_{t-2}$	−0.007 (5.84)	$E1C6_{t-1}$	0.0020 (1.89)
$\Delta CBICO_{t-3}$	−0.003 (2.43)	$E2C6_{t-1}$	0.0020 (1.98)
$\Delta CBICO_{t-4}$	−0.002 (2.25)	$\Delta YCUR_{t-1}$	−0.0070 (3.65)
$\Delta C1_{t-2}$	0.146 (1.79)	$\Delta YCUR_{t-3}$	−0.0080 (3.92)
$E1C1_{t-1}$	0.035 (2.38)	$R^2 = 0.465$	LM (1) = 0.938
$E2C1_{t-1}$	−0.164 (8.56)	DW = 1.768	LM (4) = 3.25
$\Delta YCUR_{t-4}$	0.024 (1.57)		
$R^2 = 0.656$	LM (1) = 1.695		
DW = 1.779	LM (4) = 5.869		

Sample period 1969q3–1991q3; *t*-statistis in parenthesis.
Durbin–Watson statistics (DW), Lagrange multiplier (LM) test for serial correlation of orders 1 and 4.

equations that forecast the change in C1 and C6 and, in Figures 4.8 and 4.9, show the forecasting performance of the two systems when the forecast starts from different points compared with the actual C1 and C6 series.

Both equations retain the long-run terms, although in principle this need not matter, with the degree of explanatory power relatively high (particularly for the C1 equation) for first difference equations. In Figures 4.8 and 4.9, we use the system to forecast the measures of economic activity starting from three different points. First, we forecast from 1985 quarter one (q1) onwards, testing the in-sample performance of the system. Second, we forecast from 1991 quarter four (q4) to test the out-of-sample performance. Third, we forecast from 1990q1, which gives a feel for the effect of altering the starting period on the forecast values in each case.

Figure 4.8 describes predictions for C1, with 1985q1 as the first starting point enabling an in-sample test of the system forecasting performance. The downturn in C1 from 1985 to 1986 is predicted (although the actual size of the fall was forecast to be larger) with a recovery to 1988 and a flat profile thereafter. As a result, any subsequent movements in economic activity are not forecast accurately using 1985 as a starting point. The forecast starting from 1990q1 appears to track the actual C1 quite closely up to 1991q3 and thereafter implies a continuation in the fall in activity reaching a trough in the middle of 1992. From mid-1992 onwards a recovery occurs, peaking in mid-1994. The forecast starting in 1991q4 shows a much deeper recession followed by a sharper recovery from late 1992, peaking again in late 1994. The timing of recession and of the

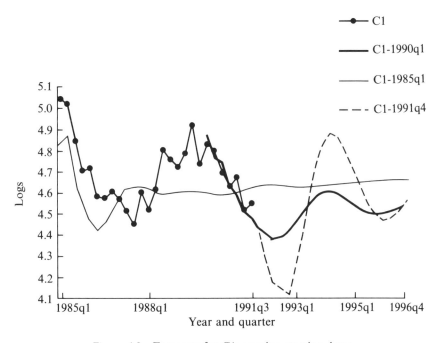

Figure 4.8 Forecasts for C1: varying starting dates

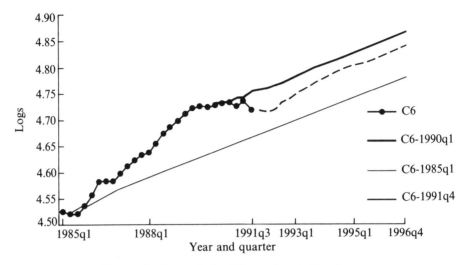

Figure 4.9 Forecasts for C6: varying starting dates

subsequent booms are very similar in these two cases. In the longer term, in 1996q4 the level of economic activity is approximately the same whatever the starting point.

Figure 4.9 plots the predictions for C6, which show differing levels of economic activity depending on the starting date. The earlier the forecast is started, the lower the predicted level of economic activity. However, the rate of change appears to be similar across the start dates. In both cases, for C1 and C6, the forecasts (or leading economic indicators) perform reasonably well for at least a 1-year horizon. The further away the start value, the less plausible are the results. Interestingly for C1, we are able to measure the current recession, and the forecast is that this bottoms out in 1992.

4.6 Conclusions

The overall conclusion we might draw from this analysis is that it is clearly important to take account of the time series properties of the data used in constructing measures of economic activity. The Stock and Watson approach adapted to allow cointegration among the variables provides a practical framework in which to do this. In the case of the C1 measure of economic activity, by allowing each variable to have a separate trend as well as a common trend, we can produce a very cyclical measure with movements close to that of the CSO variable. For the C6 measure, however, we impose the cointegrating relationship between GDP, IP and RES and produce a measure that is strongly upward-trended and, in percentage change terms, is representative of its component variables. Hence, exactly how one deals with the data affects the resulting measure of economic activity.

The measure of economic activity may then be forecast into the future such that an alternative leading economic indicator is formed which for 1-year horizons produces plausible-looking results. In particular, the forecast for C1 implies the early 1990s recession ending in 1992 with a recovery forecast through to mid-1994.

Notes

1. This format is not truly a state space one as the lag structure is more general, the move to a true state space form is, however, trivial (see Stock and Watson (1991)).
2. In the empirical application this term relates to the trend growth of GDP.
3. A preliminary investigation for the presence of lagged effects was conducted and no role was found.
4. Formally the VAR formulation is incorrect since the coincident index (C1 and C6 in this instance) contains 'signal extracted estimates', leading to 2SLS errors in variables problem. However, we choose to ignore this as the bias is likely to be small in this illustrative example.

Table 4.A1   Component series in the indicators

Longer leading index
    Financial Deficit/Surplus of ICCs divided by the GDP deflator
    CBI Survey: Changes in optimism
    Financial Times – Actuaries 500 Share Index
    Rate of interest (3 months)
    Total dwellings started

Shorter leading index
    Changes in consumer borrowing
    Gross Trading Profits of Companies (excluding stock appreciation)
    New car registration
    CBI Survey: Change in new order
    CBI Survey: Expected change in stocks of materials

Coincident index
    GDP at factor cost
    Output of production industries
    CBI Survey: Numbers reporting below average capacity utilisation
    Index of retail sales volumes
    CBI Survey: Change in stocks of raw materials

Lagging index
    Adult unemployment
    Employment in manufacturing
    Investment in plant and machinery
    Engineering industry: Index of orders on hand
    Level of stocks and work in progress, manufacturing

5 The macromodelling industry
structure, conduct and performance

Ron Smith

5.1 Introduction

Despite its importance, there has been surprisingly little economic analysis of the macromodelling industry. Most discussion of the evolution of the industry (e.g. the history by Bodkin *et al.*, 1991) has been by producers emphasising production and marketing techniques rather than wider market characteristics such as demand, value added, competition and the influence that the structure of the industry has on the incentives that the suppliers face.[1] *A priori*, one might expect that market structure would influence conduct (the process by which modelling teams operate and interact) and thus their performance in satisfying their customers. This chapter provides a discussion of the linkages.

To begin consider the production process. Econometric modelling involves assembling a large data bank full of measures, usually very inaccurate, of economic activity, and then estimating equations, more or less loosely based on economic theory, which explain the 'endogenous' variables relevant to decision-makers.[2] These equations are then put together within some theoretical and accounting framework to form a large, complicated, non-linear system, which summarises past and, with luck, future economic relationships between the variables. To produce output requires making some assumptions about the 'exogenous' variables, the ones not explained by the model (e.g. government policy), and then solving the model to obtain predictions of the endogenous variables conditional on the assumed exogenous variables. Running these models is a machine-intensive art rather than a mechanical procedure. Usually the modellers, who have a larger information set than the models, do not like the numbers that come out, so they add or subtract a bit, often on the basis of off-model calculations. This process is called judgemental adjustment and experience shows that it tends to reduce *ex ante* forecast errors substantially. These outputs are then supplied to clients who may use them to improve their decision-making.

The framework used to examine whether the models add value is shown in Figure 5.1, the basic 'value chain'. Porter (1985) links academic economists and econometricians (E), models (M), which with the addition of judgement (J), provide output (O) for decision-makers (D). The decision-makers may be in government or private firms.

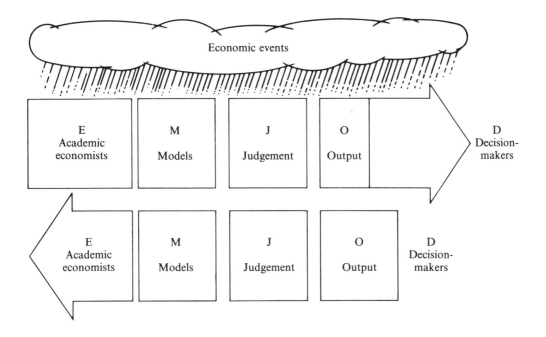

Figure 5.1 Industry value chain

This process takes place under the steady rain of economic events. The output takes a number of forms. Pure *ex ante* forecasting, trying to guess what will actually happen in the future, is the output that gets the most attention, but other forms of analysis are of equal, if not greater, importance. Policy analysis involves using the model to simulate the consequences of a number of alternative strategies in order to choose the best; this activity is sometimes automated with the help of optimal control routines. In policy analysis mode, a useful forecast may be one that provokes action that prevents it being realised, although evaluating such forecasts is difficult. Scenario analysis involves constructing alternative futures in enough detail to allow the client to develop plans to respond to those contingencies (e.g. ERM entry/exit), were they to occur. Counterfactual analysis involves re-running the past under different assumptions in order to analyse the causes of the observed events. All these activities involve constructing conditional predictions and, for brevity, I will sometimes refer to them all as forecasting, but it should be emphasised that pure forecasting is a subset of the output.

Our prime concern is with the processes in the M, J and O boxes. There are two directions of flow. Under the first, decision-makers are the customer. This fits closest to the company analogy. One might regard E as the research department or supplier of raw materials, M the manufacturing function, J marketing and D the final customer. Money flows from right to left and product flows the other way (except when obstructed by monopolistic practices). The final customer may be a private firm or the government. Although the Economic and Social Research Council (ESRC) funded models rarely provide output directly to the government, their analysis is a major input into the debate about policy, opening up, to some extent, the somewhat secretive process of UK economic decision-making. In many instances, proprietors were motivated to construct models by their policy concerns. In the competition for policy influence, individuals had to validate their prescriptions by showing that they could be derived from a theoretically consistent model which could be fitted to UK data and produce acceptable forecasts.

The second direction of flow treats academia as the final customer, buying the product either with direct money payment, e.g. through research grants provided by the state, or indirect payments – promotion, publications, prestige, etc. It is important to emphasise the existence of multiple types of customer, as their preferences over product characteristics will differ. Models can be characterised in terms of their relevance to the needs of decision-makers, e.g. forecasting and policy analysis, their consistency with *a priori* theoretical beliefs and their statistical adequacy in representing a particular sample of data. These characteristics almost invariably conflict, and differences in customer preferences will produce different rankings of models.

Whichever way value flows through the chain, it is compatible with different degrees of vertical integration. Modelling can be done in a free-standing firm, or vertically integrated into one or other of the potential customers. Analysing the two-way flow through the links in this chain involves asking questions such as whether cutting out the middle-man, by-passing the models and jumping straight from E to J, would cause a loss of value at either end. This framework questions the efficiency of the process and the value added to the two sets of customer. How rapidly does best practice academic economics and econometrics diffuse to the models? How much does work done within the models contribute to academic economics? In particular, are the models an efficient way of representing economic experience in a way that can be apprehended by the theorists? How much does the model aid the decision-making process? Could you make decisions as well without models and forecasts? How much does the process of forecasting lead to improvements in the models or would they be better models if the teams did not forecast? What one might mean by a better model is discussed in Section 5.4.

Section 5.2 discusses the various types of market structure observed, Section 5.3 discusses the conduct of the producers, Section 5.4 discusses performance, considering the range of criticisms that have been levelled at models. Within the industrial economics framework I am using, the policy-relevant questions are:

1. Does market structure matter?
2. Is there a better way than models of producing the required outputs?
3. If not, will a free market generate adequate investment in the modelling industry?

4. Given that some government support is needed, are present arrangements efficient?

Section 5.5 contains the conclusions, which are yes, no, no and probably not.

5.2 Structure

The structure of the macromodelling industry varies substantially from country to country. One can distinguish three ideal types of market structure, which are dominant in the United States, France and the United Kingdom, respectively. The structures differ in mode of finance, primary output and the extent to which modelling is a stand-alone activity or vertically integrated into one or other customer. In the United States the market structure is a commercially funded competitive industry. There are a large number of models, mainly in stand-alone firms, the bulk of which are financed by selling their output, primarily pure forecasts, to paying clients. The French type of market structure, which is probably the international norm, is of vertical integration into the government: a nationalised industry. Model building is conducted within the state apparatus for public purposes and the primary output is policy analysis. As Courbis, in Bodkin *et al.* (1991, p. 233) says 'The purpose of the French models was to enlighten government choices'. There may be many models but they tend to be highly product differentiated for particular functions, complements rather than substitutes. In the United Kingdom the market structure is based on public funding and competitive subcontracting to models vertically integrated into academia. The output is both *ex ante* forecasts and policy analysis, with the latter having relatively greater weight than in the United States. The finance is provided by the Macroeconomic Modelling Consortium of the Economic and Social Research Council, Treasury and Bank of England. Academic (or quasi academic) teams compete for Consortium money every four years. This publicly financed but competitively subcontracted structure will be extended by the proposed privatization of the Treasury modelling function.

Each of these descriptions is of course over-simplified. In the United States, despite the dominant commercial orientation there are academic (Fair) and public (BEA) models, and Public and Foundation funding were crucial in the early days of macromodelling. In France, despite the dominance of INSEE, which is the prime supplier of government demand, there are academic (OFCE and GAMA) and commercial (BIPE and IPECODE) modellers. In the United Kingdom, as well as Consortium-funded models, there are nationalised (HMT and BE) and commercial (OEF, Cambridge Econometrics, WEFA, DRI, ITEM, etc.) models, as well as many City forecasters. But, despite these exceptions, the caricatures do capture the dominant market structure.

The US system of dependence on commercial finance is probably only possible in a very large market. There is continuous evaluation of *ex ante* forecast performance, e.g. the comparisons conducted by Stephen McNees of the Boston Federal Reserve. However, as discussed below, evaluation of *ex ante* forecast performance is not

71

necessarily a good test of the models.[3] The commercial nature of the models in the United States also inhibits the disclosure of certain types information[4] and raises obstacles to neutral evaluation. Wallis (1992) discusses some of the problems this causes. The impact of structure on conduct in the United States is noted by Fair (1984). Speaking of the 1970s he says:

> The commercialisation of the models changed the focus of research somewhat. Less time was spent on what we might call basic research on the models, such as experimenting with alternative estimation techniques and statistical testing. More time was spent on the month-to-month needs of keeping the models up to date.

McCarthy (1972) also discusses the evolution of models in the United States.

In the United Kingdom, the 4-yearly Consortium competition provides the dominant market test. A third of these competitions was for funding over the 1991–5 period. In designing the competition the Consortium faces a classic agency problem. As the principal it has different objectives from, and less information than, the agents: the model teams. The Consortium then has to design a competition and contract that is robust to the asymmetric information, adverse selection and moral hazard that is characteristic of the market and elicits the desired behaviour from the teams subject to the constraint that it has very little scope to specify the output or monitor their efforts.[5] The Consortium tried to reduce the asymmetric information problem by establishing a monitoring agency – the ESRC Macro-economic Modelling Bureau at Warwick. Smith (1990) describes the origins of the Consortium and the activities of the Bureau.

Although the UK system is competitive, it is not clear what criteria determine competitive success. The Consortium finances research on the models not forecasting, which it believes should be self-supporting. The net effect of subsequent rounds has been to reduce dispersion:

> The bulk of the government's £2m budget, on top of the funds spent on the Treasury's own model, funds two other models, at the NIESR and the London Business School. Both are similar in design to the Treasury model, and all three have made very similar errors since 1985. Yet more iconoclastic (and recently more successful) forecasting teams at Cambridge, Liverpool and City universities have all had their funding withdrawn over the past decade. The public interest would be better served by a policy that promoted choice and diversity rather than a cosy cartel of like-minded clones. (*Financial Times*, editorial, 8 July 1992)

'Safe' choices could reflect either a response to the danger of adverse selection in the market or a high degree of risk aversion.

The degree of effective competition depends on the contestability of the market, which will depend on inherent entry barriers. My judgement, which many disagree with, is that the inherent entry barriers are rather low but that entry is relatively rare because the market is unattractive, possibly because it is efficient. Were it profitable, it would not be very difficult for an entrant to build a new model, produce forecasts and publicise them. It is true that modelling seems to require specialised human capital only produced by apprenticeship and most new entrants have previously worked with existing teams.[6] However, the required human capital is not that scarce and could be bought quite cheaply.

I would argue that entry is rare because the return to macromodelling is rather low, which is what one would expect in a contestable market. The academic return is low, as model-related work gains little prestige and is difficult to publish in good journals; the commercial return is low because it is difficult to make money from macroforecasting. Macro-economic forecasts are available almost free from a large variety of sources, e.g. the regular *Financial Times* summary. Thus the modeller must either rely on Consortium money to cover sunk research and development costs or be able to provide an attractive commercial product in which the forecasts are bundled with a range of other services. This has always been the case. Bodkin *et al.* (1991, p. 122) point out that the Data Resources Inc. (DRI) model, 'perhaps the most successful econometric model ever built, from the point of view of the market test of the product', was the centrepiece of a much larger information system. It was the wider information system that was central to the commercial success.

The difficulty of making money out of modelling is illustrated by the fate of the models that had their ESRC funding withdrawn: Southampton, Cambridge Economic Policy Group (CEPG), the Cambridge Growth Project, City University Business School and Liverpool. Of these only the Growth Project was able to survive commercially, though Liverpool continues to operate at a much reduced level and the CEPG is making a Lazarus-like return in another form. The Growth Project's success in continuing as Cambridge Econometrics was largely due to its near monopoly position as a supplier of consistent disaggregated forecasts.

5.3 Conduct

The size of the models makes modelling a team activity. The teams then have to establish priorities between non-model research, model-based research, model maintenance and production of output such as forecasts for clients. This section considers how size, team structure, forecasting, competition and customers influence modeller's priorities and behaviour. There are two team-related questions that I do not discuss. First, turnover in the teams is high and my impression is that many macro and monetary economists got their initial practical experience on model teams. Thus, there may be a training externality. Second, following the long tradition in industrial organisation of ignoring the internal organisation of the firm, I am going to ignore the internal organisations of the teams, e.g. the way that modelling, forecasting, selling and more academic pursuits are combined. For instance, it seems common for model construction and forecasting to be done by different people, because they require different skills. Internal organisation seems to differ substantially between teams and the Bank of England has recently restructured its modelling function, so there may be some interesting issues here.

The models tend to be large and to grow with time, although growth is subject to regular pruning. The size, teams say, reflects the complexity of the world and the need for large complicated systems to interpret it; the number of potentially important interactions that may influence the macro-economy; the extra information obtained from disaggregation; and the variety of purposes to which the models are put. Klein, in Bodkin *et al.* (1991, p. 526) gives a range of arguments for large models. Large models inevitably require team efforts and division of labour. In Mariano (1987, pp. 442–3), Klein suggests that academic incentives now discourage team efforts relative to smaller projects that produce authored publications. For the United Kingdom, Holly (1991, p. 36) comments:

> Models that depend too much on particular individuals, however brilliant, tend not to survive. Modelling groups . . . which function almost as institutions, attracting able researchers, but not being dominated by them, tend to be able to respond and change in response to pressures from developments in economic theory and method and the unravelling of economic events which continue to perplex economic forecasters.

Producing forecasts clearly meets client demands, but there is an issue of whether the process of forecasting itself leads to 'better' models. In the United States, Wharton (WEFA) was the first academic modelling group to move into commercial forecasting. There were a number of different reasons for this. Despite the fact that the *ex ante* forecasts were produced by a number of inputs of which the model was only one, it was believed that forecasting was the only real test of a model. People were willing to pay for the forecasts, so the forecasts could be used to finance academic research. The forecasting process disseminated the results of academic research in a way that was useful to the wider community. It also enabled the academics to obtain better information from practitioners in business and government about the operation of the economy. All these factors made forecasting and academic research strongly complementary activities at that time. Whether they remain complementary now is a more open question and, for a variety of reasons, WEFA was spun off from the University of Pennsylvania. Klein provides an account of the development and sale of WEFA in Mariano (1987).

Others argue that the activities can become substitutes. The demands of routine forecasting – monitoring the economy, maintaining databases, operating the model – can become all-absorbing, leaving little time for system evaluation and model improvement. Fisher and Wallis (1990), after conducting historical simulations that suggest that the models, as descriptions of the economy, suffer severe problems, comment:

> One might ask why it is that models that are in such regular use in forecasting and policy analysis exercises are so poorly validated historically. It would appear that whereas individual equations are often thoroughly tested against the historical record, once a satisfactory specification at that level is obtained and the equation

inserted into the complete model, attention is concentrated on the use of the model in 'forward-looking' forecasting and policy analysis. These may be the more pressing problems facing the model proprietor, and 'backward-looking' historical validation, system-wide, is correspondingly neglected. When the model does not perform well historically, however, and no good explanation of its failure is available, the reliability of analysis based on the model is called into question.

Modellers argue that structural and institutional changes have to be accommodated as they occur and that this worsens the model's historical tracking ability.

The form of competition between teams differs with time-horizon: forecasting in the short run, for policy influence in the medium run, and for Consortium funds in the longer-run. The relative forecasting performance of the ESRC funded teams is fairly closely monitored. As one might expect in a fairly competitive market, where appropriability of most sources of advantage is low, no team dominates (over all periods and variables) in forecasting performance. However, one effect of the strong competition is a reduction in variety: forecasts tend to be driven together (pure model forecasts diverge more than published forecasts), as it is much safer not to stray too far from the herd. In contrast, in the medium-term competition for policy influence, strongly diversifying your product from competitors may confer advantage.

The main form of long-run competition is for Consortium funds. It is difficult to judge what effect these competitions have had on the conduct of the teams, partly because the criteria for success in the competitions are not clear. More explicit criteria would increase the incentive effects and possibly improve the allocation of resources. Press comments have often attributed funding choices to political preferences, but the modellers themselves seem to put more emphasis on academic preferences. In this case the Consortium competitions may have led to a greater concern with maintaining an appearance of academic respectability. For instance one modeller commenting on the demise of another notes that:

> They neglected to take account of the developments in applied econometrics associated with Denis Sargan and colleagues at LSE, especially David Hendry. If the CEPG had been a little more discrete in describing what they actually did, and had perhaps been quicker to recognise that the use of a better set of econometric techniques would not have been at the expense of the basic messages that they wished to convey about what they considered to be the proper way to conduct macroeconomic policy in the UK, they may have not fallen foul of the coming orthodoxy in applied econometrics. (Holly (1991, p. 35))

Whether the account in the previous paragraph is correct or not, the incentives will depend on such perceptions of the criteria. Academics and decision-makers do not have the same preferences, priorities or objectives and their respective reward systems thus provide incentives for very different types of behaviour. To over-simplify: decision-makers demand rapid output that is directly relevant to their immediate problems and are not particularly interested in the process of producing it; while academics demand longer-term publications, which show methodological innovations and scholarly standards in the production process. The Consortium, of course, contains representatives of both academic and decision-making economists, though it is not clear how the two sets of objectives are reconciled.

The current market structure seems to provide incentives for the teams to adopt a two track approach. It encourages research that can get published in good academic journals (i.e. largely non-model work) or research using the existing model that will give an immediate pay-off to clients. Despite the monitoring efforts of the Bureau, my impression is that the current market structure does not seem to provide much incentive for more fundamental research on model-improvement and evaluation. As a result, relative to the past, the last few years have seen relatively less work on and relatively less change in the main models, despite their evident problems. There have been some innovations, but it appears to me that the rate of change in the last two or three years is less than in the past. It may be that I have missed many of the innovations, or that the innovations are in the pipeline and will be introduced when the models are estimated on the rebased data in 1993, or that the lack of change reflects the inability of the teams to fix the problems. But my interpretation is that the reduction in model-related work is an adaptive response to the perceived incentives from clients and Consortium. Whether these are the correct incentives depends on the objective function of the principal, the Consortium, and its expectation of the pay-off from more fundamental model research for either academic advancement or improved decision-making.

5.4 Performance

Judging the performance of a model is not straightforward because there are multiple criteria for model evaluation. These criteria can be grouped under three broad headings: (1) relevance of the model's output to the client's decisions; (2) consistency of the model's structure with *a priori* theoretical knowledge; and (3) the statistical adequacy of the model as an explanation of the sample data. Pesaran and Smith (1985, 1992) provide a more detailed discussion of the three criteria. Given that there are multiple criteria, not only will different people rank models differently according to their preference order over the three criteria but different models will be preferred for different purposes. The idea that there is a single correct model that can be used for all purposes is a misunderstanding: product diversity in modelling will be the rule, a variety of different types of models for different uses.

A major problem of judging performance is that academic economists differ in the weights that they put on consistency with economic theory as against statistical adequacy in explaining the data. The first part of this section discusses the evolution of the interaction between theory and data in econometrics. These issues are discussed in more detail in Pesaran and Smith (1992). The section then goes on to discuss performance in terms of the links to the two potential customers in the value chain used in Section 5.1: academic economists and decision-making clients.

5.4.1 Performance in terms of theory or data?

Haavelmo (quoted in Morgan, 1990, p. 242) said that 'Econometric research aims, essentially, at a conjunction of economic theory and actual measurements, using the theory and technique of statistical inference as a bridge pier'. Econometric analysis in the post-war period has been dominated by four statistical techniques or models, which have bridged the gap between theory and observation in quite different ways.

The period up to the 1970s was dominated by single equation and multivariate regression models. In the regression model the conditional mean of some endogenous variable is explained in terms of some exogenous variables. Regression was the basis of what Hylleberg and Paldam (1991) call the 'traditional strategy' of doing empirical research: of bridging theory and observations. This 'traditional strategy' emerged from the work of Tinbergen, Haavelmo and the Cowles Commission (see Morgan (1990) for details). Central to it was a dichotomy between theoretical and empirical activities: the theorist provided the model and the econometrician estimated and tested it. This proved a highly productive strategy which dominated empirical econometrics until the 1970s and still remains healthy: it is the basis of most large modelling in the United States. It was effective because the theory involved (IS-LM, static demand theory, explanations of cycles in terms of stochastic linear difference equations) could easily be cast in the form of a linear or simple non-linear regressions. The primary role of theory in this context was 'identifying the list of relevant variables to be included in the analysis, with possibly the plausible signs of their coefficients' (Tinbergen, 1939), although it also suggested linear restrictions, such as homogeneity with respect to prices, which could be tested.

The old theory focused primarily on conditional statements, such as what would happen to demand if price were to fall; decision-makers focused on conditional predictions, such as what would happen to unemployment if government spending were to increase. Regression methods, by estimating the conditional means, provided a flexible way of quantifying and testing qualitative statements about conditional moments. The testing was usually of a limited though useful sort: was the effect significant and of the correct sign? In the pragmatic application of the traditional strategy, though not in the strict Cowles Commission view, regression also allowed the empirical analyst great scope to make auxiliary assumptions to take account of the informal theory: add variables to allow for *ceteris paribus* conditions, choose functional forms, add lags for adjustment processes and experiment with proxies for unobservables. In terms of the 'Duhem–Quine problem' the theory became almost unfalsifiable: it was never clear whether the theoretical core or the auxiliary assumptions were rejected. However, this approach allowed the empirical analyst to take account of a wide range of historical, institutional and physical constraints. This increased the applicability of the theory and allowed the model to represent the data better while remaining consistent with theory. The Cowles Commission approach was characterised by the development of estimators rather than test procedures. Even without formal procedures for diagnostic and misspecification testing, the explanation (conditional prediction) provided by the model could be compared with the realisations, allowing an informal judgement of statistical adequacy.

The second statistical model was the multivariate regression model in which a number of endogenous variables were explained by the same vector of exogenous variables. The reduced form of a linear simultaneous equations model was of this form and the role of theory was then to provide the identifying restrictions that allowed the structural form to be estimated plus over-identifying restrictions that could be tested. Complete systems of demand equations, which were developed following Stone (1954), also took the form of multivariate regression models. In this case, the theory imposed a set of restrictions on the system (adding up, homogeneity, symmetry and negativity), which could be used to improve the efficiency of estimation or be tested.

The third statistical model was the univariate autoregressive integrated moving average, ARIMA (p, d, q), model. This represented a single variable (after it had been differenced sufficiently, say d times, to induce stationarity) in terms of p autoregressions (lagged values of itself) and a moving average of q lagged disturbances. Although these models were initially 'atheoretical', using no information from economic theory, there were cases where economic theory did impose restrictions on the form of an ARIMA model. For instance, efficient market theory predicted that speculative asset prices should be random walks: ARIMA $(0, 1, 0)$. However, during the 1970s it became apparent that univariate ARIMA models could outperform traditional econometric regression models in forecasting. This led to an increased emphasis on developing measures of model adequacy, a proliferation of diagnostic and misspecification tests and a shift away from emphasis on the estimation of a theoretical model.

At the same time that statisticians were arguing that traditional regressions did not represent the data, theorists were criticising them for failing to represent the theory (e.g. via the Lucas critique) and decision-makers were complaining that the models were ineffective for practical purposes of forecasting and policy. In terms of the three criteria, the models were seen as statistically inadequate, theoretically inconsistent and practically irrelevant.

The response of many econometricians to the evidence that simple time series models could, on occasion, produce better forecasting performance than econometric models was to put much greater priority on representing the data relative to the theory, which they initially saw as having relatively little to contribute, particularly for the purpose of forecasting and business-cycle research. If ARIMA models outperformed traditional econometric models, then econometric models needed to take account of both the information in the ARIMA models and the linkages between variables embodied in econometric models but ignored by univariate time series models. There were two strands to this response: dynamic elaboration of single equation regression to produce the error correction models (ECMs) associated with Hendry and his colleagues (see Gilbert (1986) for details) and the use of a multivariate time series model, the vector autoregression (VAR), the fourth of the statistical models widely used in econometrics and associated with Sims (1980). These two approaches, the VAR and the ECMs, have now been united in the cointegration approach (Engle and Granger, 1991). In both cases, the initial impetus to the research programme was statistical, a desire to represent the sample data and to forecast more accurately, but over the 1980s awareness grew that economic theory imposed restrictions on these models. We shall briefly review the Hendry and Sims approaches, before discussing the response of the theorists.

Hendry and his colleagues, in the LSE tradition (see, for example, Hendry, 1987), started from a general autoregressive distributed lag model, which explained an endogenous variable by its own lags and current and lagged exogenous variables; effectively using a moving average of observed regressors rather than unobserved disturbances as in the ARIMA. The estimated model was subjected to a battery of tests to ensure that it described the data adequately and then simplified by reparameterisation and restrictions, which reduced the number of estimated coefficients. The end result was usually a single equation ECM in which the changes in the dependent variable were explained by changes in the independent variable and lagged levels of the dependent and independent variables. Alogoskoufis and Smith (1991) discuss error correction models in more detail.

The textbook by Aris Spanos (1986) provides an influential exposition of this methodology. Spanos (1986, p. 10) notes the separation of time series modelling from mainstream econometric modelling and says that one of the main aims of his book is to complete the convergence between them begun in the mid-1970s. But in this convergence, priority is given to the development of a well defined statistical model, which adequately describes the observed data in the sense that the underlying statistical assumptions are valid. Theory enters at the first stage, with choice of the variables examined, as with Sims, and at the final stage when the estimated statistical model can be reparameterised or restricted in view of the theory so that the model can be expressed in terms of the theoretical parameters of interest (Spanos, 1986, p. 699):

> Econometric modelling is viewed not as the estimation of theoretical relationships nor as a procedure for establishing the 'trueness' of economic theories, but as an endeavour to understand observable economic phenomena using observed data in conjunction with some underlying theory in the context of a statistical framework. (Spanos, 1986, pp. 670–1)

> Modelling is seen as an attempt to characterise data properties in simple parametric relationships that are interpretable in light of economic knowledge, remain reasonably constant over time, and account for the findings of pre-existing models. (Hendry and Ericsson, 1991, p. 18)

The methodology is based on the statistical theory of data reduction. They suggest six criteria, of which five are statistical and one is 'theory consistency', which says that 'economic theory often suggests long-run relationships between economic variables', which gives a (log) linear example, and spend the rest of the section discussing cointegration. The response to Hendry and Ericsson's (HE) 1991 criticisms by Friedman and Schwartz (1991, p. 40) emphasises the difference in purpose:

> By HEs standards, the prior 281 pages of our book were mostly worthless . . . Those pages were not devoted, *à la* HE, to 'representing the joint density of [a limited set of variables] in terms of an autoregressive distributed lag model', then proceeding to simplify '[t]he conditional model to an ECM', and to evaluating it 'in the light of the model design criteria' listed in their Table 2 (HE, pp. 22–3). Instead, the first 204 of those 281 pages present our theoretical framework, our statistical framework, the basic data, and an overview of the movements of money, income, and prices over the century our data cover.

Friedman and Schwartz emphasise the importance of explaining a wider range of observations than the particular sample being analysed.

Whereas the LSE tradition largely worked within a single equation framework, the other approach to combining econometric and time series models was multivariate. Full multivariate vector ARIMA models tend to be intractable and Sims (1980), within an explicitly atheoretical approach, advocated a simplification of the VARMA model, the vector autoregression, (VAR).

The VAR is the fourth of the statistical models that has been widely adopted in econometrics. In this structure each variable (measured either in levels or first differences) was treated symmetrically, being explained by lagged values of itself and other variables, there were no exogenous variables, no identifying conditions and the only role of theory was to specify the variables included. Cooley and Leroy (1985) provide a critique of such atheoretical econometrics.

But the VAR was not necessarily atheoretical, it could provide a statistical framework within which the restrictions imposed by theoretical models could be imposed. One route was to use the VAR as the reduced form of a traditional structural model. Then the specification of the structural model could be tested by imposing the sequential restrictions necessary to generate it from a VAR: predeterminateness of some variables, non-causality, exogeneity and weak and strong over-identification conditions (Montfort and Rabemananjara, 1990). An alternative route used theoretical rational expectations or equilibrium models as a way of interpreting and imposing cross-equation restrictions on vector autoregressions:

> Rational expectations modelling promised to tighten the link between theory and estimation, because the objects produced by the theorizing are exactly the terms of which econometrics is cast, e.g. covariance generating functions, Markov processes and ergodic distributions. (Hansen and Sargent, 1991, p. 2)

Within this framework, the aim is to estimate all of the deep parameters by exploiting the cross-equation restrictions the theory imposes on those parameters.

However, this could only be done for optimising models, which take what Whittle (1982) calls the 'LQ form': linear constraints and quadratic costs. The details of this form have been extensively developed in the operations research literature and applied extensively in many fields besides economics. The decision rules take the form of a linear VAR. More complicated models of stochastic dynamic optimisation could not be solved and real business cycle theorists had to face the difficulty that analytical solutions for the decision rules of their models under uncertainty were rare. As a result of being unable to estimate these models, they adopted the explicitly astatistical approach of calibrating and simulating the theoretical models (Kydland and Prescott, 1982, 1991). Although Kydland and Prescott do not use methods of statistical inference, they regard these procedures as econometric, in the spirit of some of Frisch's exercises. Andersen (1991) provides a critique of the calibration approach. This astatistical response is strongly identified with the Lucas–Sargent research programme, which is centred on a stochastic dynamic optimisation approach. This approach requires that all the behavioural relations of the model be obtained directly from the solutions to well defined dynamic optimisation problems faced by economic agents, usually taken to be representative agents. In order to make this approach operational a large number of very restrictive assumptions have to be made about preferences, technology, endowments and information sets. The proponents of this approach are forced to use very simple functional forms; rely almost exclusively on the concept of representative agents with homogenous information (which, as Arrow (1986) points out, is odd in an explanatory model of decentralised markets where individual differences are the prime motivation for trade); and give little or no consideration to institutional constraints.

This means that a number of important problems, such as information heterogeneity, sectoral disaggregation and choice of functional forms that concern applied economists are either ignored or brushed aside. They are ignored not because they are unimportant but because they cannot be readily accommodated within the optimisation framework. Thus the theory becomes a straitjacket rather than a flexible framework for enquiry. This approach shifts the emphasis to the model of the economy rather than the economic reality itself. As Sargent states 'The internal logic of general equilibrium modelling then creates a difficulty in taking any of the model's predictions seriously' (Sargent, 1987, p. 7). Kydland and Prescott (1991, p. 169) say that:

> Without some restrictions, virtually any linear stochastic process on the variables can be rationalized as the equilibrium behaviour of some model economy in this class. The key econometric problem is to select the parameters for an experimental economy.

This is not the traditional definition of an econometric problem. The parameters of these models can be consistently estimated by the generalised method of moments (GMM) or simulated GMM, conditional on the assumption that the model is correct. However, estimation, in itself, does not generate conditional predictions, time paths for the endogenous variables, which can be compared with the actuals to assess the explanatory power of the models.

Pesaran and Smith (1992) discuss an alternative approach to estimating dynamic models. A great deal of the complexity of these models arises from missing markets which give rise to unobservable shadow prices (Lagrange multipliers in the constrained optimisation). In an Arrow–Debreu world there are complete markets for all current, contingent and future contracts. The widespread absence of forward contracts means that agents have to condition their decisions not on the known forward price but on their expectations of the price in the future. Economists have dealt with this problem by replacing the unobservable (to the econometrician) expectation of the future price by its observed determinants. The equally widespread absence of current (e.g. markets for second-hand capital goods) and contingent (e.g. contracts conditional on the agents being liquidity constrained) markets means that agents have to condition on unobservable (to the econometrician) shadow prices. We suggest that the shadow prices be replaced by their observed determinants, in the same way as expectations. A very similar approach is adopted to the estimation of a real business cycle model by Chow (1992). The effectiveness of this approach still needs to be evaluated but it may have the potential to narrow the gap between modern theory and the data.

Theory is essential in economics. It is needed to produce general, unifying insights that promote our understanding of the working of the economic system by abstracting from the complex mass of details that constitute the 'reality', thus allowing the theorist to provide tractable analysis. The theory also acts as a unifying framework within which new results can be related to what is already known. The difficulty of using much of the new theory, based on non-linear stochastic optimising models, for estimation, testing or prediction, leaves macro-econometric in an unsatisfactory position: (1) they can stick with the Cowles Commission approach, and continue to use the old theory; (2) they can adopt approaches that emphasise fitting the data but are either atheoretical or use minimal theory about simple long-run relationships; (3) they can adopt the new theory and confine themselves to largely qualitative statements that do not address the decision-makers concerns. All three approaches suffer major drawbacks.

It is interesting to contrast the position of macro-economists with financial economists, where the relationship between theory and data is very close indeed. Unlike macro data, financial data are very precise and correspond directly to the theoretical concepts. Unlike macro theories, finance theory is of great practical relevance to decision-makers. The Black–Scholes option pricing formula diffused from the *Journal of Political Economy* to dealing rooms very rapidly. In finance, theories that do not explain the observations are rapidly revised, because they are no use in the market, which is their only justification.

5.4.2 Models and academics

In the light of the previous discussion, this section examines how rapidly new academic ideas and techniques diffuse to the modellers and get embodied in the models and what modelling contributes to academic economics.

Klein (in Bodkin *et al.* 1991, pp. 530–1), who largely retains a traditional Cowles Commission methodology, takes a very positive position on the interaction. He comments on the 'mutually reinforcing role, from the outset in the 1930s to the present time, of macroeconometric model-building and macroeconomic theory', but refuses to 'attempt to buttress this assertion with examples'. As his single exception to this refusal, his example of how 'the lessons from macroeconometric model-building have served to refine macroeconomic theory and even to call into question some of its accepted propositions' is the 'time path of the standard expenditure multiplier of main stream Keynesian theory'.

In the United Kingdom, diffusion of new academic ideas to the main models seems to have been very rapid, almost certainly faster than in the United States or on the Continent.[7] Innovation tends to occur first in the academic models, followed by public sector and finally private sector models. Not all innovations are successful or diffuse and the rate of innovation in the last few years seems lower than in the past. The academic orientation of the leading teams, the academic input into the Consortium competition, and the role of the Bureau may have all contributed to the past high rate of innovation. For instance, UK models rapidly adopted rational expectations (see the discussion in Currie and Hall (1994)), whereas very few US or Continental models include them. New econometric techniques, such as general to specific modelling, diagnostic testing and co-integration were also rapidly adopted. However, it is not clear what is the optimal rate of diffusion. Barten, in Bodkin *et al.* (1991, p. 184) commenting on the Central Plan Bureau (CPB), which he describes as the centre of model building in the Netherlands, says: 'The relative insulation of the intellectual environment of CPB modelling has the advantage that there were no obvious pressures to jump on the band wagons of Scandinavian dualism, monetarism, rational expectations, supply-side economics and so on as they came and went.' The problem with such insulation is that the team cannot determine whether the innovation is a transitory fashion or a real potential improvement unless it, or some other model team, implements the innovation.

The incentives to innovate differ between commercial and ESRC funded models. The three main pressures for innovation are:

1. The existing system fails, prompting a search for an alternative. Such a search is expensive and has no guarantee of success. In general, it is much cheaper to fix-up the model by *ad hoc* adjustments, which is what commercial modellers tend to do. ESRC funded modellers have some resources and incentive to conduct such a search.
2. Academics criticise the model for not adopting the latest fashionable technique. Commercial modellers are not subject to this pressure; ESRC-funded teams are. Many of the fashionable academic techniques are difficult to apply to large models in the first place and then may not work (i.e. improve the model) in practice.[8] Given the uncertain pay-off, the ease with which successful innovations can be copied, the effort required to apply the new techniques and to determine whether they work, it is unlikely that commercial modellers would conduct this research.

3. There is a new technique which works, which is easily applied and which improves models. Commercial modellers will adopt such innovations, but they require that somebody else has done the investment to develop the application procedure and to show that the technique works.

Given the costs, uncertainty and incentives, there is a *prima facie* case that non-model-team academics and commercial modellers will under-invest in model innovation.

Whereas the impact of academic developments on the models may not always have been positive, they were clearly detectable. It is much harder to detect an impact of the models on academic developments in recent years. My impression is that most academic economists would regard the contribution of the models as either negligible or negative. The list of those who have criticised them is long, now extending well beyond the new classical and real business cycle economists like Lucas and Sargent, and Kydland and Prescott. Mankiw (1988) comments that 'the theoretical developments of the past fifteen years have had relatively little impact on applied macroeconomics' and Summers (1991) comments on the 'negligible impact of formal econometric work on the development of economic science'. Pesaran and Smith (1992) discuss these critiques.

Some of the academic criticisms reflect ignorance of the structure and function of the models, a prejudice for the analytically elegant over the realistically complex, or unrealistic expectations of what is possible. Klein (quoted in Mariano, 1987, p. 443) notes: 'Academic economists object to team effort, having a preference for the lone researcher to do his own thing apart from the team effort'. Even allowing for all this, there remains a real residue of hostility, which increases the incentive for the teams to compete in the academic market place with non-model products. However, these non-model papers are often motivated by issues that arise in modelling. In addition, as discussed above, the UK academic and public teams often act as test-beds for new econometric techniques, to find out whether they work in practice, something which neither commercial modellers nor academics have the incentive to do.

5.4.3 Models and decision-makers

The model outputs that get most attention from decision-makers are the *ex ante* forecasts. There is a large amount of research on forecast accuracy as it is, in principle, measurable. In practice, constructing and interpreting evaluations is quite difficult. Establishing a complete, comparable (e.g. in terms of timing) and consistent set of predictions over a reasonable interval for a range of forecasters is not easy. There is no absolute standard: any evaluation must be relative to some alternative forecasting method (or alternative decision-making procedure). Ranking of forecasts depends on the measure of accuracy used, and the standard measures (e.g. root mean square error) may not accurately reflect the decision-makers loss-function (see Leitch and Tanner, 1991). Past forecast performance may be a poor guide to future performance if the model or the economy changes. Forecasts may influence outcomes, becoming self-defeating. Models with no forecasting power at all may still be very useful for control purposes (e.g. in designing automatic stabilisers). Smith (1984) discusses some of these problems.

As is clear from Figure 5.1, forecasts are not purely a product of the model, they also involve a large amount of judgement, both in setting the exogenous variables and making the judgemental adjustments. The *ex ante* forecast may be wrong because the official data available at the time of the forecast was wrong, the exogenous variables were wrongly projected or the judgemental adjustments were inappropriate.[9] The Bureau decomposes the forecast errors into the components due to each of these factors and it does appear that the remaining component of the forecast error – that due to the model – has been large in recent years. As a result, the forecasting performance of the models has been subject to considerable criticism recently (Treasury and Civil Service Committee, 1991). Surveys of the UK record can be found in Wallis and Whitley (1991) and Britton and Pain (1992), and of the US record in Zarnowitz (1991).

Despite the large recent failures, there is as yet no strong evidence that the forecasting performance has got systematically worse (there were other periods when they did very badly in the past) or that models are systematically outperformed by an alternative (e.g. VARS; Fair and Shiller (1990), and Wallis and Whitley, 1991) or leading indicators.[10] That nothing does better and they have not got worse are not very strong claims. Part of the problem, emphasised by Zarnowitz, is that expectations have risen and the forecasts have failed relative to those higher expectations. It may be that we are very close to the lower bound on forecast accuracy which is imposed by the quality of the data and the inherent unpredictability of the economy. Furthermore, it may be that this lower bound was temporarily increased by institutional change such as financial deregulation.

There are two other aspects to the comparison between econometric models and the alternatives: (1) in principle, the models can encompass the alternatives; and (2) the models meet functions that the alternatives cannot fulfil. Suppose that there was fairly strong evidence that some alternative (e.g. VARs, leading indicator, time-varying parameter or non-linear chaotic models) outperformed standard econometric models at forecasting, as evidence in the mid-1970s suggested that univariate time series models then did. The specification of the models could be changed, without too much difficulty, to take account of the information that was being ignored, as it was in the 1970s. For most of the alternatives, anything they can do, econometric models could be improved to do as well or better. The only alternative I can think of for which this might not be true is technical analysis – chartism – as this does not involve a formal procedure. The reason for using econometric models, extended to take account of the information in the alternatives, rather than using the alternatives themselves is that the models do a lot of other things that the alternatives do not. For instance, VARs and leading indicators provide unconditional forecasts and for policy, scenario and counterfactual analysis conditional forecasts are required. Nor do the alternatives allow you to integrate disparate information, follow through analytical linkages, etc. These wider functions of the model are discussed below.

It has been said that investment in improving economic models is very cost-effective, as the social returns to even small improvements in economic policy (GDP 0.5% higher than it would otherwise have been) are so large relative to the investment in modelling. However, the argument can be turned on its head: if the models caused economic policy to be even slightly worse than it would otherwise have been, their value added would be massively negative. The difficulty is judging what policy would otherwise have been and the contribution of the models to policy.

Revealed preference does suggest that however much decision-makers in politics, the civil service and the private sector complain about the models, they do choose to maintain the models and pay to obtain their outputs. Their usefulness probably arises from a lot more than simply providing point forecasts: they provide a reproducible framework for systematic thought and learning about economic phenomena. Within this framework you can: assemble and store information on data and historical relationships; find out where you are now (given the data lags, forecasting the present is essential); impose consistency, e.g. make sure that everything adds up properly; follow through complicated relationships; use judgement and extraneous information in a coherent way; ask clear questions; explain the answers, i.e. provide a story about why the forecast is what it is; evaluate the forecasts subsequently to monitor your performance and learn from your mistakes; and you can do all this very quickly on a computer. Models are also probably quite cheap relative to the main alternative: skilled judgement. The spread of models probably reflects standard capital labour substitution. A new MSc or PhD and a personal computer can be bought for a lot less than the long experience required to produce skilled judgemental forecasts, and can be replaced with less disruption.

5.5   Tentative conclusions

Returning to the questions posed earlier, my main conclusion – that market structure does matter – would be unobjectionable in a micro-economics textbook but may appear objectionable in this context. Market structure matters because suppliers (the teams) adjust their behaviour to the rewards and incentives offered by academia and clients, including the Consortium. These incentives are a product of the market structure, which differs substantially internationally. The market structure in the United Kingdom has made it probably the world leader in large model development and evaluation.

My second conclusion is that no alternative production technology could replace models in generating the range of required outputs. No other approach systematically forecasts better, the models produce a range of other outputs that potential alternatives do not and they provide a framework within which improvements in economic understanding, if they occur, can be quantitatively implemented.

My third conclusion is that a free market solution (which includes public sector clients buying the outputs they require from either vertically integrated or separate producers) is unlikely to generate adequate investment in basic research and development. The immediate rewards of model development work to the clients (decision-makers and academics) are too low for them to provide enough resources to motivate the teams.

My fourth conclusion is that the present support arrangements, through the Consortium, may not be adequate. Supplier conduct (and the structure of the models) reflects a functional adaptation to the market environment and the incentives they face. However, agency problems associated with contract specification may have caused some market failures, particularly suboptimal product diversity in the market and suboptimal investment in quality assurance and production technology by producers. This last conclusion rests on my earlier judgement that the social return to model-related research is probably higher than the private return to the teams or to the clients.

Notes

1. For instance, Kmenta and Ramsey (1981, p. 10), after distinguishing between 'business' and 'scientific' models and saying that they should be evaluated according to different criteria, merely suggest judging 'business' models 'mainly on whether they provide the desired product to clients at a competitive price' before restricting the rest of the chapter to evaluation of 'scientific' models. But this begs all the interesting economic questions.
2. This makes macromodelling more difficult than purely academic econometric modelling because it has to be exhaustive, whereas academics can confine themselves to smaller more tractable subsystems, which abstract from the most difficult complications.
3. There is no equivalent general systematic evaluation of UK *ex ante* forecasting perform- ance. The ESRC Macroeconomic Modelling Bureau only examines the performance of models deposited with it and the occasional golden guru competitions in the press are no substitute. The lack of systematic assessment of *ex ante* forecasting performance may reflect the greater weight put on policy analysis relative to forecasting in the UK structure.
4. Disclosure of model structure is much more important for policy analysis than forecasting because it is well known that models with equally good forecasting performance can have very different multipliers and thus policy implications. Thus to evaluate policy analysis it is important to be able to evaluate the model structure. It is also noticeable that UK City economists, who are primarily forecasters rather than policy analysts, do not reveal their models.
5. Throughout this paper we will treat the Consortium as the principal in the standard IO model for the procurement of a public good (e.g. Tirole (1986)). This assumes that the principal's objective function corresponds to the public interest, but that the principal faces agency problems. The public choice approach would object that in cases like this the principal, the government decision maker, lacks incentives to encourage public good production. This under-supply can be ameliorated if the public good is produced by rent-seeking firms who earn excess profits on supplying it and use some proportion of the profits to bribe the Principal into procuring. The formal model is set out in Cowen and Lee (1992) for the case of congressmen and defence contractors. As my impression is that teams do not try to bribe members of the Consortium, I have not pursued this aspect.

6. This is why the history of large modelling has such a genealogical character: Klein begat Ball, who begat LBS, BofE and HMT, which begat ITEM and OEF.
7. This has made the United Kingdom a world leader in large model development and, through the work of the Bureau, in model evaluation.
8. For instance, applying rational (model consistent) expectations to a large non-linear model requires solving a range of problems not faced by the small linear systems characteristic of academic work. Further, the evidence seems to suggest that allowing for rational expectations does not improve forecasting accuracy. It does allow more interesting policy analysis, thus has been adopted by the ESRC funded models, but it has not been widely adopted by commercial forecasting models.
9. The application of judgement is more complicated in the public models, where the forecast is the responsibility of the Minister and thus may reflect political judgements.
10. Individuals claim to outperform the models, but (a) it is difficult to verify the claims in the absence of a consistent independent analysis of forecast errors; and (b) one would expect, by chance, outperformance in some sub-periods, the issue is whether they can show persistent outperformance.

6

Expectations, learning and empirical macro-economic models

David Currie and *Stephen Hall*

6.1 Introduction

Expectations have been a central issue in macro-economics from the very foundation of the subject: 'We must remember that the price of capital goods varies not only by reason of past changes but also by reason of expected changes either in gross income or in rates of depreciation and insurance' Walras (1954, p. 310). The central role of expectations effects in Keynes' general theory further illustrates this point. And yet the formal analytical treatment of expectations has only occurred over the last 20 years. During this time it has, however, been one of the most important areas of advance. This chapter has a very specific aim: to survey the development of the treatment in expectations in empirical models over this period. We will not attempt to survey the developments at a theoretical level: many such surveys already exist, for example, Shiller (1978), Begg (1982), Holden *et al.* (1985) or Attfield *et al.* (1985). Nor will we discuss the econometric issues of estimation or identification when expectations are treated explicitly (see Pesaran (1987) or Cuthbertson *et al.* (1992) for such discussions). We will focus instead on the impact that the changing treatment of expectations has had on macro-economic models, on policy analysis and on forecasting.

Much early empirical work on expectations centred around attempts to provide direct measures of agents' expectations (Katona 1951, 1958; Tobin 1959; Eisner 1965), and the thrust of much of this research was towards a psychological understanding of individual expectations formation. Direct measures of expectations were undoubtedly useful in forming economic forecasts. However, this approach was limited by two inherent problems. First, gathering direct measures of expectations was very expensive and the data rapidly became outdated. Second, and perhaps even more important, direct measures of expectations gave little insight into how expectations would change as policy changed. Thus, although the importance of expectations to economic policy was stressed by the economic theorists, direct measures of expectations helped little in determining what the correct economic policy should be. The breakthrough that allowed a more general approach to expectations modelling came with the realisation that expectations could be treated as an unobservable component. This implied that expectations could be substituted by their determinants once an explicit rule for expectations formation was assumed. One early example of this treatment was the specification of the adaptive expectations hypothesis by Cagan (1956) and Nerlove (1958): this was an important departure because it allowed the treatment of expectations to be made explicit for the first time in an empirical setting. The major disadvantage of this approach quickly emerged. It was realised that an agent who used this method to determine expectations would in many circumstances make entirely predictable errors even in the very long run. It is hard to believe that such a feature could be true of an intelligent economic agent. Hence these developments led quite quickly and naturally to the suggestion of rational expectations (RE). While there had been some early precursors to the proposal of RE (e.g. Grunberg and Modigliani 1954), Muth (1961) is widely regarded as the founder of this approach. However, RE was not widely adopted for more than a decade after Muth's work was published. Indeed, far from being viewed as a criticism of the adaptive expectations approach, the main perception throughout the 1960s of Muth's work was primarily that it justified adaptive expectations as rational under certain conditions. It was only some 10–15 years later that it began to be appreciated how restrictive these special conditions were and that an alternative empirical approach was needed.

Empirical work incorporating expectations was given an important boost by the work on the expectations augmented Phillips curve (Friedman 1968) and the empirical models that implemented such ideas (Lucas and Rapping 1969). The adaptive expectations approach both illustrated that expectations could be treated in an explicit way in an empirical model and it opened the way for alternative approaches. A rapid explosion occurred in theoretical work incorporating RE, and RE became linked very closely with the new-classical approach to macro-economics. Some main contributions in this area were Walters (1971), Lucas (1972a,b, 1973, 1975), Sargent (1973, 1976), Sargent and Wallace (1973, 1975, 1976), Barro (1976, 1977) and Kydland and Prescott (1977). The perceived connection between classical economics and RE became very strong at this time to the extent that many saw the two approaches as largely synonymous.

The late 1970s saw the development of the first macro-economic models with RE. The initial models (e.g. Sargent 1976; Taylor 1979) were essentially more elaborate versions of the simple theoretical models and not true empirical ones. The first estimated macro-economic models incorporating RE were Anderson (1979) (which included only current dated expectations of current dated variables) and Fair (1979) (a fairly large model (84 equations) including expectations of future prices in the bond and stock markets). Introducing RE terms into the Fair model required the development of new model solution procedures, which had been discussed, but not carried out, in Anderson (1979).

A clear distinction then developed within the literature between the treatment of linear and non-linear models. Blanchard and Kahn (1980) developed a closed form solution for linear models with RE. This allowed detailed theoretical analysis of the properties of linear RE models and spawned a large literature investigating the consequences of RE within a linear framework. The development of non-linear models and RE on the other hand required a range of new numerical techniques to be developed to allow their solution and analysis.

It is perhaps worth stressing that, while the formal treatment of expectations has changed enormously and has often been controversial, the importance of expectations in forecasting and policy analysis has never been seriously questioned. This is illustrated by the stress that has often been put on obtaining direct measures of expectations (for example, Klein (1987) or Pesaran (1985)).

We will begin in Section 6.2 by discussing some basic concepts in the treatment of expectations (e.g. adaptive expectations, the Lucas critique, RE, etc.). Section 6.3 will then examine the developments that have been made within a linear framework while Section 6.4 will consider the development of expectations effects in non-linear models. Section 6.5 will draw some conclusions and outline likely directions for future research.

6.2 Background to expectations mechanisms

In this section we will discuss the developments of some background concepts that underlie the treatment of expectations in both linear and non-linear models.

The hypothesis of adaptive expectations, first proposed by Cagan (1956), allowed the first explicit introduction of expectations terms into formal empirical models. If we define $(_{t-1}x_t^e)$ as the expectation of the value of x in period t formed in period $t-1$ then the adaptive expectations hypothesis states that:

$$(_{t-1}x_t^e - _{t-2}x_{t-1}^e) = \Phi(x_{t-1} - _{t-2}x_{t-1}^e) \qquad 0 < \Phi < 1 \tag{6.1}$$

That is, an individual holds a series of expectations for the variable x and at each point in time the expectation for the future is revised in a proportional way with the most recently observed error. By simply rearranging eqn 6.1 we can get:

$$(_{t-1}x_t^e) = \Phi x_{t-1} + (1 - \Phi)_{t-2}x_{t-1}^e \tag{6.2}$$

and, of course, by successively substituting out for the lagged expectation we can get:

$$(_{t-1}x_t^e) = \Phi x_{t-1} + \Phi(1 - \Phi)x_{t-2} + \Phi(1 - \Phi)^2 x_{t-3} \ldots \tag{6.3}$$

and so we may model the unobservable expectation purely in terms of past observations of x. This seems intuitively appealing, as it says that our expectations of the future are a simple extrapolation of the past. It is, however, easy to construct examples where this rule makes consistent and growing mistakes. Consider the case when x grows at a constant 10%, the adaptive expectations model would always under-estimate the level of x, and it would do so by an increasing absolute amount over time. It is, of course, possible to generalise the adaptive expectations model to overcome this specific problem, by producing an extrapolative rule that would cope with growing variables, or any other specific form of time series behaviour. There have been many such suggestions put forward for such schemes; for example, Flemming (1976) and Pesaran (1985) define a broad class of expectations mechanisms that make use of past information as extrapolative expectations. But, as a general statement, all fixed parameter extrapolative rules are liable to perform poorly in one circumstance or another. For example, if a rule is chosen which copes well with stationary behaviour in x, that rule will generally not cope if the behaviour in x changes to become non-stationary. Any fixed parameter rule will therefore be likely to perform badly in the face of a change in the regime generating x. This is the heart of the Lucas critique.

The Lucas critique (Lucas 1976) essentially emphasised the idea that policy regimes and particular policy rules will affect the reduced form solution for all the endogenous variables in a model. If agents are rational, even if only in the weak sense that they will not make systematic errors, then agents' expectations rules will change as the policy rule changes. Hence any model that either uses fixed parameter extrapolative rules or, even worse, does not explicitly model expectations at all will not be structurally stable across regime changes and will not be a suitable vehicle for policy analysis. This point can be easily illustrated in a very simple example. Suppose a government controls an instrument G and that agents want to form expectations about a variable X, which is simply the sum of G and Z:

$$X_t = G_t + Z_t \tag{6.4}$$

where we might think of X as total demand and Z as non-government demand. Assume that Z is determined as follows:

$$Z_t = \alpha X_t + \varepsilon_t \tag{6.5}$$

Now under one regime where G is simply held fixed a reasonable expectations rule to form expectations about the future value of X would simply be:

$$(_t X^e_{t+1}) = \frac{G_{t+1}}{1 - \alpha} \tag{6.6}$$

If the next period value for G was part of the information set or if this was not the case then simply:

$$(_t X^e_{t+1}) = X_t \tag{6.7}$$

In this case a simple form of adaptive expectations rule would work well. But to see the force of the Lucas critique suppose the government changed its policy rule and decided that from now on G would grow at 10% per period. Although eqn 6.6 would still be valid, eqn 6.7 is no longer appropriate, as the growth in G would now imply that:

$$(_tX^e_{t+1}) = 1.1X_t \tag{6.8}$$

The regime change has then left the structural equations unchanged but has changed the reduced form equations of the system and has altered the appropriate extrapolative rule of expectations formation. The general point is that, if agents are intelligent and avoid making consistent mistakes in their expectations, then any fixed parameter extrapolative expectations model will be unable to cope adequately in the face of policy or other regime changes. Lucas's point may also be expressed in a more formal and general framework in terms of game theory where it may be represented as steps in an extensive form of conjectural variation game, see Hughes Hallett (1986a). One answer to the Lucas critique (although as we will argue below not the only answer) is to make use of the RE assumption.

Muth (1961) introduced the notion of a rational expectation to be 'essentially the same as the prediction of the relevant economic theory'. In many formal contexts this is taken to mean the conditional expectation of the relevant stochastic system of equations, although Hall (1988) argues that in the case of non-linear systems the mathematical expectation may not always be a good measure of an agent's expectation. In the full, or strong, form of the RE hypothesis, it is assumed that the economic agent has a complete knowledge of the economic system about which they need to form expectations. This knowledge includes both the functional form, the parameters of the system and any exogenous process that is entering the system. Under this extreme assumption about the degree of information available to an agent, the optimal expectations formation mechanism becomes the model's own prediction of what will take place. In terms of the simple example above, the rational expectation of X would be given by either the structural form (eqn 6.6) or by the correct reduced form, that is eqn 6.7 for the first regime or eqn 6.8 for the second regime. By construction there is always an extrapolative rule that is equivalent to the RE, but the advantage of the RE approach is that it can cope with regime changes and other structural shifts automatically while the extrapolative model would have to be continually respecified. The main disadvantage of the RE approach is the extreme assumption that is required about the information available to the economic agent.

An alternative approach to making this extreme assumption would be to assume that agents' expectations are on average correct but not make any specific assumption about how agents arrive at these expectations: we define this as weak rationality. This represents a small generalisation of the usual notion of weak rationality (Feige and Pearce 1976), in which agents are assumed to use only a univariate model to form there expectations. The notion that agents do not make consistent predictable mistakes is an appealing one but, as noted above, it is not a property that any fixed parameter expectations rule will generally have. We must therefore move to a class of models that, while not containing full information, are able to adapt to regime changes and in effect to 'learn' about the economic environment.

The question of learning is also important in the context of the RE assumption where, in particular, the question of how agents come to know the true model is simply not addressed. As a consequence, learning has received increasing attention in the theoretical literature over the last decade. Learning can be modelled on the basis of a number of assumptions about the underlying knowledge which agents possess. The most extreme assumption, underlying much of the earlier theoretical literature, gives rise to the rational learning models (Friedman 1975; Townsend 1978, 1983; Frydman 1982; Bray 1983; Bray and Kreps 1984). The assumption made here is that the agent knows the true structure of the model but that some of the parameters of the system are unknown. As the true structural equations are known, the agent's learning problem is essentially one of estimating the parameters of the system. As long as a consistent estimation procedure is used we would expect the system to converge on a full rational expectation equilibrium (REE), and indeed most of the theoretical investigations of small analytical models have shown this to be the case. Rational learning models, however, still make very stringent assumptions about the degree of knowledge which agents have of the structure of the system.

A slightly weaker assumption gives rise to the boundedly rational learning models. Here the general assumption is that agents use some 'reasonable' rule of learning to form expectations and that the form of the rule remains constant over time. In fact, choosing a rule that all agents regard as reasonable is rather difficult and almost always the choice has been the reduced form of the whole system: for example, DeCanio (1979), Radner (1982), Bray and Savin (1986). Thus it is assumed that agents know the reduced form of the whole system as it would exist under RE but again do not know some or all of the parameters. The move to bounded rationality in this form may seem to be a rather small one and yet it has important consequences for the behaviour of the system. The reason for this is that even in the absence of regime changes the reduced form of the model is a combination of the stable structural equations and the changing parameters of the expectations rule, so that it is time varying. The boundedly rational agent is usually assumed to be attempting to parameterise a stable reduced form system and so is actually trying to estimate a misspecified model. Under this assumption Bray and Savin (1986) are able to show that, for a simple cobweb model, the model sometimes converges to the RE equilibrium and sometimes cycles or diverges from the RE equilibrium.

When we consider more realistic models and in particular when we allow for the Lucas critique, a further important complication is that the behavioural equations may themselves be undergoing structural changes. So even if the learning process is able to converge on the true model it may be, in effect, chasing a moving target and so it may not converge to a stable set of parameters.

More recently, however, we have come to appreciate that the behaviour of the parameters in the learning rule gives an important insight into the form of equilibria that may emerge from the system. Marcet and Sargent (1988) summarise the main results. The concept of learning is characterised as a mapping of the parameters of the agent's expectations rule. A fixed point of that mapping is then a situation where the parameters of the expectations rule cease changing. So suppose an agent has a rule that is a linear function of a set of parameters D and the learning process (assumed to be some form of least squares learning) is represented by a mapping S, such that $D_{t+1} = S(D_t)$, so that the learning process produces a sequence of parameters of the expectations rule. A fixed point of the mapping is represented by convergence of this sequence to some fixed value, this point is sometimes referred to as an expectations equilibrium or an E-equilibrium. Then Marcet and Sargent (1989a) demonstrate that this fixed point is also a full rational expectations equilibrium. Furthermore Evans (1983, 1986a,b), Woodford (1990) and Marcet and Sargent (1989a,b) demonstrate that the least squares learning procedure actually rules out many of the undesirable rational equilibria that can arise in conventional rational expectations equilibria. When a fixed point of the mapping is found then we not only have an RE solution, but we also have one that is not dependent on an arbitrary terminal condition.

This section has considered the conceptual developments in the treatment of expectations that underlie the empirical implementations, which will be discussed in the next two sections.

6.3 Expectations and linear models

One important strand of the literature has worked with linear models. The strength of this approach is that in many applications it admits an explicit analytic solution (following Blanchard and Kahn, 1980) permitting a greater extension of analytical ideas to model questions of credibility in policy. The disadvantage is the assumption of linearity, which excludes the additional phenomena arising in non-linear dynamics, including chaotic motion. As non-linearities in economics are usually poorly founded, and as convincing empirical examples of chaotic behaviour are not easy to find, particularly at the quarterly frequency that is the usual concern of macro-economists, this may not be too great a price to pay in return for the analytical advantages. To take advantage of the benefits of linearity, one approach to large scale non-linear models is to linearise these models, and then apply linear control methods to the linearised model. This approach is developed and applied in Barrell *et al.* (1992), in the context of an application to GEM.

Following Blanchard and Kahn (1980), consider the general linear model given by:

$$\begin{bmatrix} \mathbf{Z}_{t+1} \\ \mathbf{x}^e_{t+1,t} \end{bmatrix} = A \begin{bmatrix} \mathbf{Z}_t \\ \mathbf{x}_t \end{bmatrix} \tag{6.9}$$

where $\mathbf{Z}$ is a vector of predetermined variables (defined as variables that change only slowly, for example, the capital stock) and $\mathbf{x}$ is a vector of non-predetermined variables (such as the exchange rate or asset prices), which can change instantaneously: most (but not quite all) linear RE systems can be put in the form of eqn 6.9. Excluding unstable bubble processes, it is straightforward to show (as Blanchard and Kahn do) that the rational solution to eqn 6.9 is given by:

$$\mathbf{x}_t = B\mathbf{Z}_t \tag{6.10}$$

For an appropriate choice of B, eqn 6.10 determines non-predetermined variables (e.g. asset prices) in terms of predetermined variables, and implies a rule for private sector expectations. Then the solution to eqn 6.9 is given by:

$$\mathbf{Z}_{t+1} = (A_{11} + A_{12}B)\mathbf{Z}_t \tag{6.11}$$

which describes the dynamics of the system. These dynamics are determined by the number of predetermined (slow-moving) variables in the system.

Part of the dynamics of the system in eqn 6.9 may arise from the policy rules of the authorities (for monetary and fiscal policy, for example). Hence the rules in eqn 6.10, which specifies how expectations are formed, will depend on the form of policy rule adopted by the authorities. This represents the Lucas (1972a) critique of non-expectational macromodels: that the expectational rules implicit in such models will shift in the face of policy shifts, giving rise to instability in model structure.

The endogeneity of B also greatly complicates the problem of formulating optimal policy. As B depends on the type of policy adopted, it is necessary to take account of this in determining optimal policy: the authorities in the control problem act as a Stackalberg leader, taking account of the reactions of private sector expectations.

It also gives rise to a rather deeper problem, namely that of time inconsistency (Kydland and Prescott 1977). An optimal policy formulated at time t in full knowledge of future events may become suboptimal at a later date T simply with the passage of time and no new information. The authorities therefore have an incentive to renege on the previous policy. But an intelligent private sector can anticipate this, so that the original policy lacks credibility.

This insight has generated a rich literature on policy credibility and the scope for precommitting policy to avoid the problems of time inconsistency. As the gains from precommitted policies can often be quite large (see, for example, Currie et al. 1987), there are considerable benefits from effective forms of precommitment that enhance credibility. One means is to enhance the costs of reneging, whether by political announcements that raise the political costs or by external commitments (e.g. the ERM on G7 policy co-ordination) that may incur costs in relations with trading partners. The presence of stochastic noise also enhances credibility (Currie and Levine 1987), as may the formulation of simple rules for the conduct of policy (Levine and Currie 1987).

Four additional developments from this policy literature have also been relevant. First, there has been the attempt to relax the stringency of the RE assumption by weakening the informational requirements to only partial or diverse (across individuals) information. It turns out that the implementation of this, while retaining the rationality assumption, is highly complex, even in linear models (see Pearlman et al. 1986). The implied level of calculation by agents is therefore much higher, making its plausibility as a description of behaviour somewhat doubtful, this branch of the literature may push the rationality assumption too far.

A second strand concerns the design of robust policy rules (see Vines et al. (1983); for a discussion in a non-RE context, see also Currie (1985)). Policy rules should, if possible, preform well in a wide range of circumstances, so that uncertainty about future shocks, economic structure, and agents expectations do not seriously impair policy. Substantial work is in progress in this area (Kemball-Cook 1992), but the benefits of this research have yet to be realised.

A third area concerns the application of dynamic game theory to empirical macromodels (see, for example, Brandsma and Hughes Hallett (1984), Hughes Hallett (1986a,b) or Currie *et al.* (1987)). Multi-player games are much easier to analyse in a linear context than a non-linear one, and this represents an exciting area of research (Hughes Hallett 1987; Brandsma and Hughes Hallett 1984; Currie *et al.* 1992; Holtham and Hughes Hallett 1992). However, the benefits are more in terms of insight than precise empirical estimates: it may be that this literature pushes the empirical models rather further than their empirical basis warrants (see Currie *et al.* (1989) for a detailed survey of much of this literature).

Finally, an important area of research concerns the incorporation of learning into empirical models (see Driffill and Miller (1992) and, for a recent contribution, Kemball-Cook (1992)). This is also an active area of research in a non-linear context, as we discuss later. But an advantage of the linear framework, as Kemball-Cook demonstrates, is that it allows issues of learning to be combined with other important issues such as credibility and uncertainty. In principle, these issues could be addressed in a non-linear context, but the computational problems are considerable. The simplifying assumption of linearity allows greater richness in policy analysis along other dimensions. For this reason, we expect research on linear models to flourish alongside that on non-linear models.

6.4 Expectations and non-linear models

This section will deal with the development of expectations effects in large non-linear models. It will begin by considering some general issues of specification and assessing the importance of expectations effects. It will then consider the problem of solving models with consistent expectations and will then move on to policy formation and the time inconsistency problem. The conceptual problems of information sets, historical tracking and uncertainty will then be considered. Finally, we will examine the development of learning models of expectations formation in large models.

Fair (1979) is in many ways the natural departure point for our account. This model was the first sizeable model to be solved under model consistent expectations and so it was the first time a modeller had been faced with the new technical problems which this assumption posed. The Fair model has, however, been isolated amongst US domestic models as the only one to adopt RE as a regular tool of solution. The main focus of development switched from the United States to the United Kingdom with the publication in 1980 of the first results from the Liverpool model (Minford *et al.* 1984). From this point on, subsequent developments in solution techniques and the analysis of non-linear models with rational expectations happened mainly in the United Kingdom. Holly and Corker (1984) reported on the introduction of model consistent expectations into the exchange rate and financial sector of the London Business School model. Hall and Henry (1985, 1986) reported on the introduction of RE into both the exchange rate sector and the real side of the National Institute model. Westaway and Whittaker (1986) discussed the introduction of RE into the Treasury's model. The late 1980s saw RE spread more widely. Murphy (1989) introduced expectations effects into an Australian model and Lahti and Viren (1989) reported on the introduction of RE into a model of the Finnish economy. Masson *et al.* (1988) discussed the first introduction of RE into an international model, the IMF Multimod, and Gurney (1990) introduced RE into the global econometric model (GEM). A large amount of work then began in order to understand fully the implications of these changes for the models; surveys of some of this work may be found in Fair (1984), Hall and Henry (1988), Fisher *et al.* (1988, 1989) and Fisher (1990). We will discuss some of the main elements and results of this work below.

6.4.1 Expectations and models

It is perhaps best to begin with a simple general statement of the problems facing modellers upon the introduction of rational expectations. Let the main structural equations for a model consist of the following n equations:

$$y_{it} = f_i(\mathbf{Y}_t, \mathbf{X}, {}_t\mathbf{Y}^e_{t+1}) \qquad i = 1 \ldots n \qquad t = 1 \ldots T \tag{6.12}$$

where $\mathbf{Y}$ is the vector of current and lagged values of the n endogenous variables $(y_{it} \ldots y_{it-k}$, where k is the lag depth of the model), $\mathbf{X}$ is the vector of exogenous variables over all time periods $(x_0 \ldots x_T$, where T is the final period of the time horizon under consideration), and ${}_t\mathbf{Y}^e_{t+1}$ is the expectation based upon information available at t of Y in period $t + 1$. This expectation may, in general, be viewed as being derived from another set of relationships:

$$({}_t\mathbf{y}^e_{t+1}) = g_k(\mathbf{Y}_t, \mathbf{X}) \qquad k = 1 \ldots nl \tag{6.13}$$

Of course, if we were considering extrapolative expectations of one form or another, such as adaptive expectations, this second block of equations would simply represent a further group of essentially standard equations and no special problem arises. Under RE this second block of equations may be thought of in two ways. First, as a structural relationship, we may assume simply that:

$$({}_t\mathbf{Y}^e_{t+1}) = \mathbf{Y}_{t+1|t} \tag{6.14}$$

that is, that the expectation is equal to the actual model solution in the future period. Alternatively we may think of the expectations mechanism as the fully restricted reduced form of both eqn 6.12 and eqn 6.14. It would then be seen as just another extrapolative expectations rule, with the crucial difference that this would be the only rule that would be consistent with the rest of the model and would actually yield a forecast consistent with the final solution from the whole model. It is this second interpretation that lies behind the Blanchard and Kahn solution technique, which was discussed in the last section on linear models, but in general we are not able to solve for the reduced form of a non-linear model and so this approach is not operational for such models. The problem that Fair faced, then, was to develop a solution procedure based on eqns 6.12 and 6.14, which would allow the RE assumption to be incorporated. This involves a range of problems in terms of model solution, the use of terminal conditions, the management of the information sets in policy analysis, the time inconsistency problem and the problem of non-linearities and expectations. We will discuss these problems below, but first it is worth considering the empirical evidence for the importance of expectations effects.

6.4.2 The importance of expectations

Before considering some of the details of model analysis it is worth mentioning the empirical evidence for the importance and relevance of expectations effects. This chapter cannot even begin to attempt a survey of the full academic literature on testing and estimating rational expectations models: good introductions to the literature may be found in Pesaran (1987), Lucas and Sargent (1981) and Hoderick (1987). We would, however, stress that one aspect of the work surveyed here is that it deals with non-linear econometric models, that is to say, estimated models, in contrast to calibrated models such as those of McKibbin and Sachs (1991). This means that the various model users have had some degree of empirical justification for their use of expectations effects. In practice this varies from cases where the expectations are barely data acceptable to cases where the use of expectations has allowed a major improvement in model specification. Work has also been undertaken on the formal testing of the Lucas critique (Hendry 1988).

Perhaps the most striking example of such an area of positive achievement is the exchange rate. The fact that exchange rates are almost impossible to model in a structural way has almost become a piece of received wisdom within the economics profession and yet the exchange rate sector is one of the more obvious areas of convergence between the main large models, which include rational expectations and the empirical evidence supporting this emerging common relationship is both strong and consistent across data sets. The emerging consensus rests on the use of the uncovered arbitrage relationship to represent the fundamental behaviour of investors and attempts to estimate a model based on an augmented version of it. If we relax the risk neutrality assumption then a risk premium may be added, Z_t, and stating the relationship in logs with the general possibility of a lag structure provides a simple equation of the following form, where r_t is the interest rate:

$$e_t = \Phi_1(L)e_{t+1} + \Phi_2(L)(r_t - r_{tf}) + \Phi_3(L)z_t \qquad (6.15)$$

A series of papers have investigated structural models of this form with some success. Explicit allowance has generally been made for the expectations terms by using the Wickens (1982), McCallum (1976) errors in variables approach to rational expectations hypothesis (REH) estimation and many of the applications have also made allowance for the endogeneity of interest rates and the risk premium variable (often proxied by some form of current account effect). Estimation of this form of relationship may be found in Hall (1987b,c), Currie and Hall (1989), Gurney *et al.* (1989), Fisher *et al.* (1991), Hall (1992) and Hall and Garratt (1992b). The presence of lags may be justified in a number of ways: Hall (1987a) proposes a government that follows a 'leaning into the wind' policy of trying to slow down movements in the exchange rate; while Currie and Hall (1989) derive explicit dynamic effects as a result of the interaction of asset stocks and flows. Overall, the results lend considerable support to the risk-augmented open arbitrage view of exchange rate determination: the lags have generally been found to be short or in many cases non-existent, the coefficients on the exchange rate terms are generally very close to unity (thus confirming the unit root hypothesis of the open arbitrage model), and the interest rate coefficient is not generally significantly different from unity. The risk premium term is normally found to be significant, suggesting that risk effects are quite important in the determination of the exchange rate. Contrasting the success of this approach relative to that of the reduced form approach normally used suggests strongly to us that expectations are a crucial factor in exchange rate determination and that the reduced form treatment of expectations does not make adequate allowance for the instability in expectations formation.

A number of researchers have examined the simulation properties of models under different expectations regimes, typically RE and some form of simple extrapolative models of expectations formation. In general, the finding is that RE tends to accelerate the dynamic responses of a model and sometimes to reduce the effectiveness of policy instruments in the longer run. A typical example of this type of work would be Chapter 12 of Ghosh *et al.* (1987). We would, however, be careful to distinguish between the message coming out of this literature – that often RE gives similar model properties to other mechanisms – and the question of the overall importance of the explicit treatment of expectations. Even if all models of expectations give much the same answer, the implication may still be that the explicit treatment of expectations is important.

So while we might accept that expectations are of only marginal empirical importance in some areas, other areas such as exchange rates can not be well understood without the explicit treatment of these effects. We would suggest that this is not only true of foreign exchange markets but also true of other financial markets.

6.4.3 Solution procedures

The first applications of RE to empirical non-linear models were undertaken by Anderson (1979) and Fair (1979) and independently by Minford *et al.* (1979, 1980): the most complete statement of the solution technique used in these applications may be found in Fair and Taylor (1983). The basic Fair–Taylor algorithm consists of a two-part iteration scheme: (1) values for the expectations variables are taken as given and conventional Gauss–Siedel solution methods (Hall and Henry 1988) are used to solve the model conditional on these given values for expectations; (2) the expectations variables are set equal to the solution values from the model derived in the first stage. The whole process is then repeated until the expectations variables used in the first stage are consistent with their updated values at the second stage.

This is an intuitively appealing way to address the problem but Hall (1985) argued that it will not be computationally efficient and that the most general approach has been to set up the problem without taking account of the time dimension of the model. Conventional model solution procedures exploit the recursive nature through time of non-RE models; thus they solve the first period first and then progress sequentially to the last period. Under RE, the model no longer has this natural recursive structure and the insight of Hall was that we can effectively ignore the time dimension by restating the model from a set of n equations solved for T periods to a general set of $T \times n$ equations with no restrictions on the temporal interlinkage. Once this is done then any standard solution method may be applied to the restated general problem. Fisher et al. (1985) and Fisher and Hughes Hallett (1988) develop a family of iteration schemes that is particularly efficient within the overall Hall framework. These schemes fully exploit the sparseness of the model in terms of its simultaneous interrelationships and its dynamic structure and hence they greatly increase computational efficiency.

While the above class of solution procedures has proved to be the most widely used in practice, two other techniques should be mentioned. The first is the derivative-based procedure of Holly and Zarrop (1979, 1983), which uses an optimal control procedure to solve the model for the expectations variables by minimising the following objective function:

$$\text{Min } C = \sum_{t=1}^{T} \sum_{i=1}^{n} \Lambda_{it} ({}_{t}Y_{it+l}^{e} - Y_{it+l}) \tag{6.16}$$

where Λ_{it} is a suitable set of weights. This will reach an absolute minimum when each expectation is set equal to the actual outcome and thus is equal to the RE solution. The other technique is multiple shooting; this originates from the engineering literature and was introduced into economics by Lipton et al. (1982). This procedure essentially involves re-normalising an equation with an expectation term so that the expectation term becomes the dependent variable. The equation may then be solved recursively through time once some unknown starting condition is set. This initial condition is then chosen so that the dynamic path generated by the model hits a given condition in the terminal period, hence the name. Both of these techniques are useful in special circumstances but in general they are less efficient and general than the iterative schemes outlined above.

6.4.4   Terminal conditions

The discussion above ignored the problem of how the expectations were handled after the end of the solution period. In the section on linear models above, the analytical solution derived is for an infinite time horizon problem and the conditions on the unstable eigenvalues were sufficient to ensure a unique solution. In non-linear models an infinite horizon solution is impossible to achieve and the explicit finite solution requires an explicit set of terminal conditions to allow the solution to exist. The problem is to achieve a satisfactory form for these conditions. There have basically been two approaches to the choice of terminal conditions. The first, put forward in Minford *et al.* (1979), suggests that the equilibrium solution to the model should be used as the appropriate terminal condition; the second approach, put forward in Fair and Taylor (1983), suggested that any arbitrary condition could be used as long as it was far enough into the future not to affect the early period of interest. Both approaches are reasonable for models with rapid dynamic adjustment and it is obviously ideal to combine the two, that is to say, to use equilibrium conditions that do not affect the early part of the solution. However, much recent work has emphasised that many of the large models do not adjust quickly and that they often do not have well defined equilibrium conditions (see Fisher 1990 or Fisher *et al.* 1992). A further complication is that some of the most important uses of expectations produce a root in the model that is very close to unity (e.g. the open arbitrage condition in the exchange markets), and this means that very long time horizons would be needed to make a solution robust to the terminal condition. (An interesting alternative is that desirable policy rules may have the characteristic of moving roots away from the unit circle, but there may be severe limits on the scope for this. This may, however, emphasise important questions of long-run controllability in non-RE models and so the RE assumption may simply be making a fundamental long-run problem more obvious. In fact, Holly and Hughes Hallett (1989) show formally that RE can make a model more controllable by increasing the scope for policy feedbacks to remove long-run unit roots.) It appears that terminal conditions may be having a much greater effect on model solutions than is either desirable or than we were formerly aware of.

6.4.5   Information sets

The above two sections deal essentially with technical issues of model solution but a conceptually more difficult problem is the way information sets are used in policy analysis. For example, large models are often used in tracking exercises and to provide an analysis of historical policy (Budd *et al.* 1989). However, once RE is incorporated into such a model their use for such exercises becomes much more complex. A model such as eqns 6.12 and 6.14 may be viewed as giving a solution for $Y_t \ldots Y_T$ conditional on information at t. We can, therefore, compare the forecast for t with the out-turn for t as an indicator of the model's accuracy. We can not, however, compare $Y_{t+1|t}$ with Y_{t+1} in any simple way, as the discrepancy between the two will be a combination of the revision in the information set and the model's errors. As a concrete example, if we solve an RE model over the period 1975–80 using actual historical exogenous variables, we would expect the exchange rate to jump well above its historical values initially because the given information set would include knowledge of the rise in oil prices in 1979. This knowledge was clearly not part of the information set in 1975 and so the model fails drastically to mimic the past simply because we have given it an inappropriate information set. Analysing a historical period then entails deriving an appropriate sequence of information sets and a similar sequence of model solutions where only the first period of any solution may be compared with an actual out-turn in an unambiguous way. Hall (1987a), Matthews and Minford (1987) and Fisher and Wallis (1990) are the only attempts as far as we are aware to analyse historical periods with large RE models using successive information sets. The small number of examples of this type of work illustrates the relative complexity of the problem posed by RE in this context.

The question of differing information sets has also been investigated in a rather different way in Hughes Hallett (1993), who raises the possibility that the information set may contain errors. The RE assumption will then, by exploiting the information set to the full, make larger overall errors than the adaptive expectations assumption which makes less efficient use of the information. This constitutes an argument for the robustness of schemes such as learning and adaptive expectations over the fully efficient use of information under RE.

6.4.6 Time inconsistency

A closely related problem to the informational problem outlined above is the problem of time inconsistency, which was first highlighted by Kydland and Prescott (1977) and which was discussed at some length in Section 6.3 on linear models. Time inconsistency is not related to the question of linearity as such: it is simply the product of the expectations structure of the model and the assumption of consistent expectations. None the less, non-linearity poses some major problems in dealing with time inconsistency and as most real world policy analysis is carried out with non-linear models it is worth considering these.

The essence of the time inconsistency problem is that if an optimal policy is calculated for a model which has RE terms over a given time horizon then if we implement that policy in the first period, and even assuming that everything occurs in the first period exactly as expected, that policy will no longer be optimal from the second period onwards. The reason for this is that in the first period we achieve certain results by asserting what will happen in the future purely on the basis of expectations. In the second period we no longer have to stick to the original announcement as we have already achieved the desired results for the first period. So time inconsistency gives rise to the question of credibility on the part of the policy maker and reputational effects become important.

These issues may be formalised by following the simple illustration of Kydland and Prescott: state a general welfare function for two periods as:

$$S(x_1, x_2, \pi_1, \pi_2) \tag{6.17}$$

where x_1 and x_2 are economic outcomes in periods 1 and 2 and π_1, π_2 are government policies in periods 1 and 2, where:

$$x_1 = X_1(\pi_1, \pi_2) \tag{6.18}$$

and

$$x_2 = X_2(x_1, \pi_1, \pi_2) \tag{6.19}$$

Now, if we derive the first order condition for policy in period 2 from the standpoint of a policy maker in period 1 we get:

$$\frac{\delta S}{\delta x_2} \times \frac{\delta x_2}{\delta \pi_2} + \frac{\delta S}{\delta \pi_2} + \frac{\delta S}{\delta x_1} \times \frac{\delta x_1}{\delta \pi_2} = 0 \tag{6.20}$$

Now, if we consider the first order conditions in period 2, assuming everything occurred in period 1 as originally planned, the conditions become:

$$\frac{\delta S}{\delta x_2} \times \frac{\delta x_2}{\delta \pi_2} + \frac{\delta S}{\delta \pi_2} = 0 \tag{6.21}$$

Unless the last term in eqn 6.20 is zero, which it will not generally be, the two sets of first order conditions are different and the optimal strategy changes as we move through time. This occurs simply because the economic outcome in the first period is affected by the announced policy for the second period.

In the analysis of linear models and time inconsistency it was found to be useful to begin by describing the extremes of full reputation, which allows the government to pursue the time inconsistent policy (which is the best outcome that it can possibly achieve) and no reputation, which allows the government only to achieve the optimal time consistent policy (this will always be inferior to the time inconsistent policy but it is the best the policy maker can do when agents ignore announced policies). In the non-linear case we need to make exactly the same comparison. Calculating the time-inconsistent policy is straight forward and is the result of standard control algorithms. Calculating the optimal time consistent problem is, however, more complex: this problem was addressed in Hall (1986, 1987a) who proposed an algorithm that solved the optimal control problem for the time-consistent solution, Fisher (1990) proposed a generalisation of this algorithm. Given this algorithm, it is then possible to analyse the full range of reputational questions much as in the linear case outlined in Section 6.3.

6.4.7 Non-linearities and expectations

The usual hypothesis that underlies both the RE assumption and the analysis of linear models is that agents take the mathematical expectation of the relevant model as their measure of expectations. A further complication which arises in non-linear models is that, generally, the deterministic solution to the model will not be the mathematical expectation of the probability distribution of the stochastic model. This is due to the simple property of non-linear functions that in general:

$$Ef(y_t) \neq f[E(y_t)] \tag{6.22}$$

This means that the deterministic solution to the model (that is the solution when all the error terms are set to their expected value), will not produce the expected value for the endogenous variables. The deterministic solution will, in fact, yield a biased forecast of the endogenous variables and in so far as under the RE solution techniques outlined above we take this value as our measure of expectations we will be using a less than fully rational expectation.

The technique for analysing the probability distribution of models is known as stochastic simulations: a survey of this technique may be found in Hall and Henry (1988) and we will not discuss it here. The use of stochastic simulations has, however, shown that the bias involved in using a deterministic forecast as a measure of expectations can be considerable and, as a result, Hall and Henry (1988) term these forms of model solution as model consistent rather than rational. It is possible to use stochastic simulations to solve a model for the expectation rather than the deterministic value and thus to derive true rational solutions but this has only been done rarely. One reason for this is the complexity and computer burden involved but a less pragmatic reason is also that the non-linear model will give rise to non-normal probability distributions. Once this occurs there is no strong reason to use the expected value as a measure of agents' expectations in preference to one of the other measures of central tendency such as the median or the mode of the distribution. Hall (1988) argues that many apparent contradictions that arise because of non-linearities may be reconciled by using the median as the relevant measure of expectations along with suitable distributional assumptions. The mean of the distribution is the correct choice if agents have a quadratic loss function in expectations errors but other loss functions are quite reasonable alternatives: an absolute error loss function, for example, gives the median of the distribution. For a large class of models the deterministic model solution may be associated with the median and so model consistent solutions may be seen as having as much relevance as full rational (in the sense of using the expected value) solutions.

6.4.8 Rational expectations; an assessment

The 1980s saw the introduction of RE into a number of large forecasting models. It quickly became apparent that this innovation posed a number of technical problems of model solution and use which took some time to solve fully. We have now reached a point where these technical difficulties have been overcome and we may begin to assess the economic relevance of RE and its practical usefulness.

On the positive side few model proprietors would remain unconvinced as to the importance of expectations effects. Areas such as exchange rate modelling as well as our understanding of both company and personal sector behaviour have been improved dramatically through the use of explicit models of expectations. This is so well established that it is even an accepted part of basic economics teaching, 'Most economists accept that beliefs about the future are an important determinant of behaviour today' (Begg *et al.* 1991, p. 568). However, this does not mean that the full use of model consistent expectations is so completely accepted.

The first point to emphasise is that econometric evidence for the importance of expectations is almost uniformly based on the weak form of RE (that is that agents do not make systematic mistakes), rather than the strong form (that they use a particular model to form their expectations). It is clearly a significant step to go from the statement that agents are 'on average' correct in their expectations to the much stronger one that they use a particular model that they believe completely. Experience with RE has also been rather mixed in the sense that, while in simulation and policy exercises the presence of RE often provides rich insights, it has not been general practice to use RE in a forecasting context. The reason for this is not merely the pragmatic one of avoiding the increases in solution time during a busy forecasting round but more fundamentally that the presence of RE tends to cause jumps in the initial period value of a range of variables, most notably the exchange rate, which are considered implausible by the forecasters. A more obvious example of this problem is that it is actually impossible to analyse many policy options under RE. For example, a permanent rise in interest rates would lead to an infinitely large jump in the exchange rate under the open arbitrage condition and the model would not yield a solution. It may be argued that this is in fact correct and that governments cannot maintain interest rates above competitors' rates for ever but if a government announces that it is going to raise interest rates with no announced intention of lowering them in the future it should be possible to analyse this option with the model. The reconciliation of these two views is, of course, that agents do not believe the government's intention of raising interest rates permanently and hence the exchange rate will only rise by a modest amount. The problem with RE is that it makes no allowance for this lack of credibility. In our view this casts a serious doubt on the models, in that a good model should be suitable both for forecasting and policy analysis across a wide range of policy scenarios. To find that a particular assumption about expectations formation renders the models inoperable for one of their main purposes seriously undermines the usefulness of that assumption.

The dilemma facing model builders then is that expectations were undeniably important in the specification of individual structural relationships of their models but the assumption of model consistent expectations is too simplistic to be acceptable. If we reject adaptive expectations because it leads to systematic and long-term errors in expectations we need also to question the model consistent assumption which is implicitly ruling out the possibility of ever making any mistake about the even very distant future. We would argue that adaptive expectations and model consistent expectations are in reality both extreme assumptions and that some alternative needs to be found. One approach is to try and design policies that are robust across expectations formation mechanisms (this is proposed as a minimum requirement for good policy design by Currie (1985)) but ultimately a modeller needs to make a single choice of the best expectations formation mechanism so there was a strong incentive to find an alternative approach to these extremes. This alternative was found in the emerging theoretical literature on learning briefly surveyed in Section 6.2. We now turn to the newest strand of development in the treatment of expectations, the explicit recognition of learning.

6.4.9 Learning in non-linear models

Learning requires the specification of an expectations rule, such as eqn 6.13, and the assumption that some element of the rule is not known with certainty. This element of uncertainty is usually taken to be the parameters of the rule and the basic idea is that through time the economic agent will use some method to increase his knowledge about the true value of these parameters. So if we restate eqn 6.13 to explicitly include parameters:

$$(_t \mathbf{Y}^e_{t+l}) = g_k(\mathbf{Y}_t, \mathbf{X}, \mathbf{D}_t) \qquad k = 1 \dots nl \tag{6.13a}$$

where $\mathbf{D}_t$ is the vector of agents' estimates of the parameters at period t. Then, once a mechanism that governs the evolution of these parameters through time is specified it is possible to make the whole learning apparatus operational. This approach to the treatment of expectations was first adopted in the exchange rate sector of the London Business School model of the UK economy (Hall and Garratt 1992a,b) and it has subsequently been applied to wage behaviour in three countries in the global econometric model (GEM) (Barrell *et al.* 1992). Hall (1992) reported on the econometric specification of the learning rule and proposed using the Kalman filter as an optimal way of implementing learning. The Kalman filter is a very general estimation (or filtering) technique that can be interpreted as a minimum squared error estimator, and so it nests the least squares learning techniques of the theoretical literature, discussed in the first section, as special cases. These applications may then be thought of as direct applications of the techniques proposed in the learning literature to large non-linear econometric models.

To illustrate the way learning has been implemented in these applications it is useful to discuss the issue in a whole model context, we essentially have three blocks of equations: 6.12, 6.13a and:

$$\mathbf{D}_t = \mathbf{D}_{t-1} + e_t \tag{6.23}$$

where $e_t \sim (0, \Gamma)$. Assuming we know $\mathbf{D}_{t-1}$ we can solve eqn 6.23 for the expected value of $\mathbf{D}_t$, which is simply the Kalman filter prediction equations for $\mathbf{D}$. Given $\mathbf{D}_t$ we can solve eqn 6.13a for the expected value of $\mathbf{Y}^e_t$, and given this we can solve eqn 6.12 for $\mathbf{Y}_t$.

Γ (the covariance matrix of the errors in the equations governing the evolution of the parameters, or in Kalman filter terms, the state equation error terms) is given by the original estimation and we have an estimate for P_{t-1} (the uncertainty of the parameters or state variables). We can therefore use the Kalman filter prediction equation for P, to derive an estimate of $P_{t|t-1}$. Having solved the complete model eqn 6.12 for Y_t we can then define $V_t = Y_t^e - Y_t$, that is the error that occurs between the expectation of the vector Y_t derived from the learning model and the model's final solution for Y_t. We can therefore use the Kalman filter updating equations to derive revised estimates of P_t and D_t. The updating is done on the basis of the observed errors between the whole models solution and the original expectations model forecast.

The process can then be repeated for the next period, starting from the new updated estimates of D_t to predict D_{t+1}, and so on. In this way the learning model will adjust its own parameters to cope with any change in structure or regime of the whole model.

It is perhaps worth stressing that the underlying assumptions of this process are really still quite strong and that the spirit of the approach is not strongly divorced from that of the rational expectations approach. Agents are still assumed to process all available information in an optimal fashion and the degree of sophistication on the part of economic agents is still considerable. The only departure from the strong form of RE is that agents are not assumed to have full information and so they are likely to make mistakes in the short run, although they may well not make systematic errors over an extended period and hence the learning model may fulfil the criteria for weak RE.

As noted in the general section above, the learning model may converge on a rational expectations equilibria and a sufficient condition for this is that the parameters of the learning rule cease changing over time. In the applications cited above for both the London Business School and GEM models the learning rules did in fact converge on an expectations equilibria and so in the long run both models still reach a rational expectations solution.

Two major advantages of the learning approach are particularly important. First the assumed informational demands are weaker and therefore more acceptable in the learning case than the strong RE assumption. Second, many policy debates essentially hinge on the question of credibility and how rapidly economic agents will come to recognise a new regime. The questions raised by the United Kingdom's entry into the ERM are a good example of this. If credibility is achieved quickly the costs of ERM membership is small, while if credibility takes a long time to be built up then ERM costs may be very large. RE essentially assumes that credibility appears instantaneously and completely and so it is inherently either very difficult or impossible to address questions of how credibility may arise and what will happen before it is fully achieved. Learning, on the other hand, goes to the heart of the credibility issue and the treatment of expectation through learning models allows the satisfactory modelling of the build up of credibility to be undertaken for the first time.

This is illustrated in the application of learning to UK ERM membership, in the work of Hall and Garratt. On entry, the risk premium on sterling remained large, narrowing only gradually as private agents learnt (perhaps erroneously, in fact) about the commitment to the ERM parity. Only over time did the DM/£ interest differential narrow. The learning approach incorporates these effects with ease, and also facilitates analysis of the risk premium on sterling after withdrawal from the ERM. It also offers insights concerning the effect of the choice of initial parity on subsequent learning and credibility. By contrast, the RE assumption cannot address these questions.

6.5 Conclusion

We have reviewed the development of the treatment of expectations from three viewpoints, the general theoretical macro-economic literature, the work dealing with more complex linear models, and the developments in large non-linear econometric models. The three strands of literature have paralleled each other to a remarkable degree, although there are clear differences in emphasis. Early formal models largely ignored expectations effects although abstract discussions of the general problem often qualified the formal models by pointing to the importance of expectations. Expectations were first treated explicitly through the use of backward extrapolation rules such as adaptive expectations. It quickly became obvious that these models suffered from the problem of implying long-run predictable errors on the part of agents under certain circumstances and the early 1970s saw the beginning of a move towards the widespread use of rational expectations. This assumption has proved immensely powerful in analytical work that is more concerned with long-run equilibrium effects. More complex linear models have allowed the investigation of questions of credibility and time inconsistency under the RE assumption and have given rise to many important insights. It is perhaps the large empirical models where the weakness of the RE assumption has become most apparent: as a tool for analysing long-run behaviour in abstract RE it is both powerful and useful, but it is not a good representation of the short-run dynamic behaviour of many markets and the large models have really emphasised this weakness. The natural progression of the treatment of expectations effects is to move from the strong RE assumption to a weaker model, which gives the possibility of making errors in the short run while ruling out the implausible long-run systematic errors. This gives rise to the introduction of learning models. These have remained to a large extent a side issue in the theoretical literature but it is our view that these models will constitute an increasingly important feature of the empirical models. This represents a move back from the assumption of full rationality in expectations towards the ideas of bounded rationality more consistent with the psychological literature on learning processes.

7 Forecasting in practice

Geoffrey Dicks and Andrew Burrell

7.1 Introduction

It was Denis Healey who hoped to do for economic forecasters what the Boston Strangler did for door-to-door salesmen – but he reckoned without the forecasters themselves!

In recent years the whole process of economic forecasting has come under considerable criticism, most notably for the failure of the forecasters – all of them – to provide advance warning of the length and depth of the early 1990s' recession. It is true, definitionally, that some forecasters have done better than others, but the general impression is one of failure. Why is it that after a quarter of a century of model-building and economic forecasting at the London Business School, we were unable to meet this challenge?

This chapter does not attempt to answer the question directly; rather it describes the process of forecasting the macro-economy with the use of a large-scale econometric model, of the sort in use at the London Business School for the last 25 years. In so doing, it highlights the difficulties of forecasting the future (forecasting the past is relatively easy), and in this roundabout way provides some insight into the recent track record.

7.2 The forecasting process: an overview

Except in the case of the virgin forecast, the starting point for any forecast is its immediate predecessor. What every forecaster would dearly like to be able to do is to re-publish his (or her) earlier set of numbers, unchanged in any detail, and accompanied by a fanfare of trumpets and banner headlines of the 'we got it right' variety. In practice, no forecast, no matter what the interval between it and its predecessor, will be unchanged: there is always some new economic data or other information to invalidate the published forecast at least in some minor, if not major, regard.

The starting point in practice is therefore a post-mortem on the most recently published forecast in the light of subsequent economic developments. What new information is there? Where did the previous forecast go wrong and why? How seriously has it been wounded? In some cases, most often if the forecast interval is only a month, as it is for virtually all City-based forecasts, the published forecast may be holding up well, especially if there has been little in the way of new economic data or other news in the interim. But in the majority of instances, notably in the case of the 3–6-month interval common amongst academic and governmental institutions, there will be a considerable body of new information. Some of this may be routine updates of the economic database; some may require a major re-examination of the basis on which the forecast was made. For example, the October 1987 stock market crash led – wrongly as it happened – to a major re-evaluation of the outlook for demand in the world economy, and the withdrawal of sterling from the European Exchange Rate Mechanism in September 1992 changed the fundamental policy assumption on which most forecasts had been based prior to that date. In the worst circumstances, forecasters can even find their forecasts rendered invalid in the short period between finishing the forecast and its publication.[1]

Once the post-mortem is complete and its lessons learned, it is possible to make a start on the new forecast. There are two preliminary steps: one is to decide on the exogenous assumptions on which the forecast is to be based; the second is an analysis of the current conjuncture.

All large macro-economic models, such as are in use at the London Business School, include a set of exogenous, predetermined, variables, which have to be set in order for the model to solve out the endogenous, determined within the model, variables. The main types of exogenous variable relate to macro-economic policy and the world economy. The latter may themselves be determined endogenously within a model, for example most of the world inputs into the UK forecast are outputs of the global econometric model (GEM) (see Chapter 8 for a description of GEM), or they may be set judgementally. An example of the latter is the dollar price of oil, which is forecast in the short term on the basis of a judgemental assessment of the OPEC policy stance as well as the underlying supply and demand factors, both in the GEM and UK forecasts. In the medium term, as we do not have a well-developed model of the oil market, we make the convenient assumption that the oil price remains unchanged in real terms, that is the dollar price of oil rises in line with manufactured prices measured in dollars.

Early descriptions of the use of macro-models emphasised not just forecasting but also, and with at least equal weight, policy analysis. Models were to be used, on a forward-looking basis, to analyse the effect on the outlook of alternative policies and, on a backward-looking basis, to perform counter-factual simulations in which economic history is re-written on the basis of a different policy framework.[2] For this reason forecasts were traditionally based on the assumption of 'unchanged policy', with alternative policies explored in model simulation. The definition of 'unchanged policy', although straightforward in theory, is more difficult in practice and, following the lead of the stockbrokers, most forecasters now make their best guess of the stance of macro-economic policy and produce 'unconditional' forecasts on that basis.

A considerable amount of the forecaster's time and effort goes into what Keating (1985), in his definitive account, describes as 'conjunctural analysis'. It is important to understand exactly where the economy is at the time of the forecast, to build up a picture of the current conjuncture. The problem arises because national accounts data are only available with a delay, but other, more timely, data throw light on economic developments. By using monthly indicators and survey data, it is possible to fill in the gaps on the 'ragged edge' of the forecast.

On the basis of a set of exogenous assumptions (principally world and policy) and a rigorous assessment of the current conjuncture, the forecast proper can be embarked upon. It is the product of the model and the forecaster's judgement, as revealed by the constant adjustments (also known as intercept adjustments, residuals, fudge factors) used to modify the pure model forecast. It is here that the forecaster applies 'loving, tender care' to the model and imposes upon it priors and/or judgement. In so doing, the forecaster tends to be guided by forward-looking surveys of business intentions, plus knowledge of which areas of the model are known to be weak – generally parts of the model that have forecast badly in the past. In the short term the forecast may be swayed to a considerable degree by the forecaster; in the medium term, if the model is of any use at all, it should be the model that dominates.

It is clear from this brief outline that significant differences between forecasts can arise for a large number of reasons: different exogenous, especially policy, assumptions; a different assessment of the current conjuncture; and a different underlying economic model. Yet we also observe that the spread of the forecasts tends to be relatively limited: for all the differences, the forecasts tend to cluster. We examine the role of the consensus forecast later in this chapter.

7.3 The forecasting industry

Before we consider the London Business School forecasting methodology, we should examine the industry in which we are located.[3] Forecasts of the UK economy are produced by organisations in up to eight different categories, as shown in Table 7.1.

Within the Government, forecasts are produced by the Treasury and the Bank of England. The former are published twice a year in the Budget and Autumn Statement;[4] the latter is currently barred from publishing its forecasts, lest they conflict with those of the Treasury. In each case the forecast is produced with a full-scale macro-economic model, that of the Bank originally (in the mid-1970s) being derived from the London Business School model.

The second category of UK forecast is produced by the international organisations as part of their global forecasting and policy appraisal exercise. The forecasts are produced by a (changing) mix of judgement and model-based analysis.

The United Kingdom is possibly unique in the range of academic forecasts and models that is produced. As a generalisation, none of the academic bodies sought to enter the business for the love of producing forecasts: their original interest was policy and the models that were developed reflected in large part the policy priors of their proprietors. Indeed the proprietors generally held strong political views and the academic groups are listed in accordance with these political views: from left to right in

Table 7.1 The UK forecasting community

I.	The Government
	1. HMT
	2. BoE
II.	International organisations
	3. OECD
	4. EC
	5. IMF
	6. United Nations
	7. World Bank
III.	The academics
	8. [Cambridge Economic Policy Group, CEPG]
	9. National Institute for Economic and Social Research, NIESR
	10. [Cambridge Growth Project] Cambridge Econometrics
	11. London Business School
	12. [City University Business School, CUBS]
	13. [Liverpool]
	14. Warwick Bureau
IV.	Treasury model users
	15. ITEM
V.	UK commercial
	16. Henley Centre
	17. Oxford Economic Forecasting
VI.	Overseas commercial
	18. WEFA
	19. DRI
VII.	The City
	20. UBS Phillips and Drew
	21. Goldman Sachs
	22. Shearson Lehman
	23. CSFB
VIII.	Pressure groups
	24. CBI
	25. TUC

Square brackets have been put around those groups from which the ESRC has withdrawn funding.

terms of the political spectrum. Competition between the groups therefore tends to be aimed at the ear of the politicians and is not about the accuracy of the forecasts except in as much as these are a vehicle for policy recommendations. In contrast, in the United States the forecasting industry tends to be run more on commercial lines and competition is very much about the accuracy of forecasts; policy prescriptions take second place.

Originally all of the academic groups depended for funding on the Economic and Social Research Council (ESRC), organised over the last ten years through the ESRC's macro-economic consortium. In successive rounds, however, the ESRC has withdrawn funding from some of the groups (those shown in square brackets in Table 7.1), concentrating its support at the present time upon the London Business School and the National Institute. Despite the lack of official funding, Patrick Minford (Liverpool) and Wynne Godley (Cambridge Economic Policy Group, CEPG) are still producing forecasts. Indeed there is something of an unholy alliance between these two groups, which have been among the most ferocious critics of Government policy throughout the recession of the early 1990s.

The distinctive view of the CEPG is that there is a longstanding upward trend in import penetration, which will always constrain the ability of the UK economy to turn expansionary demand policies into real output. In its early days the CEPG argued strongly for import controls as a way of holding back this adverse trend; more recently Godley has argued for a competitive devaluation of the pound. At the opposite end of the political spectrum, Minford developed a model based explicitly on rational expectations monetarism. From this standpoint, he argued (with the support of five others, known collectively as the Liverpool Six) that policy inside the ERM was far too tight and that the pound should be withdrawn from the ERM and policy-making returned to the footing of domestic monetarism based on targets for the money supply. In terms of this particular debate, the National Institute for Economic and Social Research (NIESR) and the London Business School, though arriving at the position from historically different standpoints, supported the policy of ERM membership.

An important innovation on the part of the ESRC was the establishment in 1983 of the Warwick Bureau (ESRC Macro-econometric Modelling Bureau) as the 'watchdog' of the ESRC-funded modelling groups. Each of the publicly supported groups is obliged to deposit its forecast, the model and database with the Bureau once a year. This serves two purposes. The less important in practice is that academics outside the main groups should have access to the models; the more important is the work that the Bureau itself has carried out on comparative model properties and forecast comparisons.[5]

It was in 1975, as a result of the Bray amendment,[6] that the Treasury was obliged not only to publish its forecasts but also to make its model available to outside users. This innovation spawned at least two clubs whose 'unique selling point' (USP) was the use of the model which the Treasury itself used. The St James's Group (run by the *Economist* newspaper's Economic Intelligence Unit) is defunct but the Independent Treasury Modelling Group (ITEM) is still producing forecasts using the Treasury model.

In a growing market, a number of outside commercial companies have been able to produce and sell forecasts. These include a number of UK companies, of which the Henley Centre and Oxford Economic Forecasting (OEF) are the best known, as well as the largest US companies. OEF has in fact chosen to follow the London Business

School route by setting up its own forecasting club, in which it offers a set of linked international models in a user-friendly hands-on framework.

Perhaps the best-known individual forecasters come from the City institutions. Table 7.1 includes four from what could be a very long list.

Finally the table also lists the two sides of the labour divide, the employers and the trade unions. The latter does not produce a forecast in its own right but the CBI has a well developed quarterly model, which it uses, in combination with its economic surveys, to produce short-term forecasts. In either case the prime motivation is to sway Government policy-making in the favoured direction.[7]

One innovation is the initiative of former Chancellor Lamont, announced in the Autumn Statement of 1992, to set up an independent panel of forecasters 'to report to the Chancellor of the Exchequer three times a year on the current position of and future prospects for the UK economy'. The original members of the panel were Andrew Britton (NIESR), Professor Tim Congdon (Lombard Street Research Ltd), Professor David Currie (London Business School), Gavyn Davies (Goldman Sachs), Professor Wynne Godley (King's College, Cambridge), Professor Patrick Minford (Liverpool University) and Andrew Sentance (CBI). The panel delivered its first report in February 1993 recommending (by six votes to one) that there should be no fiscal tightening in the March 1993 Budget, as the priority should be to foster economic recovery. This view was reflected in Mr. Lamont's Spring Budget.

7.4 The starting position

The London Business School publishes forecasts of the UK economy three times a year – in February, June and October – and forecasts of the international economy twice a year – in June and December. For other groups the forecast periodicity is twice a year (Treasury, the OECD, the IMF), quarterly (NIESR, Liverpool) or monthly (most City forecasters). The period between published forecasts can be uncomfortable, especially if either the assumptions on which the forecast is based or the forecast itself are proving to be well off beam. The City institutions solve the problem by invoking the 'forecast early, forecast often' principle; at the London Business School we back up the three major economic outlooks with nine interim forecast releases. By this device we are able to react to economic developments that occur between forecasts such as the Budget (November) or other unforeseen major changes. The forecast release also enables us to examine and analyse other developments, for example the miners' strike of 1985 or alternative outcomes to the General Election.

Whatever the periodicity of the main forecast, the starting point of the forecasting round is the last published forecast. Before we return to this question, it is worth noting the concept of the 'forecasting round'. All forecasting institutions iterate towards the published forecast. It is not just a case of running the model and publishing the outcome; the model is run, a forecast is produced and examined, problems are identified (which may be trivial, for example, the latest data may not have been incorporated properly), the model is run again with shortcomings corrected and the process starts again.

In the case of most forecasting organisations, the forecasting round is an internal affair. The forecaster produces a forecast, which is then commented upon by his colleagues. This would certainly be the case at the Treasury, where the forecasting process is secret.[8] It is less true of the international bodies such as the OECD or the IMF, which produce their forecasts for the world economy after due consultation with a large number of national organisations, including the government.[9]

At the London Business School, we have taken the concept further by establishing a consortium of companies that participate in the forecasting process. The history of this development is itself interesting. For ten years, from its inception in the mid-1960s, the Centre for Economic Forecasting (CEF) at the London Business School, in common with other academic institutes such as NIESR, was funded almost entirely by the ESRC (in those days known as the Social Science Research Council, SSRC). In 1975 the ESRC took the decision that it no longer wished to fund forecasting as an activity. It viewed its remit as funding pure research, not forecasting: it was prepared to fund model developments (research) but not the use of the model to produce forecasts. Hence it suggested to the London Business School that, if it wished to continue its forecasting activities, it should seek commercial funding.[10] The Centre for Economic Forecasting responded, under the far-sighted leadership of Sir James Ball, by establishing a forecasting consortium, a group of 12–15 companies that have, since that time, supported and contributed to the forecasting process.[11]

The forecasting round at the London Business School therefore involves a dialogue with CEF consortium members. At an early stage in the forecasting round, members of the consortium are circulated with a forecast, that is a full computer print-out of the quarterly forecast, together with an agenda of items that need to be discussed. These include not only the forecast but any worthwhile alternative scenarios that should be considered. In addition, we draw on the expertise of consortium members in their own specialist fields. For example, we look to Shell for guidance on likely developments in the oil price, to RTZ and Unilever for their views on metal and soft commodity prices, to Barclays Bank for up-to-date information on credit demand, to IBM (UK) for trends in the demand for computers, to the electricity generators for current electricity demand and so on. In addition to their expertise in their own sector, we consult with consortium members on the overall shape of the forecast. The whole process is invaluable and, although the final product is the responsibility of the London Business School alone, it does mean that at the end of the forecasting round, the numbers have been examined by more pairs of eyes than is probably the case for any other published forecast.

A second spin-off from the 1975 ESRC decision was the introduction in 1976 of *Economic Outlook*, published by Gower. Before this time, the output of the CEF had been confined to academic articles and other research papers and, on the forecast side, a thrice-yearly article in the *Sunday Times*. The latter, which started in 1966 and has continued to this day, necessarily provides only a cursory treatment of the forecast. In *Economic Outlook* we are able to offer not only a lengthy analysis of economic developments and a full description of the forecast but also our (and others') views on economic policy as well as briefing papers on matters of interest. *Economic Outlook* is now into its 17th volume and is sold on annual subscription to over 500 organisations.[12]

The London Business School's UK forecast publishing schedule is focused on the end of February, June and October with a summary of the forecast appearing in the *Sunday Times* on the last Sunday of the month followed by the publication of *Economic Outlook* and wider press coverage the following day. The timetable therefore requires that the bulk of the forecasting activity is concentrated in January, May and September with a meeting of the consortium at around the third week of the month. For *International Economic Outlook*, which appears early in the months of June and December, the main forecasting periods are April–May and October–November, with consortium meetings at the end of April and October. The different periodicity of the two publications causes an immediate problem, not in the Spring/early Summer, when the international round conveniently precedes the UK round, but at other times of the year the international and domestic forecasts do not dovetail. The problem is most acute in the October UK forecast, which has to be based on the June international forecast with only a minimal amount of updating, i.e. not a fully revised set of international numbers.

The first task of the London Business School's forecasting round is to produce a forecast for discussion with the consortium.[13] This exercise can be either a major or a minor exercise. In the three months since its publication, the previous forecast might be holding up well, in other words neither the assumptions on which it was based nor the outturn of the economy in the interim have been seriously at odds with the published forecast. In this case it is a relatively minor task to update the existing forecast for the new data (which is different but only in small degree) and to inspect the (minor) changes that this will have produced.

Often, however, the need will be for a major reassessment of the previous forecast. This could be because the fundamental forecast assumptions no longer appear valid or because the performance of the economy in the interim period has not been in line with the earlier prognosis. Examples of the former include sharp changes in the oil price, such as occurred in 1973–4, 1979–80 and 1985–6, or a change in the underlying stance of economic policy, such as the withdrawal of sterling from the ERM in September 1992 and the devaluation that followed. The prime example of the latter is when the economy is close to a turning point in the economic cycle. Forecasting the precise timing of a turning point is extremely difficult, especially when confidence factors are important, and it may be that a forecast either missed a turning point or forecast one that did not happen. In terms of the early 1990s' experience, most forecasters were caught out by the length of both the upturn – the expectation was that the economy would turn down before it eventually did in the middle of 1990 – and the downturn, which continued right through 1992.

The post-mortem that is carried out on the published forecast will be able to identify such problems, both minor and major. One particular insight is of importance. We suggested earlier that the forecast is the product of the economic model and the forecaster's judgement (expressed via the setting of constant adjustments). The evidence is that for the most part the forecaster 'adds value', that is the published forecast tends to be an improvement on a pure model-based run, one in which the constant adjustments are set to zero.[14] Gratifying though this verdict is, it is important to establish in the post-mortem whether there are any exceptions in the published forecast. Are there, in other words, parts of the forecast that are both going off track and that would not have gone off track if the forecaster had not over-ruled, via constant adjustments, the pure model output? We are aware of one important occurrence of this in recent years, namely the path of consumption in 1987–8, which is worth examining in more detail.

The boom of the late 1980s is largely attributable to the strength of consumers' expenditure (model variable C), though not entirely, as investment was also extremely strong. The latest (1992 Blue Book) data are set out in Table 7.2. There are a number of technical points to be made about the data shown in Table 7.2. The first is that the data are the latest estimates and have been through several revisions since they were first published, one of which reflects the change in the national accounts base year to 1985. The second is that the equation for consumers' expenditure in the model did not change over this period, implying that changes to historical residuals reflect changes to the historical database. But the point that the table illustrates is that over a period of years we misinterpreted the recent past. Consistently from 1985 onwards the consumption function under-predicted the actual data (a positive residual). We interpreted this as a temporary aberration and most notably in the forecasts of October 1985, 1986 and 1987 lowered the constant adjustment when with the benefit of hindsight we should have run on the positive residual. What we failed to understand in this episode was that

Table 7.2 Annual percentage change (savings ratio as percentage of disposable income)

	1985	1986	1987	1988
C	3.8	6.4	5.5	7.4
RPDI	3.3	4.1	3.5	6.0
SJ£:	10.6	8.6	6.8	5.6
Forecast of C				
October 1985	2.5	3.8	3.7	3.1
October 1986	3.5	4.7	4.1	3.1
October 1987	3.7	5.8	4.0	3.9
October 1988	3.8	6.0	5.2	5.1
Constant adjustments (annual average); forecast of				
October 1985	−132	−400	−400	−400
October 1986	120	104	−75	−200
October 1987	67	396	80	−137
October 1988	601	816	927	1009

RPDI, real personal disposable income; SJ£, personal sector's savings ratio.

the consumer was prepared to borrow to an unprecedented extent, such that the savings ratio fell to an all-time low and the personal sector's overall financial balance (savings minus investment) went negative, again an unprecedented event. It may be excusable not to forecast out-turns that have never happened before, but it would clearly have been better not to have switched positive residuals to negative constant adjustments in the way we did. The post-mortems that we carried out on successive forecasts at this time revealed our downward bias on consumption, yet we persisted in our error.

7.4.1 Assumptions

The world economy

For the last 3 years the London Business School has been collaborating with the National Institute in the maintenance and development of the GEM. Forecasts of the world economy are prepared using GEM and written up in *International Economic Outlook*. The methodology of producing a forecast of the world economy within GEM is essentially similar to the methodology of producing individual country forecasts with the added advantage (discussed in Chapter 8) that trade flows, capital account flows and exchange rates can be made internally consistent. In this chapter, we concentrate on the use of world variables as an input to the UK forecast.

The United Kingdom is (relatively) a small, open economy, heavily exposed to the world environment. Approximately one-third of UK output is exported and a similar proportion of resources used in the UK economy are imported. The buoyancy or otherwise of the world economy is therefore of critical importance to the United Kingdom. This applies not just to output and trade but also to inflation – of world manufactured prices, oil and non-oil commodity prices. Indeed for much of modern history the dominant effect on the UK cycle has been the world economic cycle. The incidence of UK recession, if not its depth, over the last 20 years has coincided by and large with that in the world economy, and similarly for the boom.

There is one possible exception to the general rule, which is that the UK economy has at times been differentially affected by changes in the oil price. For the last 10 years or more, with the development of the North Sea oil fields, the United Kingdom has been self-sufficient in oil, whereas most of our main trading partners are significant net oil importers. Hence increases in the oil price have a relatively positive effect on the UK balance of payments and, for this reason, tend to push the pound higher on the foreign exchanges. This was certainly a feature of the 1980s: at the start when the oil price rose sharply and in the middle when it fell.

A second important determinant of the exchange rate and/or domestic interest rates is the level of interest rates in the world economy and/or Germany. The and/or qualification is significant in this context. Ahead of ERM entry in October 1990 and again since 16 September 1992, UK interest rates were set at the Chancellor's discretion, with the exchange rate (the sterling index is probably the appropriate variable in this context) forming a key part of the Chancellor's judgement. The task of the forecaster is to mimic this procedure, setting an exogenous path for interest rates and deriving a consistent forecast for the exchange rate. Inside the ERM, the direction is reversed. The path for UK interest rates is derived from a forecast (exogenous to the United Kingdom but consistent with the German forecast produced in GEM) of German interest rates and the need to hold the pound within its ERM parity band. Over the Summer of 1992 it was the interest rate implications of ERM membership, which were proving unpalatable for an economy entering its third year of recession, that helped focus the market attention on the pound, driving it below its ERM floor.

The description of events in the preceding paragraph offers an interesting insight into the forecasting process. It shows how the direction of causality between exchange rates and interest rates varies according to the exchange rate regime that is being operated, and that, no matter which regime, interest rates and the exchange rate have to be consistent one with another. The forecast that drops out of these underlying policy assumptions then feeds back onto the question of whether the policy stance is tenable or not. If not, and something has to give, the forecaster has to identify precisely where the weak link lies.

From this above discussion it is evident that there are a number of world series that are important for the UK forecast. These include:

1. Output and trade: for the determination of UK exports.
2. Oil prices: inflation and the exchange rate.
3. Non-oil commodity prices: inflation.
4. Manufactured goods prices: inflation and competitiveness.
5. Interest rates: exchange rate and interest rates.

UK policy

We come back to the question of forecasting exchange rates and monetary policy below but first we need to return to the philosophical question of unchanged policy versus unconditional forecasts that we raised in the overview above. At an early stage in the history of UK macro-economic forecasting, it was the norm to forecast on the basis of unchanged policy. In the 1960s, when the pound was stable against the dollar under the Bretton Woods exchange rate arrangements and when, because of this, inflation was low and reasonably stable, this was a relatively straightforward process. It was assumed that the pound would stay at $2.80 (with its implications for interest rates), tax rates were unchanged and the volume of public spending was as set out in successive White Papers. At the level of the world economy, forecasters assumed (in as much as they even bothered to make the assumption) that the oil price was stable at just under $2 a barrel.

In the course of the 1970s and 1980s these cosy assumptions had successively to be jettisoned and in the process the definition of unchanged policy came to be re-written. Following the break-up of Bretton Woods it was no longer possible to assume exchange rate stability, nor with the emergence of OPEC the stability of the oil price.

Inflation became a major problem and its effects on the tax system were explicitly recognised by the Rooker–Wise amendment, which provided for the automatic indexation of personal tax allowances (to offset what is known in American parlance as 'bracket creep'). As a result, most unchanged policy forecasts now allow for Rooker–Wise indexation and, although it is not a statutory requirement, also for the revalorisation of specific duties.

But other 'neutral' assumptions are less clear cut. Public spending is no longer planned in volume terms (which almost always led to higher-than-planned spending in cash terms); rather the planning total is set on a cash basis. The implication is that an over-run on price will lead to an automatic offset in volume, holding the total within the cash limit. Needless to say, public spending is not always kept within target despite changes and improvements over the years to the Treasury's targets – the 1992 Autumn Statement introduced a new control total that does not include demand-determined spending, such as unemployment benefit, which automatically varies with the cycle.

If, as has usually been the case, public spending is forecast to come in above target, what does this imply for tax policy? Since the introduction of the medium-term financial strategy (MTFS) in 1980, successive budgets have always shown a path for the public sector borrowing requirement (PSBR) over the medium term. This has usually been presented as a target rather than as a constraint but it opens up a difficult issue for the forecaster. If both public spending and the PSBR are forecast above the levels in the Budget Red Book, should it be assumed that taxes will be raised to fill the gap or that the overshoot will be accepted? Sensibly, with the benefit of hindsight, most forecasts have assumed the latter, though it can readily be seen that the question of what is unchanged policy has become progressively more difficult to interpret.

This conclusion applied even more obviously to the MTFS in its early days, as we were told in the 1980 Budget that 'there would be no question of departing from the money supply policy, which is essential to the success of any anti-inflationary strategy'. Again, with the benefit of hindsight, any forecast that took this statement at face value, that is to imply that interest rates would be raised to prevent the money supply (sterling M3) from exceeding its target growth range, would have made serious mistakes on the eventual out-turn of the monetary aggregates and interest rates.

For all of these reasons, therefore, the definition of unchanged policy has become progressively difficult to interpret, and most forecasters have abandoned the strict concept. What it means is that forecasters have to make clear the assumptions on which their forecast is based and this has produced two distinct strategies for policy assumptions. One is the minimalist approach of the Treasury, whose forecasts are always presented (for obvious reasons) on the 'conventional assumption that sterling remains close to recent levels' and on the 'standard assumptions of the indexation and revalorisation of taxes' and of a stable oil price (Autumn Statement, 1992, paragraphs 8, 10, 15).

For many independent forecasters, especially the stock-brokers, the alternative strategy of producing an unconditional forecast has been adopted. In this approach the forecast embodies a 'best guess' of the policy framework, covering likely changes on the monetary policy front, to fiscal policy, oil prices, tax rates and public spending.

In many ways this is a more honest approach than the alternative of spelling out the forecast assumptions. It is evident that the borderline between a forecast and an assumption is fairly nebulous – on what basis, other than what the forecaster thinks will happen, are assumptions made? The point is made more tellingly by another example from outside the policy arena. There have been occasions when some forecasters thought that it was not possible to forecast earnings with any degree of accuracy. They therefore made an 'assumption' for earnings, though obviously the assumption was bound to be their best guess of the likely out-turn: hence it was a forecast.

The London Business School approach, while fighting shy of this arcane distinction, falls between the two stools. Policy 'assumptions' are based on a reading of government policy from which we derive forecasts of the exchange rate, interest rates, the PSBR, the level of public spending and so on. On tax rates, however, we usually use the conventional assumptions of no change other than indexation to take account of inflation.

The preceding section on world forecast variables has already covered some of the issues on UK economic policy, notably the interface between world and UK interest rates and the exchange rate. This is the area, probably more than any other, where the fundamental stance of economic policy-making is decided, in as much as the assumption with regard to the exchange rate is key to much else. Certainly some of the most important forecasting errors have stemmed from a failure to predict the course of, for example, the pound in 1980–1 and the dollar in 1983–5. Purely from a forecasting perspective, it came as some relief to be able to assume in our forecasts from October 1990 onwards that the pound would be held in the ERM at or close to a central parity of DM2.95. Unfortunately, again from the narrow perspective of the forecaster, this assumption is in abeyance and the inherently more difficult task of forecasting the combination of domestic and overseas interest rates and the exchange rate is once more the order of the day.

We have at our disposal an additional input into the forecast of exchange rates and interest rates in the shape of *Exchange Rate Outlook*, a monthly publication that forecasts exchange rates one year ahead. The forecast is essentially judgemental but, into its fifteenth year, *Exchange Rate Outlook* has a body of experience not available in many comparable products. It focuses on the four major currencies ($, £, DM, ¥) each month and, three times a year, extends its analysis to other currencies of interest, for example the French franc, the Swiss franc, the Spanish peseta and the Italian lira.

Two features of the *Exchange Rate Outlook* approach stand out. One is that the database contains all 17 currencies that make up the Bank of England's trade-weighted (1985 = 100) indices. This permits us to calculate consistent trade-weighted and bilateral forecasts for all 17 currencies, including forward rates. The second important feature is the concept of competitiveness from which the analysis of exchange rate movements starts. For all 17 currencies, and again on a consistent trade-weighted basis, an underlying purchasing power parity (PPP) rate is calculated, deviations from which represent above or below par competitiveness. Thus in September 1992 the *Exchange Rate Outlook* calculations suggested that the pound was 20% uncompetitive against the dollar and 3% against the DM. This, together with an assessment of likely interest rate movements, is the main determinant of the exchange rate forecast as published in *Exchange Rate Outlook*.

7.5   The current position

The post-mortem analysis of what we referred to above as the starting position shades into the next stage of the forecast cycle, the analysis of the current position. Almost the most important contribution that the forecaster can make is to ensure that the forecast starts off 'in the right place' and 'facing in the right direction', for we can be certain that if it does not the forecast itself will quickly be proved wrong. At this stage, therefore, the forecaster needs to confront the latest data not just to see what it says about the previous forecast (the post-mortem) but also to understand what it is saying about the current cyclical position of the economy.

A major bane of the forecaster's existence is that every new data set (released in the United Kingdom by the Central Statistical Office, CSO) contains not just the latest monthly or quarterly data but invariably also revisions to historical back data. And very often these revisions, as Table 7.2 has already made clear, are not small: indeed they may require a radical re-interpretation of the past, if not a complete re-write of recent economic history. The path of consumer spending between 1985 and 1988 is a recent example of how, with virtually every new set of quarterly data, the back data were revised upwards. In his autobiography, Nigel Lawson (1992) cites the example of the course of the trade figures in 1988, which, as originally published, failed to provide adequate indication of how rapidly the deficit was in fact widening.

A further example of how early CSO data can be seriously misleading is the recovery from the recession of 1980–1. According to the latest CSO data, the trough of the recession occurred around the turn of the year 1980–1. This was not readily apparent at the time, or even in March 1981, when the notoriously deflationary Budget of that year aroused the wrath of 364 economists. Nevertheless by June of that year we were sufficiently convinced that a recovery was under way to forecast GDP growth in 1982 in excess of 2% (Table 7.3). Over the next year, successive national accounts updates suggested that this view was over-optimistic and, by October 1982 (that is with data for the first half of 1982 to hand), we had scaled back the forecast. In fact we wrote

Table 7.3   Output in 1982

Annual % change	June 1981 Forecast	October 1982 Forecast	Blue Book 1983 Data	Blue Book 1984 Data
GDP(E)	2.2	1.3	2.3	1.4
Adj (%GDP)	0.6	−1.0	−1.2	0.6
GDP(O)	2.8	0.3	1.1	2.0

E, expenditure measure of GDP; O, output measure of GDP.

an article in *Economic Outlook* asking 'What Happened to the Recovery?' The output measure of GDP (O in the table) was now expected to rise by only 0.3% in 1982, though the expenditure measure (E in the table) was apparently holding up better. The change in sign in the discrepancy between the output and expenditure measures was confirmed in the 1983 Blue Book,[15] though both had apparently risen more rapidly in 1982 than seemed to be the case at the time. A year later, the picture had changed again. The output measure was revised up to show growth of 2% – it still does – though this time the expenditure measure was revised down. Furthermore, the level of GDP(O) in 1981 was raised so that the actual level estimate for 1982 was now 1.3% higher than had been published the previous year. In terms of the level of GDP(O) in 1982, therefore, the original June 1981 forecast was close to the mark, closer than the forecast made in October 1982!

Once the latest data is in place, and revisions to back data taken on board, the new information needs to be interpreted. The main task here is the analysis of the conjuncture (see page 127), backed up by a comparison of the latest data and the previous forecast (the post-mortem) and a comparison of the latest data with the output of the model.

The core of the London Business School model of the UK economy is a set of equations for a number of key variables such as consumer spending, investment, exports, prices and earnings. These equations have been estimated quarterly over a data set extending backwards over 20–30 years, usually in a regression framework (ordinary least squares estimates or more complex methods). The basis of this approach is to minimise in some sense the equation errors, that is the gap between the data and the fitted value of the regression. But this is revealing: the errors are minimised not eliminated. For every quarterly observation therefore there will be a residual, the difference between actual and predicted. The art of the forecast, as we suggested earlier, lies in the setting of the residuals into the future.

For those without experience of running models it might be thought that, once a model has been estimated and the exogenous assumptions made, all that has to be done is to run the model forwards with zero constant adjustments. While this would make everybody's life much simpler, it does not happen in practice, though the Warwick Bureau performs the exercise as a measure of the value added by the forecaster.

With the latest data in place, the forecaster runs the model to obtain a set of up-to-date residuals, that is the difference between the latest data and the pure model predictions. The residuals contain information on how well the model is performing with regard to the latest data, where this includes revisions to back data. The interpretation of these residuals is important, both with regard to the development of the economy and the performance of the model. For practical purposes models are not continuously re-estimated every time a new piece of data becomes available. At the present time most of the main model equations have been estimated up to the fourth quarter of 1985 or later. Thus an important question is whether the model equation has tracked well or badly in the recent, out-of-sample, period. In the case of the consumption episode already referred to, we found that the model was tracking the latest data badly, consistently under-predicting the out-turn, especially in the course of the upward revisions to the data (see the October 1988 constant adjustments in Table 7.2).

Where the latest data suggest that parts of the model are going off track, one strategy is to re-estimate the offending equation in its existing functional form (to obtain a different set of parameter estimates) or, more radically, to re-specify the equation. In the case of the consumption function, we adopted the latter course, introducing housing and non-housing financial wealth and demographic factors into the specification.[16] More generally, however, and for less critical parts of the model than consumer spending, the forecaster attempts to compensate for the weakness of the model through the setting of the constant adjustments. Hence, if an equation is consistently under- or over-predicting the data, this can be allowed for by maintaining positive or negative (respectively) constant adjustments over the forecast period.

The approach is not, however, as mechanistic as the preceding paragraph might suggest. In terms of the consumption example, the forecaster has to consider whether the under-prediction is likely to continue over the whole of the forecast period[17] or whether to 'run off' the constant adjustment, so assuming that the bias is temporary and that in due course[18] the equation will come 'back on track'.

The analysis is complicated in that nearly every important variable in the London Business School model[19] is estimated with a lagged dependent variable. In the case of a simple first difference equation the value of the lagged dependent variable is one; in other equations, estimated either by cointegration techniques or in an error correction framework, the coefficient on the lagged dependent variable (or variables) is estimated.[20] This means that future values of the variable in question (and thus of all model variables) will depend on the current value of the variable and hence on the current value of the constant adjustment. In practice this is less important than it might appear, except in the case of first difference equations. For example, the equation for personal income tax payments, which is not estimated but derived from the parameters of the tax system, is in first difference form so that any change to the starting position will affect all future outturns. Thus a constant adjustment of say £1bn in the first forecast period will raise the level of every quarter by £1bn (ignoring the small feedback), that is it would lower the PSBR by £4bn a year in perpetuity. Obviously such adjustments need to be used with caution.

Another important role of constant adjustments is where it is known (or thought) that there has been a genuine change in the structure of the model in the period since it was estimated but where there has not been sufficient time to change the specification of the model to allow for this. One example is the privatisation programme, under which various public sector companies were put into the private sector, thereby introducing a structural break into a number of series, for example business investment, both manufacturing and non-manufacturing. In the absence of a better method, most forecasters coped with these changes by the judicious use of constant adjustments.

A more important example of this is where equations have been estimated with time trends and where the forecaster has reason to believe the time trend may have shifted. The obvious example of this is exports of manufactures, where for most of the post-war period the UK share of world trade in manufactured goods has been on a declining trend. In many models this is captured by a negative time trend. Similarly import penetration of the United Kingdom has been rising and may be explained in the model by a positive time trend. What, therefore, should the forecaster do if he believes that the time trend has shifted: the UK share of world trade in manufactures has been reasonably stable over the last ten years? One answer is to offset the time trend by a constant adjustment of the opposite sign so that, for constant competitiveness, the United Kingdom holds its share of trade over the forecast period.

While the main purpose of residuals is to draw attention to parts of the model that are not performing well, 'one-off' residuals are also important. These occur as a result of specific events which it is known in advance are not captured by the equation. In the estimation procedure, they may be 'taken out' by dummy variables, which is how we have explained, for example, the increase in consumer spending in various periods ahead of pre-announced changes to VAT or other taxes, most notably in the second quarter of 1979 when VAT was raised to 15%. More recently, following the Budget of 1991, it was necessary, using the earlier experience, to estimate how big an effect the increase in VAT to 17.5% would have in bringing forward consumer spending.

In all of these instances, therefore, the use of constant adjustments may be second best to a re-specification of the model but in practical terms they offer the easiest way forward.

The constant adjustments for the main model variables used in producing the June 1993 forecast are shown in Table 7.4. They are multiplicative adjustments in the main, as the equations are estimated in logarithmic form. For most of the variables shown in the table the data set runs up to the fourth quarter of 1992. Hence prior to that period the residuals are erratic, varying in both size and sign. In the true forecast period, the constant adjustments tend to be smooth, either zero (e.g. manufacturing production, PRODMF), flat (volume of manufacturing exports, XMAN, price of manufacturing exports, PMMAN) or smoothly trending (average earnings in manufacturing, AEM).

In general, a new set of data (especially quarterly national accounts data) provides a new set of residuals both for the latest quarter and, where the data has been revised, for previous quarters. The new residuals have to be analysed for unforeseen developments and for indications that the model is going off track. The forecaster then has to decide how to extend the historical residuals into a series of constant adjustments over the forecast.[21] The important point is that, depending on how the recent history is interpreted, different sets of constant adjustments can produce radically different forecasts.

The setting of constant adjustments is complicated by model interactions, for example if prices are affected by wages and wages by prices, especially if there is simultaneity in the relationships. In this example a change to the constant adjustment on wages will affect prices and thence feed back onto wages. The position is even more complicated where model equations contain forward-looking variables, such that wages are affected by expected prices and vice versa. Where this applies a constant adjustment set at a future date will affect wages and prices at earlier time periods which, given wage–price interactions, makes residual setting a difficult process. At the present time the London Business School model has only a very limited set of forward-looking variables and the practical problems are small, though it was not the case in an earlier version of the model, which included a financial sector based on full rational expectations.

7.6 Conjunctural analysis

Most of the UK macro-economic models are quarterly with their framework corresponding in large part to that of the national accounts. GDP is both the sum of the expenditure components, the consumption + investment + government expenditure + exports–imports, of the textbook, and the sum of various categories of output (oil, manufacturing, services etc).[22] The data appear with a considerable lag, preliminary estimates of output appearing one-third of the way through the following quarter and full national accounts statistics appearing towards the end of that quarter. But though the complete picture is only available with a delay, it is possible to build up a partial picture of the conjuncture through other data sources.

The most important of these are the monthly indicators produced by the CSO itself. These include retail sales, industrial production, unemployment and vacancies, producer and retail prices, exports, imports and the balance of trade, the PSBR, money supply, bank and building society lending, and consumer borrowing. Retail sales, which account for approximately 40% of consumers' expenditure, are published in the third week of the following month; most of the other series listed above also appear in the course of the month after that to which they refer with the exception of industrial production and manufacturing output which lag by around six weeks.

In addition to the official monthly series there are three main supplementary sources: survey data (whose role in the forecasting process is discussed in the next section), trade data and market data.

The best source of survey data is the CBI, whose monthly and quarterly surveys of manufacturing industry have a long historical record and which have been supplemented in recent years by surveys of the distributive trades (in combination with the *Financial Times*) and of the financial sector (with Coopers and Lybrand). These have been joined in recent years by surveys from the Chambers of Commerce, the Institute of Directors and the Institute of Purchasing Managers, whose methodology mimics the long-running and successful National Association of Purchasing Managers Survey in the United States. Additionally there used to be the official (DTI) survey of industry's investment intentions (which has been discontinued) and the surveys of the various trade associations including the Engineering Employers Federation and various parts of the construction industry. Outside the industry surveys listed above, which give a good barometer of business confidence, the monthly Gallup survey conducted for the EC provides the same sort of information for the consumer and for the standing of overall consumer confidence. What these surveys bring to the forecaster is not so much a picture of future economic developments as a very good snapshot of where the economy is and where it has recently been. As such they both anticipate and complement the official statistics rather than provide genuine information about where the economy is heading.

Table 7.4 Summary of constant adjustments

	AEM	C	EEBARN	EEMF	IMAN	INMAN	KIID	OSWI	PC	PIMO	PRODMF	PMMAN	PXMAN	XMAN
	% 85=100	Levels £M85	% 0005	% 0005	% £M85	% £M85	% £M85	% 85=100	% 85=100	% 85=100	% 85=100	Levels 85=100	% 85=100	% 85=100
1989:1	−0.7	0.00	−1.6	−0.7	−3.8	13.2	−3.4	−0.5	−0.2	−1.0	0.0	−0.01	−0.4	4.1
1989:2	−1.5	0.01	−2.3	−0.8	0.7	9.7	−1.3	−0.4	0.7	−1.0	0.0	−0.02	−0.2	3.0
1989:3	−2.8	−0.01	−3.0	−0.5	−4.6	2.9	−1.2	−0.9	0.0	0.4	0.0	0.00	0.1	3.9
1989:4	−2.1	0.01	−2.6	−0.7	−6.1	2.7	−1.5	0.6	0.1	0.7	0.0	−0.01	−0.4	3.6
1990:1	−1.8	−0.01	−2.0	−1.6	−1.7	6.6	−0.6	0.6	0.0	0.8	0.0	0.00	−3.0	1.5
1990:2	−1.9	0.01	−2.4	−1.6	−11.4	4.8	−2.9	0.9	−1.9	1.2	0.0	−0.00	−3.1	2.6
1990:3	−0.9	−0.01	−0.7	−1.9	−13.8	1.0	−1.9	−1.4	0.5	0.3	0.0	−0.01	−3.7	−1.4
1990:4	−1.6	−0.01	−1.9	−2.5	−11.2	−2.6	−2.2	−2.4	0.1	0.7	0.0	−0.03	−4.7	1.6
1991:1	−0.6	−0.01	−1.5	−2.8	−8.9	−3.4	−1.1	0.4	−1.2	2.1	0.0	0.01	−3.6	0.2
1991:2	−2.1	−0.02	0.7	−2.6	−8.0	−11.3	−2.0	−1.9	1.5	2.0	0.0	0.01	−2.5	2.7
1991:3	−2.5	−0.01	−1.1	−2.4	−6.8	−12.8	−1.0	−2.5	−0.1	2.1	0.0	0.01	−2.6	0.4
1991:4	−1.0	−0.02	−0.7	−1.5	−4.1	−13.0	−2.6	−1.4	−0.1	2.3	0.0	0.01	−2.7	−0.6
1992:1	−0.1	−0.02	0.9	−1.2	−12.9	−9.8	−0.2	1.0	−0.8	2.5	0.0	−0.02	−2.4	−0.5
1992:2	−4.2	−0.01	0.7	−1.2	−4.3	−11.7	−4.0	−3.1	0.0	2.2	0.0	−0.01	−2.0	0.6
1992:3	0.0	−0.01	−1.7	−3.0	−4.9	−10.2	−1.3	−1.0	0.5	2.3	0.0	−0.02	−2.7	−0.9
1992:4	−0.7	−0.02	0.0	−2.3	−4.2	−12.0	−0.5	−2.2	0.5	1.5	0.0	−0.01	−0.5	3.7
1993:1	−4.0	−0.01	0.3	−1.9	−6.0	−13.0	−2.0	−0.5	−0.8	3.6	0.9	−0.01	−1.0	0.5
1993:2	−3.5	−0.01	0.0	−1.4	−6.0	−13.0	−2.0	−2.0	0.2	3.5	0.0	−0.01	−1.0	0.5
1993:3	−2.7	−0.01	1.0	−0.9	−6.0	−13.0	−2.0	−1.0	0.2	2.5	0.0	−0.01	−1.0	0.5
1993:4	−2.1	−0.01	−1.0	−0.9	−6.0	−13.0	−2.0	−1.0	0.2	2.5	0.0	−0.01	−1.0	0.5
1994:1	−2.5	−0.01	−1.0	−0.9	−6.0	−11.0	−2.0	−1.0	0.2	2.5	0.0	−0.01	−1.0	0.5
1994:2	−2.6	−0.01	−1.0	−1.0	−6.0	−11.0	−2.0	−1.0	0.2	2.5	0.0	−0.01	−1.0	0.5
1994:3	−2.7	−0.01	−1.0	−1.1	−6.0	−11.0	−2.0	−1.0	0.2	2.5	0.0	−0.01	−1.0	0.5
1994:4	−2.8	−0.01	−1.5	−1.1	−6.0	−11.0	−2.0	−1.0	0.2	2.5	0.0	−0.01	−1.0	0.5
1995:1	−2.9	−0.01	−1.5	−1.1	−6.0	−11.0	−2.0	−1.0	0.2	2.5	0.0	−0.01	−2.0	1.0
1995:2	−3.0	0.00	−1.5	−1.2	−6.0	−11.0	−2.0	−1.0	0.2	2.5	0.0	−0.01	−2.0	1.0
1995:3	−3.1	0.00	−1.5	−1.3	−6.0	−11.0	−2.0	−1.0	0.2	2.5	0.0	−0.01	−2.0	1.0
1995:4	−3.2	0.00	−1.5	−1.3	−6.0	−11.0	−2.0	−1.0	0.2	2.5	0.0	−0.01	−2.0	1.0

Table 7.4 continued

	AEM	C	EEBARN	EEMF	IMAN	INMAN	KIID	OSWI	PC	PIMO	PRODMF	PMMAN	PXMAN	XMAN
	%	Levels	%	%	%	%	%	%	%	%	%	Levels	%	%
	85 = 100	£M85	0005	0005	£M85	£M85	£M85	85 = 100	85 = 100	85 = 100	85 = 100	85 = 100	85 = 100	85 = 100
1996:1	-3.3	0.00	-1.5	-1.3	-6.0	-11.0	-2.0	-1.0	0.2	2.5	0.0	-0.01	-2.0	1.0
1996:2	-3.4	0.00	-1.5	-1.4	-6.0	-11.0	-2.0	-1.0	0.2	2.5	0.0	-0.01	-2.0	1.0
1996:3	-3.5	0.00	-1.5	-1.5	-6.0	-11.0	-2.0	-1.0	0.2	2.5	0.0	-0.01	-2.0	1.0
1996:4	-3.6	0.00	-1.5	-1.5	-6.0	-11.0	-2.0	-1.0	0.2	2.5	0.0	-0.01	-2.0	1.0

C = consumer's expenditure (£ million, 1985 prices)
EEBARN = non-manufacturing employment (1,000s)
EEMF = manufacturing employment (1,000s)
IMAN = manufacturing investment (£ million, 1985 prices)
INMAN = non-manufacturing investment (£ million, 1985 prices)
KIID = stock level; distribution (£ million, 1985 prices)
OSWI = average earnings in non-manufacturing non-government sector (index, 1985 = 100)
PC = consumers' expenditure deflator (index, 1985 = 100)
PIMO = producer prices; manufacturing output (index, 1985 = 100)
PRODMF = manufacturing production (index, 1985 = 100).

In addition to their surveys, trade organisations also provide hard data which go into official statistics and which are therefore helpful to the forecaster. An obvious example is the information on car sales provided by the Society of Motor Manufacturers and Traders.

The final source of non-national accounts data is that provided by the markets on a daily basis. A number of market variables are important components of any macro-economic model, such as the exchange rate (trade-weighted, $:£, DM:£), interest rates (base rates, mortgage rates, long rates), equity markets (FTSE-100) and so on. Indices of commodity prices are also available on a daily basis.

The availability of this wide range of information is exhaustively explored by Keating (1985), who tracks the life of the macro-economic forecaster over an eight-week period. While we do not wish to subject the reader to a repeat of this experience, the message is clear. On a daily basis there is a barrage of new information, which needs to be processed and with which the forecaster has to confront his forecast – whether it be the published forecast or the latest iteration of the forecast round. Of course there is a great deal of 'noise', especially in the market data, but repeatedly the forecaster has to ask what information is there in the latest data, to assess whether his or her underlying analysis of the conjuncture is correct and if not why not. This applies not just to the big picture but also to the small detail of the computer print-out.

7.7 The short-run outlook

For many forecasters, notably those in the City, the short-run outlook is the limit of their aspirations. As such, some firms of stock-brokers have let it be known that they have abandoned the use of a formal model[23] in preparing their forecasts – a reflection of their disenchantment over the failure to forecast the severity of the early 1990s' recession. What this is saying is that one-year ahead forecasts can in principal be put together without a formal model, as we ourselves attempt in *Exchange Rate Outlook*. A spreadsheet approach, which can be made to ensure that the national accounts adding-up constraints are satisfied, backed up by judgement may suffice. We do not believe this because, without the estimated parameters that a model embodies, it is not possible to work out what would be the effect of (say) a 1% cut in interest rates or of the fall in the pound which took place after 16 September 1992.

Be that as it may, it is certainly the case that the forecaster's informed judgement – informed by both their model and their analysis of the conjuncture – is of paramount importance for the short-term forecast. The aim of this section is to describe the complex interaction between the model and the forecaster in producing a short-term (one year to 18 months) forecast.

With or without a model, the forecaster approaches his task with a set of priors as to precisely where the economy is and the general direction in which it is heading. These priors, we have suggested, represent the informed judgement of the conjunctural analysis, interpreted through the model. But they are more than that. Survey data ask forward-looking questions and, even though the evidence suggests that the answers to these questions tell us more about where the economy is or has recently been, it would be rash to ignore what businessmen or consumers are telling us about their likely short-term behaviour. We examine the future information content of the surveys in detail in the next section.

It is also, unfortunately, the case that no forecaster operates in a vacuum and that all forecasters are inevitably influenced to a greater or lesser degree by what other forecasters are saying. This is perfectly legitimate when a forecast contains new information (as is often the case with the Treasury forecasts, which can include changes in the Budget or to public spending plans) but generally it reflects a desire on the part of forecasters not to distance themselves too much from the consensus. Especially in the City, the cost of being very wrong may be greater than the benefit of being very right. A good example of this is a recent survey by the *Financial Times* of forecasting performance over the early 1990s recession. What the FT survey claimed to do was to provide a ranking of forecasts in terms of how well they had forecast the path of GDP in 1990–2. What in fact the survey showed was a remarkable clustering of forecasts with the gap between the best and worst forecast smaller than the gap between the best forecast and what actually happened: all forecasts were bad; some were just worse than others.[24] The cynical conclusion would be that individual forecasters do not like to depart too far from the consensus. This may in fact be a valid strategy as there is evidence to show that the consensus will outperform any one individual forecast through time. It is because of this that there has sprung up a number of publications covering a wide range of forecasts and showing the consensus. We examine this development in a later section.

It has taken us a long time to get here but we are now ready, as it were, to start forecasting with our model. Our preparation has been thorough, including:

1. A post-mortem on earlier forecasts.
2. A new set of policies and other exogenous assumptions (including the world economic environment).
3. An examination of the latest data.
4. An interpretation of the current conjuncture.
5. An assessment of the latest survey data.
6. An updated set of constant adjustments.

All that remains is to run the model and examine the output.

As far as the short-term outlook is concerned, the first step is to fill in the blanks over the ragged edge, that is to make sure the recent past is as coherent as possible. At one level this is simply to be certain that the quarterly output of (say) industrial production is consistent with the monthly numbers already available, i.e. if two months' data have already been published the quarterly number is not implying an unlikely out-turn in the third month. A second straightforward task is to make sure that adding up constraints apply. Thus, the data on the PSBR appear before its components, which requires that the full set of public sector accounts has to be made to add up to the published number. Similarly the data on unemployment appear before those on employment and the working population.

Once the model is run with an up to date database, the output for the immediate future can be examined. Most forecasters, using a quarterly model, will proceed quarter by quarter, though there are two obvious problems with this. The first is that, although the short-term forecast may by itself be sensible, it may have distinctly unpalatable medium-term implications. This is why the London Business School has always run its models over the medium term to confront the medium-term implications of the short-term forecast. The second problem is the technical one that some models have forward-looking variables, often (rational) expectations in a number of equations. This means that it is not possible to solve the model recursively – period by period – because future values affect the current period. Thus the model has to be solved over the complete time horizon, not on a quarter-by-quarter basis. This obviously makes life difficult for the forecaster, though at the present time, with the exchange rate system in the model based on learning (which does not assume full rational expectations), it is possible to solve the model recursively. (See Chapter 6 for a full treatment of expectations in macro-economic models.)

We referred above to examining the model output. What does this mean in practice? Leaving aside the medium-term picture, which we come back to below, having run the model, we examine the output. At a trivial level, this operation may reveal mistakes but at a more fundamental level, the forecaster needs in some sense to be satisfied with each and every number on the print-out. For a model with 700 variables, run quarterly over ten years, this is no small task. In practice the forecaster looks at a number of key variables and relationships and asks whether they are 'sensible', whether they conform to his priors and so on. Does the picture which the numbers are describing make sense? – in broad outline? – in detail? When the forecast is written up (in *Economic Outlook* in the London Business School case), will it be coherent and convincing? and if not why not? Which bits of the forecast look implausible and why? It is clear that the forecasting process proper involves asking a number of searching questions of the model output and trying to understand why the model is saying what it is saying and, more importantly, why the forecaster feels uncomfortable with it. Once this process has been carried out, remedial action can be taken.[25]

An example will make clear what we are talking about. Suppose we ran the model and found that manufactured exports were shown rising 10% in the year ahead.[26] This is a large number in a UK context, though not without precedent. Since the mid-1960s manufactured exports have risen by an average of 4.4% a year, ranging from a peak of 14% in 1968 to an absolute decline of 6.1% in 1981. Manufactured exports are an important variable in the context of the UK economy (and hence of the model) and it is therefore important to understand why the model is indicating such a large increase. This involves examining two aspects of the forecast: the forecast for the explanatory variables and the equation residuals.

In the London Business School model (and most macro-economic models) manufactured exports are explained principally by the path of world trade and the competitiveness of exports. In the 1960s and 1970s the UK share of world trade declined steadily; in the 1980s it was reasonably stable. Thus in the context of a forecast

10% increase in world trade, 10% growth of UK exports may appear reasonable. This throws the question back onto the forecast of world trade: is 10% growth likely? Alternatively the forecast may imply a considerable increase in the UK share of world trade: is this likely? The answer depends on what has been happening to competitiveness. If, as occurred on and after 16 September 1992, the UK exchange rate fell around 15%, improving competitiveness in the short term by a similar amount, an increase in trade share may be appropriate. But how big an increase? What was the experience in 1968 after the November 1967 devaluation or in 1981–2 when the severe over-valuation of the pound was removed? The last question hints at another aspect of the calculation: is the absolute competitive position of the United Kingdom important, or just the fact that it has improved?

In principle, the model (which has been estimated over a period of history) which takes in these experiences and many more, should provide answers to the questions. But this leads onto the second aspect: the setting of constant adjustments. Suppose the equation left to itself results in a steady decline in the UK share of world trade, reflecting the experience of the 1960–70s rather than that of the 1980s. If this is the case, we may find that the equation has been under-predicting the data, i.e. there is a positive residual in recent quarters. Should we therefore run on the latest residual(s) to allow for the recent under-prediction in the forecast and if so at what level? The obvious possibilities would be to run on the latest residual, to set a constant adjustment at the average of the last four residuals or even to set adjustments to maintain the UK trade share at constant competitiveness. It is clear that there is an element of arbitrariness about the procedure.

Moreover, we can assume that we faced most of these problems in the June 1992 forecast, so that the forecast is simply the product of the lower value of the pound, which we did not anticipate in June 1992. So the question becomes: are we happy with the implied elasticity of demand for UK exports or was there a mistake in the June forecast that we are carrying forward? This is, we should say, a hypothetical example but it does provide a good illustration of the forecasting process, with the added benefit at the London Business School that the sort of questions that we have raised here are asked of a wide group of outside economists with a variety of experience.

In this description, particularly the reference to earlier devaluations, we have also touched on another weapon in the forecaster's armoury, the use of off-model information. In this example the information is implicitly contained in the model (by way of the historical estimation), but there are many instances where we call on estimates from outside the model to inform our judgement.

7.8 The role of survey data in economic forecasting

In addition to the official monthly indicators produced by the CSO, conjunctural analysis can be complemented by a range of additional information. An important component of this is survey data collected from questionnaires (see Table 7.5 for UK examples). These numbers are most often of qualitative rather than quantitative

Table 7.5 Survey indicators

Confederation of British Industry
The employers' federation initiated the questionnare survey in the United Kingdom in the late 1950s. At present, the published surveys are:

The Industrial Trends Survey (respondents 1400–1500)
A monthly enquiry into the current general business environment for manufacturing. Questions are asked about the state of order books, stock levels, output and prices. The survey is also published at quarterly intervals with a more detailed series of questions referring both to the previous 4 months and to projections for the next 4 months

The Distributive Trades Survey (respondents 500)
Formerly with the *Financial Times*. A monthly enquiry into the distribution sector, retailing in particular, but also wholesale and motor trades. Started in 1983 in order to give manufacturers better information on their main markets. It includes questions on sales, stocks and orders. Results can be compared to official retail sales statistics. A more detailed quarterly enquiry is also undertaken

Non-CBI surveys include
Gallup Consumer Confidence Survey
A monthly review of economic sentiment amongst consumers published by the prominent market research company

European Economy
A European survey of economic confidence which includes the CBI survey results for firms, the NEDO construction industry surveys and also the Gallup consumer confidence indicator

Chamber of Commerce, Institute of Directors and Institute of Purchasing Managers Surveys
Methodology mimics the long-running National Association of Purchasing Managers Survey in the United States which covers economic sentiment

---

indicators, unlike official statistics, and as such are not generally incorporated into macromodels. However, the information provided by tendency surveys is used extensively on an informal basis during the forecasting process.

Qualitative surveys involve a series of questions directed at a sample of economic agents, generally a group of firms or consumers. The form of the enquiry is usually 'What has been the trend with regard to output (say) over the past x months?' (often with the addition, 'relative to what is normal'), to which the response is either up, down or unchanged. These results are processed so that each category can be cumulated and the percentages for each response calculated. The usual practice is then to subtract the 'down' percentage from the 'up' percentage to get a 'balance' number which is used to summarise the results. Forward-looking questionnaires merely substitute 'in the next x months' for 'in the past x months'.

Survey results have a number of important advantages over official statistics. First, they are collected and disseminated far more rapidly than official numbers. In the case of the CBI industrial trends enquiry, publication is up to a month prior to the CSO manufacturing output data. Second, survey figures also provide some benchmark to assess the reliability of current CSO data if, for instance, the evidence from government series is conflicting. The CBI claims its surveys have forewarned of significant revisions in CSO statistics, in 1964 and 1974, when the two sources diverged significantly. Third, qualitative data can give information on an economic agent's intangible, but crucially important, subjective perceptions such as confidence levels and expectations. This aspect has attracted much academic investigation to establish just what information can be extracted from survey data. Last, the balance in qualitative surveys is not suitable for quantifying trends precisely although it is seen as valuable in discerning the timing of cyclical turning points. It may be no accident that the CBI was one of the first to predict a fall in output during 1991 (but there is certainly no evidence to show that their forecasts out-perform their rivals systematically).

How do we interpret quantitative data and what information do these numbers actually contain? Of all the UK sources, the CBI's Industrial Trends Survey (ITS) has been subject to the most detailed and systematic scrutiny. The monthly ITS has been going since 1958 and, although the form has undergone significant changes (see Junankar 1988), provides the richest source of back data. It gives, via a simple postal questionnaire, representative coverage of UK industry with 1400–1500 respondents sampled. This covers about 3 million employees and includes half of the UK's exporters. There is also a more detailed quarterly (tri-annual before 1972) enquiry run along similar lines and this data set has been used most frequently for research. All results are weighted according to industry, employment and output then carefully assessed before being published. An important advantage of CBI data is that it is on a micro level, all its questions are firm-specific and it is less likely to be subject to external influences, which may produce a bias in perceptions in macro-orientated surveys.

Interpretation poses important methodological problems for qualitative survey data particularly when comparing such data with official statistics (Klein and Moore 1981). Most attention is paid to the percentage balance figure, which approximates to the first derivative, or rate of change, of the corresponding economic indicator. To compare the net balance to a quantitative variable it must be cumulated unless the question refers to future changes. In this case the forward-looking net balance should be added to the cumulated actuals to allow for the correction of past forecast error. Use of the balance as a summary statistic involves certain assumptions on the nature of the statistical distribution of the responses. Such suppositions, while convenient, are not testable and may invalidate inferences.

Many questions ask for an assessment relative to what is 'normal'. The problem with this is that such perceptions are not time-invariant. The balance in the case of these surveys is not analogous to the rate of change but to whether the variable is above or below the accepted level. Thus it is the change in the balance which relates to the change in the indicator. Further problems in dealing with surveys include the overlap of survey periods, which tend to cover four month periods, the 'automatic' seasonal adjustment that is asked for by the CBI, and the phrasing of questions (e.g. the CBI changed from asking about values to volumes in the mid-1970s).

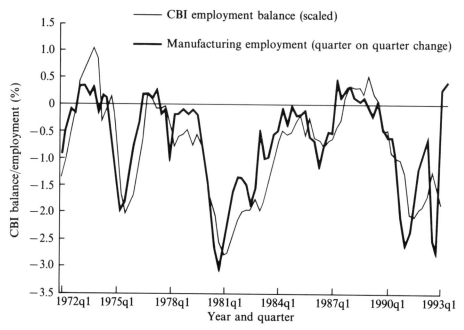

Figure 7.1 Manufacturing employment and the CBI survey

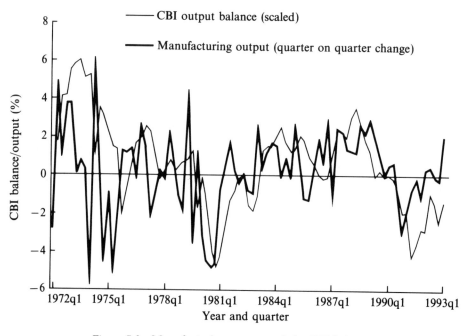

Figure 7.2 Manufacturing output and the CBI balance

How well does the CBI's ITS track the official statistics? The graphs show that there is a reasonably good fit of survey numbers to the official outturns for manufacturing employment and output (see Junankar 1988; Walsh 1991). More systematic work by Klein and Moore (1981) found that the CBI net balance series for orders, stocks and profit margins conformed closely to UK growth cycles and quantitative data. They conclude that such surveys are important for increasing our ability to forecast the present at the very least.

It is perhaps not surprising that industry insiders have more timely information than official statistics. A more important question is do the balances in the CBI survey questions relating to the future contain useful information. Savage (1975) regressed survey information on investment intentions, from the DTI and the CBI, but found that neither forecasts investment particularly well and so should only be used as a complement, not an alternative, to existing econometric relationships.

The 1970s saw the ascent of new classical economics and the rational expectations hypothesis (REH) and since then increasing attention has been paid to modelling expectations formation. This has led researchers to search for a proxy for these unquantifiable perceptions in survey data. Wren-Lewis (1985a,b) used the CBI's forward-looking output series in a model of UK manufacturing employment and found that they encompass specifications with adaptive expectations. He concludes that such numbers provide an under-utilised source of information about expectations, albeit with a very short time horizon, and an alternative to the strong assumptions of the REH. Pesaran (1987) utilises another approach for quantification of qualitative data. The regression technique uses the relationship between actual outcomes and past perceptions surveys for this purpose. This has a number of advantages over the probability method, common in earlier work, and the underlying assumptions are, in principle, testable. Pesaran uses the future price trend responses from the CBI Industrial Trends Survey to examine inflation expectations, to compare the regression and probability methods and to test them against the REH, which is strongly rejected.

In summary, it is important to distinguish the forecasting and modelling uses otrend surveys. The great advantage of survey data for forecasters is that they provide economic information some weeks before official publications. They can be used, in conjunction with CSO numbers, to help obtain a richer picture forecast of the present conjuncture. Surveys appear to track the relevant time series well and they are especially useful for indicating turning points or as a check for seemingly conflicting numbers.

However, qualitative data are not extensively used in econometric models because converting tendency surveys into qualitative expectations series is fraught with difficulties. Though research indicates that CBI data do provide useful information, such expectation series suffer from two fundamental flaws. First, CBI questions give a very short time horizon of only four months. Second, some structural equation to capture the evolution of expectations through time must be devised before survey results can be used for forecasting purposes. This means that the more general rational expectations formulation, for all its faults, is unlikely to be challenged as a paradigm in macromodelling usage.

7.9 The medium-term outlook

In principle the medium term forecast is no more than an extension of the short-term outlook; in practice it raises a number of extra issues, such as sustainability, and thereby acts as a check on the short-term forecast. An outlook that appears sensible in the short term may be implausible if it stretches out over a number of years. For example, it may be possible to run a deficit on the current account of the balance of payments equivalent to 4% of GDP, as the United Kingdom did in 1989, or a PSBR of 8% of GDP, as the government is forecasting for 1993–4, but a forecast that projected such deficits into the medium term would be lacking in credibility. Something would have to give.

It may be that there are forces in the model that correct such unlikely out-turns, especially if the model has been estimated in the error correction framework, which builds in desirable medium-term properties or the answer may be that policy will have to change. This is an example of the use of forecasts in guiding the policy-making process. We know that inflation today is the product of yesterday's policy stance and that tomorrow's inflation is determined by policy today: the forecast may therefore highlight the need for a change in policy today if it contains unwanted inflationary implications.

For the non-governmental forecaster without access to policy-makers, the task is to guess how and when the government might respond to the implications of this forecast. This is an especially taxing task in the case of monetary policy outside the ERM, where the interaction between interest rates and the exchange rate is very difficult to forecast in the short term let alone over the medium term.

The medium-term forecast also provides a useful check on the validity of the short-term forecast by way of the economy's 'great ratios'. Many of these are embodied in the model by way of the estimation process but it is important to monitor their output in the forecast. We have referred to some of these ratios above, for example the share of UK exports in world trade, the current account and budget deficit as a share of GDP (and the related debt:income ratio), and the personal sector savings ratio. Other important ratios are the share of imports in total final expenditure, which has an upward trend over the historical data set, the money supply to GDP (inverse velocity) ratio and so on. As a general rule, any variable that is the difference between two large numbers, or is a residual in the model, needs to be looked at closely.

In the current London Business School model, two such residual variables are of extreme importance: total company profits, which are the difference between the income and expenditure measures of GDP (they are measured in this way in the national income accounts), and imports, which are the difference between demand for GDP and domestic. Thus any 'implausible' forecasts for expenditure or income will show up in company profits and for the components of demand and domestic output in imports. As before, it is the forecaster who has to decide what is implausible in this context and to consider what adjustments need to be made to produce a more plausible outlook. Depending on the stage of the forecast, these adjustments could be simply to correct obvious mistakes in the forecast input, to require large adjustments to some of the forecast's underlying assumptions or marginal adjustments to the forecast output.

The same process applies to the important balances in the model, such as the balance of payments, the PSBR and the financial surpluses and deficits of the company and personal sectors. Questions as to their size and sustainability need regularly to be addressed.

7.10 Consensus forecasts

The idea of a forecasting consensus is a well established one. It is usually represented by the unweighted average of all predictions for a macro-economic variable made at a particular time. Such consensus measures are published on a monthly basis from surveys of a wide range of institutions by *Consensus Forecasts* and *Economic Forecasting* magazines. In addition to these explicit calculations, the Treasury produces a comprehensive survey of domestic forecasts and there are regular reviews of the state of expert opinion published in the *Financial Times*.

There is a theoretical reason for the interest paid to measures of the consensus. The forecast combination literature has shown that the accuracy of any predictions can be substantially improved by the combination of a number of individual forecasts (see Clemen (1989) for a survey). Furthermore it has been demonstrated that simple averages often perform as well as more complicated weightings of numbers when defining the consensus.

If combined forecasts are superior to single efforts then consensus numbers provide valuable information to the analyst. However, this proposition requires unbiased forecasts, that is predictions being made independently of each other. In practice this is not likely to occur. The rapid dissemination of information between groups and the easy access to consensus numbers mean that the economist can never be truly independent when framing a new forecast. Once reference is made to a combined forecast the nature of any consensus is changed (McNees 1992). If analysts actually aim for these measures then the consensus itself becomes a meaningless indicator.

One criticism of macro-economic forecasters is that their concentration on consensus measures fosters risk-aversion and reduces variety. Conservatism is the result of a highly competitive environment where forecasters, keen to preserve their credibility, are afraid to deviate from the conventional wisdom. However, the exercise is then reduced to producing a (misleading) consensus forecast rather than an independent assessment. This behaviour is seen by some as the cause of the failure of experts to accurately predict the economic changes during the late 1980s and early 1990s. In Figure 7.3 the out-turn for the percentage growth in GDP in each year is plotted against the forecasts made in the previous year. The lines represent aggregate predictions from the City, the academic modelling groups and other commercial

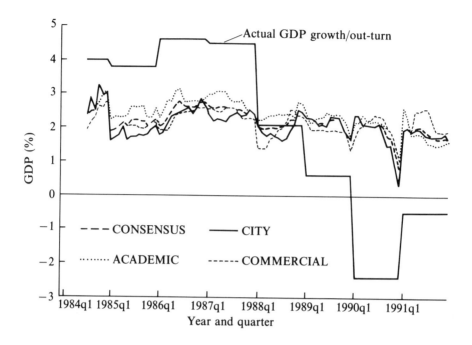

Figure 7.3 The forecasting record

institutes. The chart shows clearly that the difference between the highest and the lowest forecast is typically far smaller than the difference between the best forecast and the out-turn. Clearly there is a close bunching of forecast numbers around the consensus.

It is difficult to see why there is this consensus-seeking when it is not necessarily the most sensible form of behaviour. It is possible to argue that forecasters have an interest in differentiating their product and producing numbers at the extreme ends of the range of possibilities away from the pack. This is because only 'correct' predictions receive any attention and 'incorrect' numbers are quickly forgotten. However there is no evidence that such an approach is widely used. Commercial forecasters could perhaps gain from this strategy but most macromodels are still partly funded by public money and subject to systematic academic evaluation. The wide swings in opinion that such maverick behaviour could imply would seriously undermine their credibility.

An explanation for the malaise in macro-economic forecasting is probably to be found in the volatility of the last economic cycle rather than any consensus or variety-seeking behaviour. All short-term predictions are made on the basis of some form of macro-economic model, explicit or otherwise, and these are known to perform less well in more turbulent periods. The situation has been further complicated by important structural changes in the UK economy, which have yet to be fully understood and assimilated.

7.11 Why do forecasts differ?

The preceding section provides good reason why forecasts might cluster; if this is the case, what then makes forecasts differ?

The forecast is the product of the model, which will embody the main theoretical priors of the forecaster (and his institution), the assumptions on which it is based, the forecaster's analysis of the conjuncture, their intuitive sense of where the economy is heading and a whole range of external inputs, such as business surveys and, it has to be admitted, what everyone else is also saying. Differences between forecasts can arise in any of these areas.

There is a wide variety of model used to generate forecasts of the UK economy. Within the 'academic' community some models emphasise rational expectations monetarism (Liverpool) or supply side factors (City University Business School) or the trends in exports and imports (CEPG, Wynne Godley). Even amongst the more mainstream models (London Business School, NIESR, HMT, Bank of England), there are different parameters providing, for example, different elasticities for UK exports with respect to growth in world trade or an improvement in competitiveness, or for consumers' expenditure or company investment with respect to a change in interest rates. In some cases these inherent model differences may be offset by the setting of different constant adjustments or by different exogenous assumptions; in some instances, the natural model differences may be exaggerated by these factors.

As a general impression, however, it is not in these areas that forecasts differ: if anything policy assumptions and residual setting tend to bring forecasts closer together rather than drive them further apart. What seems to distinguish forecasts one from another is their reading of the conjuncture and their intuitive sense of where the economy is heading. This is particularly important at turning points in the economic cycle, as a very different forecast can result from a disagreement over the precise timing of either the peak or the trough of the cycle.

There is another point, which is more important in the UK context than elsewhere. We noted earlier that virtually all of the academic model-builders in the United Kingdom set up their models not to produce forecasts *per se* but as a handle on which to base their policy analysis and recommendations. There is therefore a subtle interaction between the forecast and the policy recommendation, nowhere more obviously than in recent years. The forecasters are polarised about the operation of domestic monetary policy between those who believe in the ERM link to the Deutschmark and those who believe in the operation of monetary policy with respect to domestic monetary targets and favour a floating exchange rate. The latter group was very critical of the pound's entry into the ERM in 1990 and forecast continuing recession as a result. While critics of policy were correct in this instance, the more general point remains. Any forecaster who is fundamentally critical of policy will tend to produce a forecast which shows a worse outturn than those who favour the government's approach.

Notes

1. The problem is acute for those forecasters, mainly the international bodies, which have a long institutional delay between finalising the forecast numbers and their eventual publication; for most other organisations, the advent of desk-top publishing has reduced, though not eliminated, this hazard. Our October 1987 forecast, for example, was completed, though not published, before Black Monday, which occurred on 19 October 1987.
2. For an early example, using the London Business School model, see Ball and Burns (1978).
3. For a more wide-ranging discussion, see Smith (1992).
4. With the consolidation of the Budget and Autumn Statements from late 1993 onwards, it is uncertain whether the Treasury will publish one or two forecasts a year.
5. See the surveys of Wallis *et al.* (1984, 1985, 1986, 1987). The Warwick Bureau is included on Table 7.1 as a member of the UK forecasting community: it does not, however, produce its own forecasts; nor does it have a political stance.
6. Named after Jeremy Bray, Labour MP for Motherwell.
7. See, for example, the CBI's *Making it in Britain* report, CBI (1992).
8. This may change if the Chancellor's initiative to involve outside help in the forecast or even to privatise the process takes off.
9. The London Business School is regularly consulted on the outlook for the UK economy by the OECD, the IMF and the EC.
10. Interestingly, this change of policy was not applied to other recipients of ESRC funding such as the National Institute. It may have been the case that the ESRC thought that a business school would have been better placed to attract commercial funding than an independent research institute. At a later date the ESRC extended the remit to the Cambridge Growth project, which established Cambridge Econometrics as its independent commercial arm.
11. The present members of the consortium are: Barclays Bank; British Telecom; IBM United Kingdom; National Grid; National Power; Peat, Marwick, McLintock; PosTel Investment Management; PowerGen; Prudential Portfolio Managers; RTZ; Salomon Brothers International; Shell UK; Sun Life of Canada; TSB; Unilever.
12. Other CEF forecast publications – *Exchange Rate Outlook*, *International Economic Outlook*, *Financial Outlook* – are discussed below.
13. In practice the forecast sent to the consortium is the product of a sequence of internal iterations; other forecasting groups will go through the same process, but only internally.
14. This is the conclusion that Whitley (1992) reaches in regard to recent London Business School forecasts.
15. The annual Blue Book, published in September of each year, is the main source of national accounts data.
16. See Currie *et al.* (1989).
17. The model is usually run for ten years into the future; forecasts are published in *Economic Outlook* for four years ahead and for the full ten years in *International Economic Outlook*.
18. For which the forecaster again has to exercise judgement.
19. And in all other serious models too.
20. It must be (sum to) less than one.
21. In practice, given how quick it is to run the model on modern computers, the setting of constant adjustments involves a degree of trial and error.
22. In the London Business School model as currently specified it is imports which are the residual, accounting for the difference between domestic output and total final expenditure.

23. Because, to our knowledge, no firm of stock-brokers has ever published a formal model, it may not be sensible to read too much into this development.
24. See Burrell and Hall (1993) for a more detailed analysis.
25. The London Business School forecast is being studied by Scott Moss and colleagues at the Metropolitan Museum of Manchester with a view to providing an 'expert system' of the forecasting process, i.e. a model of the forecaster.
26. As in the Treasury's March 1993 forecast.

8 Modelling bilateral trade*

Chris Allen and John Whitley

8.1 Introduction

Economies in multi-country models tend to be linked directly through trade flows as well as via exchange rate and interest rate transmission paths. Yet, in practice, the role of trade flows in simulation analysis appears to be minor (see, for example, Whitley 1992). One motivation for further empirical analysis of trade is to test whether the bilateral modelling approach enhances the role of trade linkages. Much of the literature on bilateral trade models (Italianer 1986) has focused on a demand explanation of trade where the allocation of imports by source is made separately from the determination of total imports. The common bilateral approach is based on conventional utility theory and requires import shares to be explained by identical factors across different sources. In this chapter we show how the various restrictions embodied in this approach are rejected by the data and how a more general approach can be developed which retains some of the advantages of the bilateral framework. In particular we extend the bilateral trade model to include non-price factors. These are in turn explained by relative investment patterns and this has important implications for the explanation of growth differences between countries as transmitted through trade flows.

These considerations are given empirical weight by examination of the different bilateral trends in import and export shares, which suggest that there may be different features underlying trade performance in different economies that are not explained simply by relative price differentials. The modelling of trade can have important policy implications. For example, closer integration within Europe might be expected to increase trade flows between the EC members and it is only in a more detailed framework that these phenomena can be captured. The incorporation of different responses across countries makes simulation analysis of alternative economic policies and scenarios more relevant. A further interest in understanding the trade flows between different economies comes from the attempt to explain differences in growth

---

* We are grateful to Andries Brandsma of the European Commission for his help in allowing us access to the EU bilateral trade data set.

between economies and the role of trade in promoting or eliminating these differences through technological innovation or the non-price characteristics of goods.

The first section of the chapter surveys the literature of trade modelling, particularly in the bilateral context. This involves setting out the underlying theory and its assumptions. One of the key assumptions in bilateral approaches is that of separability, which supports a two-stage approach to modelling imports. Tests of this assumption are reported and the rejection of separability is used to develop an approach in the second section of the chapter, which is based on a single-stage explanation of imports. This approach incorporates specific supply-side or non-price factors. In particular we emphasise the role of technology in explaining changes in non-price competitiveness. The bilateral model of trade is then applied to the trade flows between the G7 economies. The results are used to reject the idea of separability and to support the role of disaggregation. The final section then discusses the implications of the results.

8.2 A survey of existing approaches

One standard approach to modelling trade in multi-country models is through a set of aggregate equations to determine the volume of import demands. These are then summed to produce total world import demand and a set of export relationships then used to share out these imports across the main exporting countries. A separate set of equations determines trade prices and together the volume and price equations produce the value of imports and exports that enter into the balance of payments of each country.

Most of these systems do not ensure consistency automatically between total imports and exports (volumes or values) especially if other variables such as time trends or capacity variables enter into either or both of the import or export equations. In practice this means that some scaling of one or the other world aggregates is necessary to ensure global consistency. A further complication is the need to deduct the various coverage adjustments from imports of goods and attribute it then to the invisibles account. The specification of the aggregate equations is usually fairly *ad hoc* and the interpretation of these equations may be either as a set of demand equations or as reduced forms. If the correct interpretation is the former then the price equations are the corresponding supply side of the trade framework. Otherwise the price equations are also reduced forms and hence should be simply a renormalisation of the volume equations.

An alternative approach is based on bilateral trade flow models and this in turn is based on a model of demand derived from standard utility theory. This approach is adopted by the EC's multi-country model (QUEST) for example. In the bilateral approach the price equations usually represent the supply side of the system. In the rest of this section we spell out the bilateral approach in some detail, emphasising its derivation from theory and the importance of some of the assumptions that it makes. We begin with the theoretical framework.

145

8.2.1 The theoretical framework

Work on the determination of bilateral trade flows originates with the work of Armington (1969) and Barten (1971) in the late 1960s and early 1970s. They proposed very simple demand-system models for the exports of each country. Export supply considerations were entirely neglected.

The Armington and Barten models are predetermined price models. Exporters supply differentiated products which are infinitely elastic at a given price. Trade volumes between different countries are therefore determined entirely by the demand for the various products in each country.

Given a set of prices and domestic income, the set of bilateral import volumes can be entirely determined by a standard demand system. Export volumes, of course, can then be derived by simply adding up bilateral import demands.

Armington and Barten consider the choice problem for the representative consumer. They maximise a utility function, given the level of income and the set of prices that they face.

Two crucial assumptions are made. The first assumption is that each country's exports can be treated as a separate commodity. Hence for each exporting country we can define price and quantity indices relative to a particular market. We define the price and quantity indices of the ith exporting country to the jth importing market as P_{ij}^x and X_{ij}, respectively. Note that this will cause difficulties if different importing countries' trade patterns are significantly different. For this reason, Armington advocates product disaggregation of trade flows.

The second assumption is that imports are weakly separable from domestic output. This means that the demand for relative quantities of imports is independent of domestic prices. Hence, we can characterise the consumer's decision as a two-stage budgeting process. In the first stage overall expenditure on imports and on domestically produced goods is determined. In the second stage, the consumer decides on their expenditure on the various sorts of imports.

Under weak separability of preferences, and assuming homotheticity, we can define aggregate price and volume indices for imports as a whole. For the jth importing country we will denote these as P_j^m and M_j, respectively. Of course, these will only be conventional price and quantity indices (i.e. linear combinations of the individual prices and volumes) in the special case of a Leontief utility function. We can thus characterise the first stage of the consumer's budgeting process as resulting in an aggregate demand function for imports of the form:

$$M_j = F_j(P_j^m, P_j, Y_j) \qquad (8.1)$$

where P_j is an aggregate domestic price index and Y_j is nominal domestic income. In principle there will be a counterpart equation for domestic demand for domestic output (see Dinenis *et al.* 1989).

The second stage of the budgeting procedure determines the demand for the exports of individual countries. In general we will have a set of demand functions of the form:

$$X_{ij} = f_{ij}(P_{ij}^x, P_{kj}^x, \ldots)v_j(M_j) \quad \text{for all } i \tag{8.2}$$

where $P_{kj}^x, \ldots$, etc. are the price indices of other exporter countries.

What are the problems with this separability assumption? Italianer (1987) cites the example of the impact of North Sea oil production on UK imports. Domestic oil production, and hence lower relative domestic oil prices, switched imports towards domestic production. This did not of course leave the relative geographical distribution of trade unchanged, as the majority of the substitution was obviously against the OPEC oil-producing countries. In general, whenever tested, this separability assumption has been rejected (Winters 1984; Italianer 1986).

8.2.2 Empirical bilateral trade models

Despite the length of time since the original papers of Armington and Barten, relatively little work has actually been done on bilateral trade modelling as such. The majority of the work has instead focused on aggregated international trade linkage models which are discussed in the next section.

Armington's theoretical paper suggested the use of a nested constant elasticity of substitution (CES) utility function to derive the aggregate and individual import demand functions. Hickman and Lau (1973) followed this suggestion to estimate trade relationships between 27 countries or regions.

Taking a CES subutility function, it can easily be shown that the demand for the ith country's exports is:

$$X_{ij} = a_{ij}^{\sigma_j} M_j \left(\frac{P_{ij}^x}{P_j^m}\right)^{-\sigma_j} \tag{8.3}$$

where σ_j is the elasticity of substitution. P_j^m is a CES price index of import prices defined as:

$$P_j^m = [\Sigma_i a_{ij}^{\sigma_j} P_{ij}^{x(1-\sigma_j)}]^{1/(1-\sigma_j)} \tag{8.4}$$

Letting $P_{ij}^x = P_j^m = 1$ in the base period, we can identify $a_{ij}^{\sigma_j}$ with α_{ij}^0, which is the base period's value share of the ith country's exports in the jth country's imports.

In principle, we could estimate equation sets 8.3 and 8.4 using non-linear methods. Given the number of equations to be estimated, however, Hickman and Lau decide to linearise. Using a first-order Taylor expansion around $P_{ij}^x = P_j^m = 1$, we obtain:

$$X_{ij} = \alpha_{ij}^0 M_j [1 - \sigma_j (P_{ij}^x - P_j^m)] \tag{8.5}$$

where the aggregate price index has become:

$$P_j^m = \Sigma_i \alpha_{ij}^0 P_{ij}^x \tag{8.6}$$

If we finally linearise the cross-products we obtain:

$$X_{ij} = \alpha_{ij}^0 M_j - \sigma_j (P_{ij}^x - P_j^m) M_j^0 \alpha_{ij}^0 \tag{8.7}$$

where M_j^0 is base period total value (= volume) of imports.

Equation 8.7 contains only one unknown parameter, σ_j, which is the constant elasticity of substitution. This was estimated for each country using pooled time series and cross-sectional data.

An advantage of this specification is that the overall elasticity of demand for a good can be derived as:

$$\eta_{ij} = -[\sigma_j - \alpha_{ij}^0(\sigma_j - \varepsilon_j)] \tag{8.8}$$

where ε_j is the elasticity of demand for imports as a whole (Branson 1972).

Other studies following the Hickman and Lau formulation are Artus and McGuirk (1981) and Weale (1984). The former was used to derive the so-called weights for the International Monetary Fund (IMF) estimates of real exchange rate indices, whilst the latter is in the context of a linear global model.

Italianer (1986, 1987) notes that the assumption of a constant elasticity of substitution between imports of potentially very different countries is highly restrictive. He instead uses a slightly more general elasticity specification, the constant ratios of elasticities of substitution (CRESH) aggregation function based on Hanoch (1971).

The CRESH aggregator function defines the volume of aggregate imports as:

$$\Sigma_i d_{ij}\left(\frac{X_{ij}}{M_j}\right)^{-r_{ij}} - 1 = 0 \tag{8.9}$$

where the d_{ij} and r_{ij} are parameters. Consumers are assumed to minimise the cost of a given quantity of these real imports, defined in the first stage of the budgeting process. The bilateral import demand equation can then be defined as:

$$\log X_{ij} = a_{ij} + \log M_j + b_{ij}\log(P_{ij}^x/P_j^m) \tag{8.10}$$

Italianer proxies the M_j and P_j^m by simple weighted averages.

Other approaches are Johnson (in an unpublished PhD thesis, cited in Helliwell and Padmore (1984)) who apparently used a linear expenditure system to model country demands.

8.2.3 Trade linkage models and the problem of adding up

As a result of the informational requirements of bilateral trade models, most international modellers have turned to more aggregated trade linkage models. Within these models, bilateral trade equations are aggregated up to explain total export equations for each country. The advantages of such equations are obvious from an estimation or forecasting perspective.

The major problem that emerges is the one of consistency between total world imports and exports using such aggregative equations. The restrictions required are analogous to the 'adding up' restrictions in demand-system theory.

The earliest model of the trade linkage type was suggested by Hickman (1973). This provides the theoretical basis of subsequent contributions and therefore will be discussed in detail.

The Hickman model explicitly built upon the linearised bilateral trade equations estimated in Hickman and Lau (1973), which were discussed earlier (see page 147). It therefore ensured consistency between world exports and imports, unlike most subsequent contributions.

Hickman and Lau's bilateral trade equation for the trade flow between the ith exporting country to the jth importing country is given in eqn 8.7. We reproduce it here for convenience:

$$X_{ij} = \alpha_{ij}^0 M_j - \sigma_j (P_{ij}^x - P_j^m) M_j^0 \alpha_{ij}^0 \tag{8.11}$$

Aggregating over all importing countries j, we obtain the ith country's aggregate exports as:

$$X_i = \Sigma_j X_{ij} = \Sigma_j \alpha_{ij}^0 - \Sigma_j [\sigma_j \alpha_{ij}^0 M_j^0 (P_{ij}^x - P_j^m)] \tag{8.12}$$

Hickman now makes the assumption that a country's export prices are the same to each and every other country. Hence there is assumed to be no price discrimination between countries, nor any bilateral differences in price owing to different transport or tariff rates. Hence $P_{ij}^x = \bar{P}_i^x$ for all countries j.

This assumption of course means that we cannot model the effects of say Japanese firms pricing specifically to the US market, nor the effects of discriminatory tariff regimes such as the EC.

Now define the export market weighted elasticity of substitution as:

$$\bar{\sigma}_j = \Sigma_j \sigma_j \left(\frac{X_{ij}^0}{X_i^0} \right) = \Sigma_j \sigma_j \lambda_{ij}^0 \tag{8.13}$$

where λ_{ij}^0 is the share of country i's exports going to country j in the base year.

We can also define weighted competitors' prices in the ith country's export markets as:

$$P_i^{xc} = \frac{\Sigma_j \sigma_j \lambda_{ij}^0 P_j^m}{\bar{\sigma}_i} = \frac{\Sigma_j \sigma_j \lambda_{ij}^0 \Sigma_k \alpha_{ij}^0 P_{kj}^x}{\bar{\sigma}_i} \tag{8.14}$$

Using these two definitions, we can write total exports as:

$$X_i = \Sigma_j \alpha_{ij}^0 M_j - \bar{\sigma}_i X_i^0 (P_i^x - P_i^{xc}) \tag{8.15}$$

It will be seen that the sum of these export equations aggregates exactly to the sum of total exports. There is thus no adding up problem within the Hickman system.

Unfortunately the availability of this form of aggregation has the cost of having to estimate the entire set of bilateral trade equations in order to be able to aggregate. Equation 8.15 requires the separate estimation of all the elasticities of substitution of each country (the σ_j). We cannot, therefore, directly estimate eqn 8.15.

As a result of this problem, subsequent investigators such as Klein and van Peeterssen (1973) have chosen to simplify the Hickman system. Their principal additional assumption is that the elasticities of substitution between imports are approximately the same for all countries. Hence competitors' export prices are re-defined as:

$$P_i^{xc} = \Sigma_j \lambda_{ij}^0 P_j^m = \Sigma_j \lambda_{ij}^0 \Sigma_k \alpha_{kj}^0 P_k^x \tag{8.16}$$

The aggregate export equation for estimation is therefore of the form:

$$X_i = a_{0i} + a_{1i}(\Sigma_j a_{ij}^0 M_j) + a_{2i}(P_i^{xc}/P_i^x) \tag{8.17}$$

where $P_i^{xc}/P_i^x \approx P_i^{xc} - P_i^x$ for $P_i^{xc} \approx P_i^x \approx 1$.

Later trade linkage models have had a similar structure, but have usually adopted a log–linear specification. Amongst these are Beenstock and Minford (1976) and Samuelson and Kurihara (1980). It forms the basis of the current version of the global econometric model (GEM), OECD Interlink, and IMF Multimod models.

None of these models are compatible with the adding-up restrictions of demand theory and hence in simulations there is no intrinsic restriction which would stop world aggregate estimated imports and exports from diverging. A number of ad hoc methods have been suggested to deal with this problem.

Two solutions to this problem have been suggested in the literature. The first is simply to change exports in proportion to their shares in world trade. This effectively mimics the procedure used for updating input–output tables. The technique was first suggested by Moriguchi (1979) and has been implemented in the GEM model. A second technique, which involves weighting exports by the standard errors of the residuals on the various equations, has been suggested by Italianer (1987) and was implemented in the EC Quest model.

8.2.4 Models of export supply

To complete the world trade models discussed above, we need some model of export supply. There are broadly two approaches to this.

The first approach embodies explicit export supply functions as in the work of Haynes and Stone (1983) and Holly and Wade (1989). Generally the estimated supply functions are of the form:

$$\log P_i^x = \log C_i^x + \beta(\log Y_i^x - \log K_i^x) \tag{8.18}$$

where C_i^x is domestic variable costs, and K_i^x is the capital stock in the export industries.

How might these supply functions be integrated in an international model? We could keep the paradigm of each country supplying a differentiated product, but assume that the export industry within each country is perfectly competitive. For instance, it is assumed that a Taiwanese TV is a different commodity from a Korean TV, but that all Taiwanese exporters supply the same product.

Within any given 'small' export market, producers will supply a product at a given price. However, the aggregate supply of any export will depend on an increasing marginal cost supply function.

A second approach stresses the importance of differentiated products and price competition in supply. This is based on the early work by Kravis and Lipsey (1971) and Isard (1973), which found:

> There were persistent differences between prices of similar goods in international trade produced by different countries and while careful econometric studies of data for a long sample period might indeed find that the relative price changes associated with any given exchange rate movement are completely offset over long periods of time, in reality exchange rates are rarely stable over long periods of time and thus for practical purposes, products at the 4- to 5-digit Standard Industrial Classification (SITC) level are not close enough substitutes to preclude substantial and persistent changes in relative common currency prices. (Isard 1973)

Modellers following Samuelson (1973) have seen export prices as depending on a linear combination of domestic costs and competitor export prices. Occasionally, capacity utilisation terms are added into these equations. Import prices are determined just as trade weighted averages of importer export prices.

In the GEM model, for instance, manufacturing export prices depend in the long-run on a linear combination of domestic wholesale and relative competitor export prices (as defined in eqn 8.16), together with separate short-run effects from exchange rates. All of the country models have equations of this form with the exception of the United States, whose export prices are assumed only to depend on domestic prices. This results in a dollar inhomogeneity in the model.

A slightly more sophisticated version of this model has been proposed by Herd (1987) in which attention is also paid to competition from importer domestic prices. Export prices into each market are assumed to be a linear combination of domestic costs, foreign import prices into that market, and the domestic prices in that market:

$$P_{ij}^x = a_i C_i^x + (1 - a_i)[b_j P_j^m + (1 - b_j)P_j] \tag{8.19}$$

The aggregate export price equation is therefore also a linear combination of domestic costs, and weighted competitor export and foreign prices:

$$P_i^x = a_i C_i^x + (1 - a_i)\Sigma_j \lambda_{ij}^0 [b_j P_j^m + (1 - b_j)P_j] \tag{8.20}$$

where λ_{ij}^0 are base-weighted export shares.

We can also define the jth country's aggregate import price as a weighted average of domestic prices and foreign costs:

$$P_j^m = \theta^{-1}[\Sigma_i \alpha_{ij}^0 C_i^x + (1 - b_j)(\Sigma_i \alpha_{ij}^0(1 - a_i))P_j] \tag{8.21}$$

where $\theta = 1 - b_j(\Sigma_i \alpha_{ij}^0(1 - a_i))$.

151

Herd's formulation thus allowed aggregate import price equations to exhibit pricing to market effects. He estimated sets of equations, such as eqns 8.20 and 8.21, for the aggregate trade price indices of the principal OECD countries. The cross-equation restrictions were informally imposed using an iterative technique.

8.2.5 Testing for separability and homotheticity

A major motivation for bilateral rather than multilateral trade modelling is that the assumptions of separability and homotheticity do not hold in practice.

Most of the work surveyed above has taken the Armington and Barten approach of assuming that the demand for imports is derived from an underlying utility function, which is both homothetic and separable between imports and domestic output. If preferences are separable, then the demand for relative quantities of imports is independent of the consumption of domestic output. The representative consumer's decision can therefore be characterised as a two-stage budgeting process. In the first stage the division between overall expenditure on imports and on domestically produced goods is determined; in the second stage, expenditure on various sorts of imports are calculated. If preferences are also homothetic, then relative demands for goods are also independent of the overall level of real expenditure. This allows us to define aggregate price and quantity indices for imports as a whole.

If the joint assumptions of homotheticity and separability were accepted therefore, then there would in principle be no advantage in modelling individual bilateral import flows, if all that is required is a model of total imports. Instead, we should model aggregate imports directly, using aggregate price and volume indices for imports as a whole. We could then model bilateral trade, if we wished, conditional on aggregate import expenditure and relative import prices.

Clearly it is therefore important to test whether indeed consumer preferences exhibit separability and homotheticity.

8.2.6 Testing for separability

The form of the test we use is derived from consumer demand theory. Let us define the representative consumer's indirect utility function as:

$$U = \phi(p_1, \ldots, p_m, p_n, y) \tag{8.22}$$

where the $p_1, \ldots, p_m$ are the individual prices of the m imports, p_n is the price of domestic output, and y is nominal income. We assume this function has the usual regularity properties and is twice continuously differentiable.

The indirect utility function is a complete representation of consumer preferences. In particular, it can be shown that $\phi(p_1, \ldots, p_m, p_n, y)$ will be separable in import prices and homothetic in prices if, and only if, the direct utility function is itself separable and homothetic (see Blackorby et al. 1978, theorem 4.6). For the moment, however, let us assume that ϕ is completely general.

The consumer's demand for individual imports can be derived using Roy's identity:

$$x_i = -\frac{\partial \phi / \partial p_i(p_1, \ldots, p_m, p_n, y)}{\partial \phi / \partial y(p_1, \ldots, p_m, p_n, y)} \tag{8.23}$$

where x_i is the demand for the ith country's goods.

The demand for the ith country's goods, divided by total imports can therefore be derived as:

$$\frac{x_i}{M} = \frac{\partial \phi / \partial p_i(p_1, \ldots, p_m, p_n, y)}{\Sigma_k \partial \phi / \partial p_k(p_1, \ldots, p_m, p_n, y)} \tag{8.24}$$

In general therefore the ratio of the imports from any individual country to total imports will depend on all individual import prices, domestic prices, and total income.

We can now restrict eqn 8.1 to show the impact of increasing amounts of structure.

Preferences separable but not homothetic

If preferences are separable but not homothetic, we can write the indirect utility function as:

$$U = \phi(f(p_1, \ldots, p_m), p_n, y) \tag{8.25}$$

The ratio of individual to total import demands will now be independent of domestic prices, i.e.:

$$\frac{x_i}{M} = \frac{\partial f / \partial p_i(p_1, \ldots, p_m, y)}{\Sigma_k \partial f / \partial p_k(p_1, \ldots, p_m, y)} \tag{8.26}$$

Preferences homothetic but not separable

If preferences are homothetic but not separable in imports, we can write the indirect utility function as:

$$U = \phi(p_1, \ldots, p_m, p_n)g(y) \tag{8.27}$$

The ratio of individual to total import demands will now be independent of income, i.e.:

$$\frac{x_i}{M} = \frac{\partial \phi / \partial p_i(p_1, \ldots, p_m, p_n)}{\Sigma_k \partial \phi / \partial p_k(p_1, \ldots, p_m, p_n)} \tag{8.28}$$

Preferences both separable and homothetic

If preferences are both separable in imports and homothetic, we can write the indirect utility function as:

$$U = \phi(f(p_1, \ldots, p_m), p_n)g(y) \tag{8.29}$$

The ratio of individual to total import demands will now be independent of both domestic prices and income, i.e.:

$$\frac{x_i}{M} = \frac{\partial f/\partial p_i(p_1, \ldots, p_m)}{\Sigma_k \partial f/\partial p_k(p_1, \ldots, p_m)} \tag{8.30}$$

This is the highly restrictive case discussed by Armington and Barten. Clearly this case is the conjunction of preferences separable but not homothetic and preferences homothetic but not separable.

8.2.7 The test procedure

We have implemented a test of separability and homotheticity by estimating a general equation for each individual import demand relative to the demand for total imports. Our general equation has the form of eqn 8.3 with the addition of capital stock variables, whose inclusion is explained below.

We have run log–linearised equations of the form:

$$x_i - m = \alpha_0 + \alpha_1(p_i - p^c) + \alpha_2(p^c - p) + \alpha_3 y$$
$$+ \alpha_4(k_i - k^c) + \alpha_5(k^c - k) \tag{8.31}$$

Our test of separability in prices is $\alpha_2 = 0$, whereas that in capital stocks is $\alpha_5 = 0$; the test of homotheticity is $\alpha_3 = 0$. Our global test of both homotheticity and separability assumptions is that all these co-efficients are zero (we can in principle test several equations at the same time).

8.2.8 A structural test of separability using an almost ideal demand system (AIDS) function

As is well know, log–linear demand functions cannot be integrated up into a well-behaved utility or expenditure function. In particular, the property of the 'adding up' of demands to total expenditure is only satisfied if there is both a unit own-price elasticity and a unit income elasticity (see Lau 1986).

A more satisfactory method of testing for separability is therefore to use one of the many 'flexible' functional form cost or utility functions and to derive the demand functions directly from this. The restrictions of separability can then be directly derived and tested from a set of theoretically consistent demand functions.

Unfortunately, as analysed by Blackorby et al. (1975) for the case of the 'generalised quadratic' functional form (which includes the translog as a special case), almost all of these functional forms themselves impose restrictions on the forms of separability allowed. The AIDS function is itself a generalisation of the 'generalised quadratic', but as we will see it is not immune to this problem.

To illustrate, we examine the popular AIDS demand system, introduced by Deaton and Muellbauer (1980). The consumer demands are generated from the following cost function:

$$\ln C = \alpha_0 + \Sigma_k \ln P_k + \tfrac{1}{2}\Sigma_k \Sigma_l \gamma_{kl} \ln P_k \ln P_l + u\beta_0 \Pi_k P_k^{\beta_k} \tag{8.32}$$

Consumer demands can be derived by Shepherd's Lemma and substitution as:

$$w_i = \frac{P_i X_i}{C} = \alpha_i + \Sigma_j \gamma_{ij} \ln P_j + \beta_i \ln(C/P) \tag{8.33}$$

where P is an aggregate price index defined as:

$$\ln P = \alpha_0 + \Sigma_k \alpha_k \ln P_k + \Sigma_k \Sigma_l \gamma_{kl} \ln P_k \ln P_l \tag{8.34}$$

which, it will be noted, is independent of the β_i. The AIDS function can be seen as an extension of the translog function.

We utilise the Leontieff–Sono differential definition of separability of goods i and j from s which implies:

$$\frac{\partial}{\partial P_s}\left(\frac{\partial C/\partial P_i}{\partial C/\partial P_j}\right) = 0 \tag{8.35}$$

and which is equivalent to:

$$\frac{\partial^2 C/\partial P_i \partial P_s}{\partial C/\partial P_i} = \frac{\partial^2 C/\partial P_j \partial P_s}{\partial C/\partial P_j} \tag{8.36}$$

Evaluating the left-hand side of this expression, we have:

$$\frac{\partial^2 C/\partial P_i \partial P_s}{\partial C/\partial P_i} = \frac{[\gamma_{si} + \beta_i \beta_s u\beta_0 \Pi_k P_k^{\beta_k}]P_s^{-1}}{\alpha_i + \Sigma_k \gamma_{ik} \ln P_k + \beta_i u\beta_0 \Pi_k P_k^{\beta_k}} \tag{8.37}$$

Condition (8.15) therefore implies that the necessary conditions for separability are:

$$(\gamma_{si}\alpha_j - \gamma_{sj}\alpha_i) + \Sigma_k(\gamma_{si}\gamma_{jk} - \gamma_{sj}\gamma_{ik})\ln P_k + u\beta_0 \Pi_k P_k^{\beta_k}[(\gamma_{si}\beta_j - \gamma_{sj}\beta_i)$$
$$+ \beta_s(\beta_i\alpha_j - \beta_j\alpha_i) + \beta_s \Sigma_k(\beta_i\gamma_{jk} - \beta_j\gamma_{ik})\ln P_k] = 0 \tag{8.38}$$

Using the interpretation of the AIDS function as a second-order log approximation to any arbitrary cost function, and assuming the expansion is taken round $P_i = 1$, this simplifies to:

$$(\gamma_{si}\alpha_j - \gamma_{si}\alpha_i) + u\beta_0[(\gamma_{si}\beta_j - \gamma_{sj}\beta_i) + \beta_s(\beta_i\alpha_j - \beta_j\alpha_i)] = 0 \tag{8.39}$$

For the left-hand side to be zero, we require each of the terms in round brackets individually to be zero. We therefore essentially have three necessary conditions for separability, though they are not independent. Essentially they boil down to the following two equalities:

$$\frac{\alpha_i}{\alpha_j} = \frac{\gamma_{si}}{\gamma_{sj}} = \frac{\beta_i}{\beta_j} \tag{8.40}$$

These are non-linear restrictions, but are very easy to impose. This is an extension of the result in Blackorby *et al.* (1975).

It is obvious that there are also some simple sufficient conditions for separability, these are:

$$\gamma_{si} = \gamma_{sj} = 0 \quad \text{and} \quad \beta_s = 0 \tag{8.41}$$

These are easily testable conditions, although highly restrictive. They result in additive separability of the cost function. In terms of their implications for the form of demands, they imply that the *absolute* demand shares for goods i and j are affected by price changes in s only through income effects (as is s by i and j) and that the budget share of good s is entirely independent of real income. In terms of our import example, where s represents domestic consumption of domestic goods, this latter condition entails that only price changes are allowed to explain movements in import penetration.

Winters (1984) and Brenton (1989) examine separability in the context of an AIDS demand function. Each find that it is rejected, although they do not use the proper structural tests proposal above.

8.2.9 An alternative non-parametric test

All of the separability tests above have depended on the estimation of specific functional forms. As Blackorby *et al.* (1975) note, even so-called 'flexible' functional forms impose very tight restrictions on the types of allowable separability. This is certainly the case with the AIDS function as is discussed above. It is therefore important to examine alternative tests which are more robust to functional structure.

Such a test is the non-parametric test proposed by Varian (1983). The test is not statistical, but instead allows us to examine the data to see whether it contains any inconsistencies incompatible with the joint hypothesis of separability and the rationality of choices.

Varian's test is based on revealed preference analysis as developed and extended by Afriat (1967). Essentially the data are tested for inconsistencies with the generalised axiom of revealed preference (GARP). Varian proposes the use of an algorithm due to Warshall to test whether the set of demands, prices, and total expenditure are compatible with GARP.

The test is a joint test of rationality and of separability. First we test whether the entire data-set is compatible with GARP. If not, then no test of separability is possible. The separability test comes from the following property of separable utility functions. If a certain subset of goods are separable from the others, then we can also define a subutility function over this set of goods alone. (This is a clear consequence of the fact we can characterise the problem as a two-stage budgeting problem.) This subutility function should also be compatible with GARP. The test is to examine the resultant choices amongst the subset of goods to ensure this is the case.

On time series data, Varian's test is clearly somewhat weak. The data is characterised by relatively small changes in relative prices and large changes in real income. Most of the data will be clearly revealed preferred to each other. In fact, only over two brief periods (of the two oil shocks) does our data provide preference reversals.

We have tested the US data for compatibility with GARP. Somewhat surprisingly, we find it compatible with rational choice overall. We then test the set of import functions alone to see if they are compatible with a subutility function. Here, one inconsistency was found, which occurs during the second oil crisis period between 1980q1 and 1981q1. Taking the set of imports alone we find both that:

$$P'_{80q1}Q_{81q1} < P'_{80q1}Q_{80q1} \qquad (8.42)$$

and:

$$P'_{81q1}Q_{81q1} > P'_{81q1}Q_{80q1} \qquad (8.43)$$

Hence from the first inequality, the imports bought in 1981q1 could have been bought (but were not) in 1980q1, whilst the goods bought in 1980q1 could have been bought in 1981q1, but were not chosen. In fact, taking into account different prices and quantities bought of domestic goods, the choices of 1980q1 and 1981q1 can be rationalised as compatible with rational choice. However, the divergence between the two observations is very small, of the order of 0.2% (Table 8.1). This might be accounted for by measurement error.

8.3 An amended bilateral trade model

In this section we describe how we modify the bilateral trade approach and apply it to trade flows between the G7 economies. Following rejection of the separability assumptions we choose to model imports as a single-stage process using a log–linear framework, where imports from the jth country to the ith country depend on the domestic price in the importing country (relative to the weighted average of competing export prices, expressed in dollars), the relative export price of the jth country (again relative to other exporters) and the level of demand in the ith country. Ideally, we would use this as a description of the demand side and estimate price equations that represent the supply schedule. However, two considerations persuade us to modify the

Table 8.1 Divergence between import costs and demands in 1980q1 and 1981q1

Import costs	Demands 1980q1	Demands 1981q1
Prices 1980q1	1.0000	0.9984
Prices 1981q1	0.9979	1.0000

demand equation for supply factors directly giving it a reduced-form interpretation. First, bilateral price data were not available and hence we would be unable to capture country/exporter specific features such as pricing to markets. Second, we wish to attempt to capture the role of innovation and technology improvements and some of these are likely to appear as non-price competitiveness (or quality improvements) rather than as changes in price competitiveness – this partly reflects the common problem of incorporating quality improvements in price data but it also reflects a divergence from the traditional neoclassical view of technological innovation where innovation is assumed to lead to cost reductions. The alternative view, which we espouse here, is that technological improvements are embodied in the product itself in terms of improved quality.

The fact that economic growth may have led to a divergence of growth rates across economies has been interpreted by some as a violation of the predictions of neoclassical growth theory. At the centre of the new theories (for an excellent survey see Crafts (1991)) is the role of factor accumulation, both of physical and human capital. It is possible that innovation can lead to a technological gap between countries and that a virtuous circle is begun whereby the higher profits that emerge stimulate further innovation. Greenhalgh et al. (1990) argue that the most important implication of the technology gap theory is that the country with superior techniques will export that commodity irrespective of its factor endowments. The technology itself is not exogenously determined but comes from innovatory activity. Usually research and development expenditure (R & D) is used to measure the scale of this activity. However, there are some problems with this measure. There is a time lag between R & D expenditures and innovation incorporated in products. In the United Kingdom in particular there is the problem that much R & D expenditure is concentrated in the defence industry where trade is not subject to normal market conditions. Patents data have also been used and encouraging results reported for industry-level equations in the United Kingdom by Greenhalgh et al. (1990), although there are also problems in interpreting patents data (because the significance varies from industry to industry and may reflect strategic decision making by firms rather than innovatory activity). As the main purpose of our work is to investigate the use of the bilateral approach in an empirical multi-country model we wish to avoid the use of measures which are both difficult to collect and which would then have to be explained within the model. Consequently we have adopted a second-best solution by using statistics on business investment in the G7 economies. This assumes that all new investment is technologically enhancing, which is an extreme assumption. We have chosen not to attempt to construct measures of the capital stock because this involves problems with the assumed rate of depreciation. Following the arguments of Scott (1989) we use cumulative gross investment as the most useful measure of the capital stock, as it avoids attempts to allow for depreciation based on arbitrary non-economic procedures. This variable has also been used by Owen and Wren-Lewis (1993) to explain aggregate UK exports.

Our approach is very much an approximation but it does make an effort to explain both trade flows by specific supply side factors rather than exogenous shifts in export and import shares through time trends, etc., and also provides a link between technology, investment, trade and growth. Our cumulated measures are based on a fairly arbitrary starting point of 1966q1. Both domestic investment and the cumulated level of the exporter's investment are then included in the bilateral trade equations.

The model of bilateral trade flows developed in Section 8.2 is applied to flows between the G7 economies using trade data (in goods) supplied by the EC over the period 1966–90. Estimation is usually over the period 1968q3–1989q3 in order to allow the use of lags and to make forecast tests possible. Only an aggregate export price index is available so that the value flows from each country are deflated by this index irrespective of the destination of the exports.

The underlying basic model is of the form:

$$\ln m_{ij} = \alpha_0 + \alpha_1 \ln(p_j/p_c)$$
$$+ \alpha_2 \ln(p/p_c) + \beta_1 \ln(CI_j/CI_c) + \beta_2 \ln(CI_i/CI_c) + \delta \ln Y \qquad (8.44)$$

where m_{ij} is the flow of imports to country i from country j, or in other words the exports of j to i. Aggregating gives:

$$\sum_{i=1}^{n} m_{ij} = M_i$$

$$\sum_{j=1}^{m} m_{ij} = X_j \qquad (8.45)$$

for total imports of country i and total exports of country j. There are two relative price terms: (1) the ratio of domestic prices to the weighted average of competitors' prices; and (2) the ratio of the exporter's price (j) to the weighted average of all exporters. We would expect the former ratio to be positively signed (a rise in domestic prices encourages higher imports) and the latter ratio to have a negative influence (if country j has a higher export price than other exporting countries then country i will substitute away from country j in favour of exports from another country, say country k). There are also two cumulative investment ratios (these are expressed in the log of the relative cumulative investment so that scale does not matter). The first of these relates to the cumulative investment of the importing country and stronger domestic investment performance would be expected to lead to a reduction in imports since domestic goods are of higher quality (non-price competitiveness has been improved). The second term is also analogous to the relative price term, and relates cumulative investment of the exporter (j) to an average of other exporters. Higher investment is expected to improve export performance and hence, *ceteris paribus*, increase the imports of country i from country j. The final term is that relating to domestic demand, here proxied by total final expenditure.

The equations are estimated in dynamic form using the general to specific methodology.

Before discussing the empirical results we describe some basic features of the data, which are relevant to the nature of bilateral relationships and provide some further evidence on the question of separability and homotheticity.

Some of the trade flows imply quite strong trends in the shares of imports from particular countries (see Figures 8.1–8.3). Thus the share of imports into the United States and Germany, respectively, from Japan has increased quite sharply over the 25-year period whereas the shares of imports into Japan from these other two economies has not shown the same sort of movement. The increasing level of Japanese penetration into the other G7 economies is quite dramatic (Figure 8.1) but we note that other bilateral import shares also show trend changes in share over the period. Given that relative price movements are not trended, homotheticity would seem to be clearly rejected. Some other trending variable(s) are required in the cointegration framework. Using the Johansen method we tend to find only one cointegrating vector between import flows and final demands. In some cases, however, the residuals in the cointegrating relationship are not $I(0)$ and the inclusion of one or more of the cumulative investment variables is necessary to achieve this.

The price variables are measured net of tariffs. Collection of tariff data on a quarterly basis is a very extensive process and the proper concept that is required is not the *ex-post* tariff based on revenue data but the effective tariff. For example, a tariff that is prohibitive will prevent any imports and hence generate zero tariff revenue suggesting a low tariff. Estimates of effective tariff rates are even more difficult to

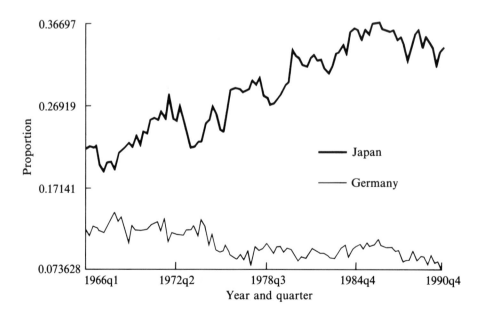

Figure 8.1 Shares of Japan and Germany in total US imports

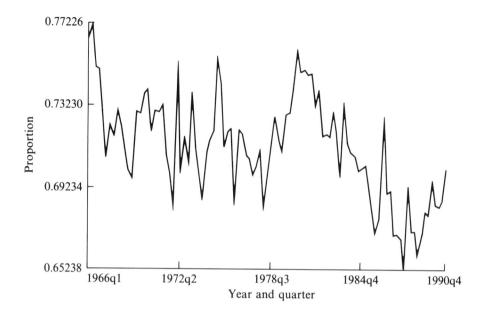

Figure 8.2   Share of United States in Japanese imports

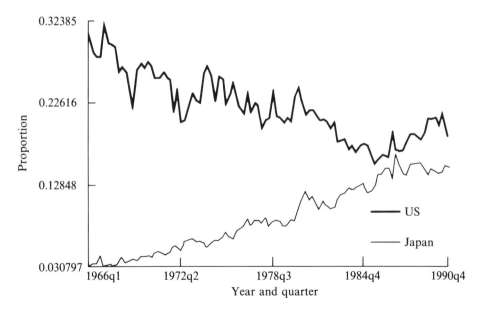

Figure 8.3   Share of United States and Japan in total German imports

collect. It is probable that non-tariff barriers, for example specific restrictions such as safety regulations, which deter foreign imports, may be as important as tariff barriers.

The results are summarised in Table 8.2 where the long-run elasticities of bilateral imports are given.

Where price or investment variables have been found to be statistically insignificant they have been dropped from the equation. Additional tests are made to see whether the two relative price terms can be collapsed into one single term; this involves testing the restriction that the price elasticities are equal and opposite and the results of the χ^2 test of this restriction are reported in Table 8.2.

Table 8.2 Bilateral import equations

Importer	Domestic price (p/p_c)	Relative exporter price (p_j/p_c)	Domestic demand (Y)	Relative domestic cumulative investment (CI_i/CI_c)	Relative foreign cumulative investment (CI_j/CI_c)	Restrictions
United States						
Japan	1.41	−0.82	2.92	−0.95		
Germany	1.74		3.48	−2.67	5.77	
France		−1.87	2.51			
Italy	1.14	−2.60	3.64		1.90	
UK	1.25	−0.31	1.75			
Canada	0.54		2.01			
Weighted average	1.04	−0.54	2.57	−0.61	0.69	Chi²
Japan	1.33	−1.33	3.02	−0.73		0.73
Germany	1.10	−1.10	3.89	−2.72	6.59	0.50
France						3.88
Italy						3.46
UK						16.30
Canada						6.84
Japan						
US		−1.48	5.03	−5.84		
Germany	1.38		3.94		9.88	
France	0.60	−0.68	2.84	0.00		
Italy	2.71	−3.98	4.19			
UK	1.10	−1.44			9.46	
Canada	0.38	−0.95	1.00			
Weighted average	0.31	−1.33	4.12	−4.00	1.19	
US	0.26	−0.26	4.89	−5.45		
Germany						
France	0.47	−0.47	2.80			

Table 8.2 continued

Importer	Domestic price (p/p_c)	Relative exporter price (p_j/p_c)	Domestic demand (Y)	Relative domestic cumulative investment (CI_i/CI_c)	Relative foreign cumulative investment (CI_j/CI_c)	Restrictions
Italy	1.65	−1.65	3.42			
UK	1.05	−1.05			9.22	
Canada	0.46	−0.46	1.17			
Germany						
US		−0.99	0.92	−2.41		
Japan	0.59	−1.75	2.63		1.53	
France	0.21		1.14			
Italy	0.62		2.55	−2.28	7.02	
UK		−0.94	1.77			
Canada		−1.21	0.44			
Weighted						
average	0.27	−0.59	1.73	−0.91	1.80	Chi^2
US						4.60
Japan						8.40
France						
Italy	0.61	−0.61	2.45	−2.47	6.34	0.33
UK						4.93
Canada						5.40
France						
US		−0.76	1.92	−0.90		
Japan		−0.73	3.62			
Germany	0.18	−0.85	1.98	−0.51		
Italy		−1.67	2.94	−1.34		
UK		−0.57	2.65			
Canada		−1.28	1.28			
Weighted						
average	0.08	−1.05	2.46	−0.61		Chi^2
US						14.10
Japan						
Germany						18.30
Italy						3.85
UK						1.76
Canada	0.51	−0.51	1.55			2.44
Italy						
US		−0.87	0.60			
Japan	2.72		2.75			
Germany	1.34	−0.59	1.79			

Table 8.2 continued

Importer	Domestic price (p/p_c)	Relative exporter price (p_j/p_c)	Domestic demand (Y)	Relative domestic cumulative investment (CI_i/CI_c)	Relative foreign cumulative investment (CI_j/CI_c)	Restrictions
France			1.67		0.50	
UK		−0.34	1.74	−1.64	3.31	
Canada		−1.68				
Weighted average	0.62	−0.41	1.60	−0.21	0.57	Chi²
US	0.78	−0.78	0.64			2.00
Japan						6.00
Germany						6.22
France	0.09	−0.09	1.65		0.54	0.94
UK	0.23	−0.23	1.71	−1.54	2.64	2.71
Canada	1.48	−1.48				2.32
United Kingdom						
US		−0.83	2.04			
Japan	1.88		2.79			
Germany*	0.41	−1.90	3.97	−3.98		
France*	1.29	−1.32	5.00	−8.83		
Italy		−4.22	3.92			
Canada		−1.17				
Weighted average	0.54	−1.60	3.41	−2.83		Chi²
US	0.66	−0.66	1.78			0.17
Japan						3.88
Germany	2.56	−2.56	8.08	−15.16		0.70
France	1.85	−1.85	6.80	−13.32		0.08
Italy						5.09
Canada	0.89	−0.89				1.51
*Canada**						
US	1.03	−2.50	1.07			
Japan	2.49	−1.78	1.82			
Germany	1.63	−0.86	1.25			
France	1.69	−0.66	1.53			
Italy	1.80	−1.52	1.73			
UK	1.69	−1.20	0.72		5.81	
Weighted average	1.21	−2.29	1.14		0.22	Chi²
US	1.22	−1.22	1.13			2.46
Japan	2.07	−2.07	1.72			0.61
Germany	1.08	−1.08	1.14			0.89

Table 8.2 continued

Importer	Domestic price (p/p_c)	Relative exporter price (p_j/p_c)	Domestic demand (Y)	Relative domestic cumulative investment (CI_i/CI_c)	Relative foreign cumulative investment (CI_j/CI_c)	Restrictions
France						3.50
Italy	1.64	-1.64	1.71			0.12
UK	1.40	-1.40	0.73		6.33	0.08

Estimation period: 1973:3–1989:3.
*Estimation period: 1979:2–1989:3.

A summary of the results is given in Table 8.3 where the number of significant parameters for each importing country are presented. The domestic price is statistically significant and of the expected sign in just over half of the bilateral flow equations and the foreign relative price significant in over three-quarters of the cases. In about half the equations the restriction required to collapse the two price terms into one are accepted. The cumulative investment terms are significantly different from zero and of the expected sign in about one-quarter of the cases. Separability is rejected in most cases due to the significance of the price variable, whilst the demand variable is almost invariably positive and significant, thus rejecting homotheticity. Equation diagnostics are shown in the Appendix. In general the equations satisfy standard tests; the main exception is that of normality where the principal cause is typically outliers in the data due to special factors. The normality test is often failed for French exports.

Exports to the United States, Germany and Italy appear far less price sensitive to the exporter's price than the other G7 economies. The weighted average elasticities for foreign prices are around 0.5, in contrast to an average response of around unity for

Table 8.3 Summary of results: number of significant parameters per importing country

Import country	Domestic price	Foreign price	Price restrictions	Domestic investment	Foreign investment
US	5	4	2	2	2
Japan	5	5	5	1	2
Germany	3	4	1	2	2
France	1	6	1	3	0
Italy	2	4	4	1	2
UK	3	5	4	2	0
Canada	6	6	5	0	1
Total	25	34	22	11	9

exports to Japan and France and around 2 for the United Kingdom and Canada. Domestic prices are least important for French imports where only German exports are influenced by French domestic prices. US imports reveal more sensitivity to domestic prices as do those of Canada and the United Kingdom.

There is no simple pattern in the comparative investment influences on trade suggesting that institutional factors may be important. Trade between the United States and Japan and between the United States and Germany is influenced by investment performance in the home country but trade between Germany and Japan is influenced by investment in the exporting country. For example, exports from Japan and Germany to the United States depend on investment in the United States, whereas exports from Japan to Germany depend on investment in Japan. The only other case where there is some symmetry between import and export bilateral behaviour is in trade between Italy and France. Italian exports to France depend on French investment performance as do French exports to Italy. There is a considerable divergence between estimates of the trade elasticity with respect to cumulated investment with long-run elasticities ranging from around 0.5 to just under 9. With the exception of the United Kingdom, where the highest elasticities are found, the general conclusion appears to be that it is G3 trade where investment performance is most important in determining bilateral trade flows. UK exports to Japan and to Italy depend on UK investment with quite large long-run elasticities, but it is in the explanation of UK imports from Germany and France that the most striking results occur. Here there is some evidence of structural change in the 1980s and this is consistent with the previous work of Holly and Wade (1989). When estimated over the full sample period imports from Germany and France depend on cumulated UK investment with long-run elasticities of over 13. However, over the period post-1979 these elasticities are reduced to -4 and -9, respectively. The elasticities with respect to cumulated investment are not easy to interpret, especially as they also incorporate the lags in adjustment. They imply that a 1% rise in the cumulated level of investment in the United Kingdom relative to the rest of the G7 will lower UK imports from France by nearly 9% in the long run. However, this change in cumulated investment to occur would require the United Kingdom to increase its rate of increase in business investment by some 10% a year more than its competitors over a 5-year period. This compares with the historical average growth of 6% a year in business investment between 1979 and 1990. Figure 8.4 shows the historical performance of UK investment relative to the other G7 economies. Relative cumulative UK investment was falling until the 1980s, after which the trend was reversed. This suggests a possible explanation for the reversal of the trend decline in the UK export share (for a summary see Whitley et al., 1992). Our empirical results imply that it is the combination of the increased importance of non-price factors, as well as the change in investment trends, which have been responsible for the different import penetration from France and Germany in the 1980s given that the cumulative investment terms are either statistically insignificant or weaker in size in the 1970s. However, comparable structural breaks are not observed in respect of UK export performance between the United Kingdom, Italy and Canada, where investment is also a determinant of trade flows.

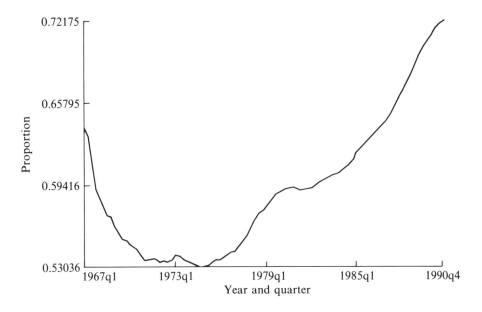

Figure 8.4   Relative cumulated investment in the UK (log)

We do not have a full explanation of why some flows are sensitive to investment and not others but it is the case for some flows that relative cumulative investment is highly colinear with total final demand and hence their separate contributions cannot be easily disentangled.

We now turn to a more detailed discussion of the results. We begin with a description of US imports. Domestic prices are statistically significant for all import flows with the exception of France, the long-run price elasticities varying from 0.5 for Canada to 1.7 for Germany. The exporter's relative price is negative and significant in five cases with the smallest long-run elasticity recorded as −0.3 for UK exports to the United States but with a greater price responsiveness for Italian and French exports (with long-run elasticities of −2.6 and −1.9, respectively). Long-run demand elasticities are very high, ranging from just below 2 to around 3.5. US cumulated investment explains the behaviour of US imports from Japan and Germany and the exporter's investment behaviour is important in Germany and Italy.

In the case of imports to Japan we also find that trade with the United States is influenced by cumulated investment as are imports from Germany and the United Kingdom. However, whereas US exports to Japan depend on investment in Japan, German and UK exports depend on investment in these economies. German exports are insensitive to their relative price (the same finding holds for German exports to the United States). Otherwise the export price elasticities are higher for exports to Japan than to the United States but the sensitivity of Japanese imports to domestic prices is less than for US imports, ranging from 0.4 for imports from Canada to 2.7 for Italian imports.

German domestic prices are only significant in the case of three flows and the exporter's price significant and negative for four flows. In only one case, imports from Japan, are both prices relevant. Investment affects imports from the United States, Japan and Italy.

French imports only depend on domestic prices in one case; imports from Germany (hence France is closest to accepting the separability hypothesis). However the exporter's price is always significant and lies between −0.6 and −1.7 (the United Kingdom and Italy, respectively). Investment explains imports from the US, Germany and Italy.

Italy also reveals only a small number of flows where imports are sensitive to the domestic price but the price elasticities are relatively large where these price variables are statistically significant (Japan and Germany). Foreign price elasticities tend to be low and investment is a determining factor in trade with the United Kingdom and with France.

UK imports from Japan, Germany and France are highly sensitive to the UK domestic price level but Japanese imports do not depend on the Japanese export price. Exports from the United States are least sensitive to the export price whereas those from Germany and Italy are highly price-sensitive.

Canadian imports are always determined by both domestic and foreign export prices with an average domestic price elasticity in the long run of 1.2 and a corresponding average foreign price elasticity of −2.3.

The dynamics of the equations imply quite rapid speed of adjustment. Typically adjustment is complete within 2 years and often shorter. More protracted adjustment processes in some flow equations suggest up to 4 years before complete adjustment to a shock is made.

Table 8.4 gives estimates of aggregate import equations for each G7 economy, estimated in the same way as the bilateral equations together with the results from the bilateral equations themselves, weighted by 1985 import shares. Aggregation tends to exclude investment variables as the disaggregated results show that this is a country-specific result and is hence weighted out in the aggregate.

Disaggregated price elasticities tend to be higher than those from the aggregate equations but not always. The most striking result is in the case of France where prices do not enter into the aggregate import equation. We conduct formal aggregation tests along the lines of that proposed by Lee *et al.* (1990). This involves constructing an aggregate dependent variable which is the sum of the logs of the bilateral flows rather than the more usual log of the sum. The disaggregated equations are always preferred to the aggregate equations on the criterion proposed.

Finally we can also present the results in terms of aggregate export elasticities. This involves weighting the parameters of the bilateral equations by export weights rather than import weights. The results are shown in Table 8.5, calculated using average 1985 weights.

Table 8.4

Total import equations

	Domestic price (p)	Competitor's price (p_c)	Relative investment (CI_i/CI_c)	Domestic investment (CI_j/CI_c)	Final demand (y)
US	1.02	−1.19	−0.74		2.46
Japan	0.53	−1.31			2.63
Germany	0.20	−0.26	−1.67		1.78
France			−0.71		2.33
Italy	0.63	−0.60			1.58
UK	0.50	−0.26			1.94
Canada	0.39	−0.93			1.83

Bilateral weighted

	Domestic price (p/p_c)	Competitor's price (p_j/p_c)	Domestic investment (CI_i/CI_c)	Foreign investment (CI_j/CI_c)	Final demand (y)
US	1.04	−0.54	−0.61	0.69	2.57
Japan	0.31	−1.33	−4.00	1.19	4.12
Germany	0.27	−0.59	−0.91	1.80	1.73
France	0.08	−1.05	−0.61		2.46
Italy	0.62	−0.41	−0.21	0.57	1.60
UK	0.54	−1.60	−2.83		3.41
Canada	1.21	−2.29			1.14

GEM import equations

	Relative prices (P_c/P)	Final demand (y)
US	−0.84	2.25
Japan	−0.63	1.29
Germany	−0.07	1.70
France	−0.60	1.50
Italy	−0.73	1.50
UK	−0.36	2.00
Canada	−0.19	2.00

Table 8.5 Aggregate export price elasticities from the bilateral approach

Country	Export price elasticity
US	-1.49
Japan	-0.89
Germany	-0.17
France	-0.67
Italy	-1.76
UK	-0.61
Canada	-0.11

These average export price elasticities are comparable in ranking to those used in the aggregate export relationships in GEM but tend to be a little larger in size.

8.4 Summary and conclusions

In this chapter we have outlined the standard bilateral trade model and shown that its theoretical assumptions are violated by the data. However, the bilateral approach to modelling can still be sustained by using a single stage procedure to estimate trade flows. We have also shown how the bilateral approach does not have to be based solely on a demand system and have demonstrated how the bilateral system can be modified to include specific factors that might influence non-price competitiveness. The results are encouraging. Most of the equations have significant and correctly signed coefficient estimates and satisfy most of the standard statistical criteria. The supply side innovations variables (cumulative investment) are significant for some flows and appear to be quantitatively important. These variables imply that economies need to invest at least as rapidly as their main competitors in order to maintain their export performance. Given that estimated demand elasticities are high a failure to innovate could result in a substantial increase in import penetration following a domestic demand boost. This characterisation does seem to explain recent UK import behaviour quite well. Whilst further research is required to explain why supply side factors are relevant in some cases and not in others and to estimate comparable price relationships (this would test whether technological innovation does also reduce costs and prices) the results do go some way to endogenising the growth process in the context of a full multicountry model. The inclusion of cumulated investment variables and the increased price elasticities potentially increase the role of trade flows in multicountry models. The results so far are consistent with both theories that attempt to explain persistent growth differences between economies and those which use the catch-up hypothesis. In both cases the essential ingredient is the transfer of technology through the trade process (another alternative not considered here is the direct transfer of technology through direct investment). Further work is underway to evaluate the impact of the bilateral system on the simulation properties of GEM.

Appendix

Equation diagnostics

Table 8.A1 US imports. An asterisk indicates statistically significant at the 5% level

	auto(4)	het(1)	norm(2)	pred(5)	funct(1)
Japan	9.2	0.3	4.0	12.8*	1.8
Germany	4.1	0.4	0.7	6.3	0.3
France	5.0	0.5	0.9	4.7	1.9
Italy	7.6	3.2	0.3	3.7	0.1
UK	5.8	0.3	0.8	1.4	0.1
Canada	11.2*	0.3	6.2*	2.6	0.5

Table 8.A2 Japanese imports. Asterisk as in Table 8.A1

	auto(4)	het(1)	norm(2)	pred(5)	funct(1)
US	11.4*	0.0	10.9*	0.0	0.0
Germany	5.3	0.1	0.2	0.5	0.2
France	2.4	0.0	24.7*	1.6	0.1
Italy	12.7*	0.1	0.9	0.0	0.5
UK	10.8*	1.6	1.5	1.2	0.9
Canada	7.7	3.7	0.3	0.8	0.8

Table 8.A3 German imports. Asterisk as in Table 8.A1

	auto(4)	het(1)	norm(2)	pred(5)	funct(1)
US	7.6	14.5*	0.0	2.3	2.2
Japan	1.9	1.9	1.1	8.9	0.3
France	7.0	1.3	23.7*	21.8*	2.8
Italy	7.4	1.4	1.9	11.4	5.9*
UK	1.8	0.0	4.7	4.7	1.2
Canada	4.6	0.0	6.1*	3.5	0.3

Table 8.A4 French imports. Asterisk as in Table 8A.1

	auto(4)	het(1)	norm(2)	pred(5)	funct(1)
US	7.6	1.9	15.1*	1.1	7.0*
Japan	6.6	0.0	43.8*	0.6	0.5
Germany	6.2	0.1	0.4	12.2*	5.6*
Italy	6.9	0.0	1.4	3.0	9.3*
UK	3.6	0.4	5.1	4.5	0.6
Canada	2.2	0.1	0.4	3.7	3.8

Table 8.A5 Italian imports. Asterisk as in Table 8A.1

	auto(4)	het(1)	norm(2)	pred(5)	funct(1)
US	4.0	2.6	1.5	0.7	0.1
Japan	3.4	1.7	27.4*	0.2	4.3*
Germany	1.0	0.2	1.1	3.5	0.1
France	3.1	0.0	14.5*	1.7	1.9
UK	3.0	1.6	4.0	6.5	1.5
Canada	10.6*	4.6	1.1	3.3	0.1

Table 8.A6 UK imports. Asterisk as in Table 8A.1

	auto(4)	het(1)	norm(2)	pred(5)	funct(1)
US	10.7*	0.6	3.5	2.5	0.1
Japan	13.4*	0.7	0.6	2.8	0.1
Germany	1.4	1.3	1.0	1.2	0.1
France	1.8	2.0	2.5	11.1*	0.2
Italy	5.1	0.1	0.8	3.5	0.3
Canada	7.9	2.7	4.7	2.1	1.1

Table 8.A7 Canadian imports. Asterisk as in Table 8A.1

	auto(4)	het(1)	norm(2)	pred(5)	funct(1)
US	4.5	10.4	7.1*	2.0	0.4
Japan	4.4	2.7	3.7	3.3	1.1
Germany	3.6	0.6	0.7	4.2	0.3
France	1.3	3.8	8.5*	10.3	8.9*
Italy	5.5	0.1	1.4	2.3	0.1
UK	5.5	0.1	1.4	17.1*	0.5

9 Learning about monetary union

an analysis of boundedly rational learning in European labour markets

Ray Barrell, Guglielmo Maria Caporale, Stephen Hall and *Anthony Garratt*

9.1 Introduction

In this chapter we address the issue of learning in macro-economic models in the context of European labour markets. Individuals form expectations about the future level of prices when bargaining over wages, conditional on their perception of the current economic environment or regime and the possibility of it changing. Monetary union in Europe is one example of a change in regime likely to effect the evolution of the price level in individual European countries and it is therefore important to be able to analyse developments and to understand the problems facing policy makers. In this context we argue that the use of policy analysis conducted on a large macro-econometric model, based on the assumption of strong rational expectations may be misleading and that modelling explicit learning behaviour is more appropriate.

The exercise conducted here is an example of bounded rational learning and is discussed in more detail in Chapter 6. The large macro-econometric model used is the global econometric model (GEM) developed by the National Institute and jointly maintained with the London Business School. In this exercise we compare consistent rational expectation solutions with the bounded rational outcomes.

Following Hall and Garratt (1992b) we assume that agents learn using a Kalman filter based process for updating their expectations conditional on prior errors made when forecasting the price level. We first estimate a time varying parameter model for forecasting prices and this defines the information set of economic agents. This and the structural equation in which the expectations are embedded (see Anderton *et al.* 1992a,b) are then incorporated into the GEM. The outcomes of a set of simulations where the learning mechanism is in operation are then compared with those under rational expectations and a fixed parameter adaptive expectations mechanism. The simulations are the realignments of the franc, lira and pound within the ERM, and an oil price rise.

Section 9.2 outlines the implementation of bounded rational learning presenting a set of filters for price expectations in the United Kingdom, France and Italy and their introduction into GEM where the filters are combined with forward looking wage equations. Section 9.3 reports the results of simulating GEM for two different shocks under the three expectations schemes. They are designed to investigate the role of learning in a monetary union in response to price and supply side shocks. This section also contains a comparison of the properties of a model that uses Kalman filters in place of full model-consistent solutions. Section 9.4 contains concluding comments.

9.2 Implementation of boundedly rational learning

In this section we describe the implemention of model consistent boundedly rational learning using the Kalman filter (which nests ordinary least squares and recursive least squares) to update time varying coefficients relating model variables to expectations terms. Agents are modelled as using an 'incorrect' rule to generate expectations while they are learning about the true structure. In our example we focus on price expectations. The first stage involves estimating time varying mechanisms, which represent economic agents using partial historical information to form expectations. In the second stage the expectations formation mechanisms and the forward looking behavioural equations in which they are incorporated are introduced into a large scale macromodel (GEM).

9.2.1 Estimation of time varying parameter learning mechanisms

In the context of bounded rational learning, the criteria used to decide which variables are included in the time varying price expectation rule will, by definition, not follow from a tightly formulated theory. However, the selection used here is not completely *ad hoc* and two criteria are used in this application. The set of variables used to instrument the one period ahead price expectations terms in the wage equations described below seems an obvious starting point. We also decided to include a set of variables that is likely to be relevant in the proposed simulation and that captures important endogenous linkages operating in the model. This would enable the price expectation equation to adjust the coefficients on existing variables in accordance with movements in other variables that were not included in the instrumenting equation.

The dependent variable for the price expectations equations in each of the three countries (United Kingdom, France and Italy) is the change in the log of consumer price inflation one period ahead. The information set, or the independent variables in the time varying estimation, are of the same structure for each country (with the exception of France where German inflation is also included) and are as follows: ΔP^h home country inflation measured by the difference in the logs of consumer prices, CU the log of capacity utilisation, R the 3-month interest rate and Δe the change in the log of the relevant spot nominal exchange rate, with respect to the Deutschmark. We use information dated at period $t - 1$ and $t - 2$, representing the most recent information available. Where current period information does exist it would be desirable to include it, but in most cases information is only available after a lag.

Table 9.1 reports the expectations equations estimated by OLS. This is intended to give some guide as to the approximate form of the price equations when estimated with time varying parameters. In all three cases, price expectations appear to be autoregressive with the most significant term being the home country inflation. The other variables are for the most part insignificant. However, because they may play an important role in capturing the endogenous interactions of the model, they are retained.

Table 9.2 reports the hyperparameters and residual diagnostics for each equation when estimated using the Kalman filter. The hyperparameters determine the speed of learning and reflect the signal to noise ratio for each variable and hence affect the rate of convergence of the model. For example, if the hyperparameters were exactly zero the learning model would collapse to the standard case of OLS updating of an underlying fixed parameter rule; alternatively if the hyperparameters were all infinite then this would become a very fast form of learning where the parameters would be free to move about to an infinite extent in each period. Hence the large hyperparameters associated with the autoregressive terms imply that learning will occur rapidly with respect to

Table 9.1 OLS regressions of price expectations equations

Variables	UK	France	Italy
	(1970q2 to 1989q1)	(1969q3 to 1990q3)	(1969q3 to 1990q3)
Constant	0.005	0.002	0.070
	(0.75)	(0.02)	(0.56)
Δp_{t-1}^{H}	0.409	0.663	0.50
	(3.66)	(7.23)	(4.02)
Δp_{t-2}^{H}	–	–	0.20
	–	–	(1.63)
Δp_{t-1}^{G}	–	0.364	–
	–	(3.32)	–
CU_{t-1}	0.0135	0.0005	−0.014
	(0.47)	(0.03)	(−0.50)
R_{t-1}	0.0009	−0.0002	–
	(1.47)	(−0.57)	–
Δ_{t-1}^{e}	−0.067	−0.041	0.0059
	−(1.7)	(−1.83)	(0.17)
$\bar{R}^2$	0.24	0.653	0.401
s.e.	0.0148	0.0057	0.0110

t-statistics in parenthesis. Δ_t^h home country inflation; Δ_p^g German inflation; variable definitions in text.

Table 9.2 Hyperparameters and equation diagnostics from time varying Kalman filter estimation

Variables	UK	France	Italy
	(1970q2 to 1989q1)	(1969q3 to 1990q3)	(1969q3 to 1990q3)
Constant	0.22E-04	0.29E-07	0.4749
	(0.019)	(0.28)	(1.50)
Δp^H_{t-1}	55.73	233.33	150.32
	(0.317)	(0.124)	(0.75)
Δp^H_{t-2}	–	–	124.97
			(0.57)
Δp^G_{t-1}	–	305.33	–
		(0.516)	–
CU_{t-1}	0.749E-04	0.0098	0.103E-10
	(0.015)	(0.69)	(0.10)
R_{t-1}	0.0018	0.0053	–
	(0.966)	(1.977)	–
Δ^e_{t-1}	0.47E-19	4.896	0.057
	(0.00)	(0.429)	(0.11)
BJ normality*	4.29	0.15	3.86
LB(1)	1.70	0.07	0.01
LB(4)	13.89	2.02	0.64
LB(8)	22.72	11.94	5.31

t-statistics in parenthesis.
* Test proposed by Jarque and Bera (1980) for testing the validity assumption.

changes in these variables and in contrast learning with respect to the other variables will be relatively slow.

The estimated time varying coefficients show a reasonable degree of variation over the period and by the end of the estimation period show a positive relationship with respect to expected future inflation (for an example see Figure 9.1). Two points are worth noting. First, interpretation of the parameter values is not straightforward. Second, although coefficients may not vary much or in some cases are observed to be close to zero, this will not necessarily be the case in model-based policy analysis with learning where other variables such as interest rates may play an important role.

9.2.2 Wage behaviour in GEM

The following wage equations are estimated under the assumption of rational expectations. In this chapter the expectations components of the wage equations are modelled in simulations using the Kalman filter. The wage equations on GEM are in

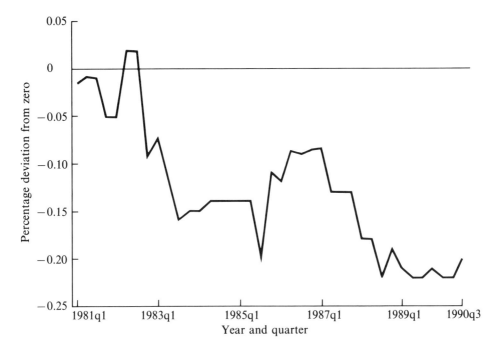

Figure 9.1 Coefficient on lagged French inflation: French filter

general forward-looking. We have used the bargaining approach to wage determination advocated by Layard *et al.* (1991). The bargain is struck over the expected real wage, and allowance is made for institutional differences between countries. The background to our approach and the econometric specification is discussed in Anderton and Barrell (1992). The effect of forward-looking wages on model properties is discussed in Anderton *et al.* (1992b), and an analysis of a monetary union with forward-looking wages is set out in Anderton *et al.* (1992a). Our approach has been to estimate wage equations that include both the long-run factors affecting the wage bargain and also the factors affecting the dynamics of the wage bargain. Particular attention has been paid to variable inclusion and exclusion restrictions and to testing for structural change. We have, therefore, avoided using co-integration techniques as they presuppose the absence of systematic structural change. The equations are estimated in an error correction form and are specified using the general to specific principle. The producer wage equations are:

$$\Delta \log W = a + b_1[\log W(-1) - \log PP(-1)] \tag{9.1}$$

$$+ b_2 \log PROD + b_3 WED + b_4 U(-1) \tag{9.2}$$

$$+ b_5 PE + \text{Dynamics} \tag{9.3}$$

177

where W is total compensation per employee hour, PP is our index of the producer price of output, $PROD$ is a measure of average labour productivity in the economy, WED is the wedge between our producer price index and the consumers' expenditure deflator (CED), U is the level of the unemployment rate, and PE is the rate of consumer price inflation expected over the next quarter.[1]

The dynamics in the equation includes past terms in the rate of change in the CED and this depends in part on import prices and on indirect taxes. The equation determines the real wage in the long run, but the short-run bargain is over the expected real wage. There are a number of propositions to test in this framework. If the supply of labour were fixed, or if all wages were determined by the bargain we would expect real wages to rise in line with productivity in the economy.[2] We would expect the wedge effect to be positive or zero, and in this chapter we have followed Layard et al. (1991) and taken our null hypothesis to be that the effect is zero. We have assumed that there should be a role for price expectations, and that the coefficient should be less than or equal to one.

We are interested in testing our relationship for structural stability, but our task is made non-standard by the presence of expectation effects. We do not have data on expectations, and hence we have to take as part of our maintained hypothesis the assumption that individuals hold expectations that are consistent with the outturn. This does not mean that they have to have perfect foresight, but rather that they should not on average be wrong. This allows us to use actual inflation as a proxy for expected inflation. However, we know our proxy measures the actual with error, and hence there can be problems in estimation by ordinary least squares. Even if the errors in the proxy variable are independent of the errors in the equation, the proxy variable will in general have a lower variance (and a different covariance structure) than the true variable, and hence under OLS the estimates of the parameter vector and the variance/covariance matrix of the parameters will be inconsistent. We have estimated our equations by instrumental variables techniques (IV) in order to be able to test hypotheses on individual parameters and on the equation as a whole.[3] We have instrumented price expectations with current and lagged inflation and capacity utilisation.[4] Table 9.3 reports our results for the major European economies. The results are discussed in detail below, but their overall structure is of some interest. In all cases we can validly accept the restriction that real wages rise in line with productivity in the long run, and generally we find a significant and negative long-run role for unemployment. We test for wedge effects, and can only find a role for them in Italy, and then only if we use a narrower definition of the indirect tax rate than that used in the equation in Table 9.2.[5] All equations have been tested for stability using a Wald deletion test on a set of dummied variables included for half of our sample period. All equations (except that for Italy) pass this test.[6] However, recent developments in Germany may change the nature of wage bargaining but it is too early in the process of unification to make any estimate of its effect.

We found no significant role for price expectations in our German wage equation, and it shows no sign of structural instability. Given that wage inflation has been low and steady in Germany over our estimation period we would not expect a strong role

Table 9.3 Forward-looking wage equations ($\Delta \log(W/E)$)

Variables	Germany	France	UK	Italy
Constant	−1.355 (5.89)	0.2326 (1.22)	0.741 (3.7)	1.618 (2.29)
Error correction	−0.279 (6.06)	−0.051 (1.39)	−0.171 (3.79)	−0.135 (2.33)
Δ Compensation (−1)	−0.349 (3.77)			
Δ Compensation (−2)	−0.211 (2.02)		0.338 (4.3)	
Δ Compensation (−3)	−0.304 (3.14)			
ΔCED(−1)		0.608 (4.03)	0.197 (2.5)	
ΔCED(−2)				0.707* (4.35)
ΔCED(−3)				
ΔCED(−4)			0.281 (3.94)	
Unemployment (−1)	−0.0070 (7.68)	−0.0025 (4.32)	−0.00074 (1.84)	−0.0013† (2.33)
Expected inflation	−	0.419 (1.65)	0.309 (2.51)	0.586 (2.31)
Standard error	0.0106	0.0057	0.008	0.0148
Serial correlation (LM(4))	7.77	1.66	2.494	2.247
Sargan test of instruments	−	12.86 ($\chi^2(8)$)	2.404 ($\chi^2(4)$)	13.26 ($\chi^2(10)$)
Data period	1970q2–1991q1	1971q2–1990q1	1969q4–1990q2	1972q3–1990q1

* Before 1982q1; † current period after 1982q1.
The dependent variable is the change in the log of compensation per person hour, the error correction term is the divergence between the log of real producer wages per person hour and average productivity.
All variables, except unemployment, are in logs.
t-statistics in parenthesis.

for expected inflation, and past wage bargains and the level of unemployment may contain all the information that bargainers need. In the long run in Germany, real wages rise in line with productivity, but the speed of pass-through of prices to wages is slower in Germany than in any other European economy. This is clearly the result of the low degree of persistence of German inflation. (See Barrell (1990) for a discussion of signal and noise in wage determination.) All of our other European wage equations do display a role for forward-looking inflation, and all have a significant role for unemployment (although the evidence is weak for the United Kingdom). Only in the case of Italy do we find some structural change, and our Italian equation differs significantly between the pre- and post-1982 periods. Our final equation contains a backward-looking inflation indicator for the period prior to 1982, and over this period there is no role for unemployment. The change in the system of wage bargaining in Italy in the early 1980s[7] is associated with a sharp change in the estimated wage equation. After 1982 we do find a role for forward-looking expectations, and there is a role for unemployment. The long-run test statistics for these equations are set out in Table 9.4.

It is possible to produce indices of real and nominal wage flexibility. These so-called sacrifice ratios will depend upon the interaction of wage and price determination processes and are difficult to calculate from reduced form equations. It is, however, possible to produce some indices of wage flexibility. Table 9.5 sets out our overall results. The first row gives an indication of real wage flexibility in response to a rise in unemployment. The second gives the long-run coefficient on unemployment. The sacrifice ratio indicates the percentage point rise in unemployment that is required to reduce inflation by one percent in the first year. The long-run coefficient on unemployment indicates the effect on the real wage of a permanent one percent rise in unemployment. The third row gives an indicator of the degree of forward-looking behaviour in prices. The fourth and fifth give various indicators of the speed of response to increases in prices (given constant expectations). Germany has a systematically slow impact and long-run response to increases in prices. This reflects a great deal about the success of the Bundesbank policy over the last decade.

Table 9.4 Tests on long-run coefficients (Wald tests and χ^2)

	Germany	France	UK	Italy[f]
Productivity[a]	0.20	1.22	0.006	0.403
Unemployment[b]	36.18*	16.94*	2.57†	3.58†
Wedge[ac]	0.32	1.17	0.61	1.69
Expectations[d]	1.72	2.89*	5.32*	6.31*
Structural change[e]	5.87 (6)	9.66 (6)	15.6* (7)	5.67 (6)

(a) A Wald variable addition test on a productivity term entered into the final equation
(b) A Wald variable deletion test on the parameter in the final equation
(c) Tax wedge effect, using a Wald variable addition test on the final equation
(d) A deletion test for France, Italy and the UK and an adition test for Germany. In each case the instrument set is adjusted accordingly.
(e) A variable deletion test with degrees of freedom in parenthesis
(f) Figures are for the post-1981 period
* Significant at 95%; †significant at 90%.

Table 9.5 Wage flexibility

	Germany	France	UK	Italy[2]
Sacrifice ratio[1]	0.591	0.827	0.625	1.93
Long-run unemployment coefficient	−0.026	−0.014	−0.0043	−0.0096
Ratio of backward to forward expectations	no forward	5:5	5:3	switches in 1982
Mean lag in prices (in quarters)	6.26	4.63	1.08	7.41 (2.17)
Median lag in prices (range between two quarters)	[4–5]	[1–2]	[2–3]	[4–5] [1–2]

1. Sacrifice ratio: mean lag in prices divided by long-run unemployment coefficient, and re-scaled by 0.0025 for comparability with Layard *et al.* (1991).
2. Italian figures are for the post-1982 period, those in parenthesis beneath these figures are for the pre-1982 period.

9.2.3   GEM with price expectations in wage equations

The four bargaining equations for wages that are described above have been embedded into the most recent version of GEM. The rest of the model is described fully in the May 1992 Manual (NIESR 1992). This chapter is designed to look at the role of learning about price inflation in the labour market and its implications for policy in a European monetary union.

The wage equations described above are an integral part of the model. They have been programmed up in three alternative ways. First, they have been implemented with model-consistent expectations. This requires the use of a terminal condition for each forward-looking variable and we have implemented a standard constant rate of growth condition on the price level. Our solution method is a variant of forward shooting and is described in Barrell and Gurney (1991). Our second approach avoided the assumption of strongly rational expectations in the labour market. We estimated our equations by IV, and the auxiliary instrumenting regression can be seen as a description of a data-consistent expectations generating mechanism that is on average accurate over the past. A fixed parameter version of this mechanism has been programmed up, and its predictions are used as the expectations variables. Our third approach has been to implement three Kalman filters in GEM, one for each of the wage equations where expectations occur. We have undertaken three sets of simulations on the model, with two types of shock applied.

The standard method of solving models with expectations in them is to assume that individuals' expectations are the same as the predictions of the model. In the results presented below we have attempted to ensure comparability between models, and we have used the backward-looking equations for all other variables where there is a possibility of forward solution. In particular, long-term interest rates, equity prices and bond prices are all backward-looking in these runs. These runs are directly comparable with our fixed coefficient expectations generating mechanisms. These are based on the set of instruments used in the IV estimation of the forward-looking wage equations.

The Kalman filter expectations generating mechanisms have been described above. They are based on our IV equations, but they do not contain either contemporaneous information or such a rich lag structure. However, as the filter updates the coefficients, including the stochastic constant, we do not see this as a major drawback. In our early experiments in this research we implemented the filters one at a time, and then two at a time in order to check that there were no dynamic instabilities introduced by the use of more than one filter. We found no significant problems.

Our two experiments involved a realignment of the ERM, with each country in turn changing its nominal exchange rate by 10%, and also an oil price shock. In each case a monetary union remained in place after the shock, and interest rates were set by a Community-wide feedback rule that targets inflation and GDP. This rule is discussed in Anderton *et al.* (1992a), and has been used by the Commission in *'One market, one money'* (CEC 1990). Its advantage over money-base targeting is that it allows step changes in price levels but no permanent increases in inflation.

Our experiments have been designed in order that we can investigate the effects of learning filters. A realignment followed by fixed rates should cause the price level in the realigning country to rise, and the real effective exchange rate to return to base. We do not expect the domestic price level to rise by 10% in response to a 10% devaluation. In a world model a devaluation in one country is an appreciation in another, and the price level there may fall (especially if we have some elements of pricing to markets in our model). This effect is reinforced in our simulations because the policy response to the realignment affects all members of EMU. Aggregate inflation and output in the Union rise in response to our realignments (because the ECU also depreciates) and hence interest rates rise everywhere by the same amount in line with our feedback rule. This causes some deflation in the rest of the Community, and hence adjustment takes place through price level changes throughout the Community. If we undertake this experiment in full forward-looking mode we are assuming that individuals in the labour market are acting as if the inflationary success of the monetary union were fully credible. They act as if they were certain the monetary union would survive. This is in contrast to the experiments with Kalman filters in place. If inflation rises in response to a realignment then we would expect that anticipated inflation will rise. However, because the filter is not forward-looking, reactions might be slower but more persistent. Alternatively the estimated filter may reflect the lack of credibility on the part of the authorities. If, say, the UK or Italian authorities have had little success in sticking to their monetary stance then actors may read a lot of signal into a rise in inflation, and hence wages could rise more than in a situation where the authorities have full credibility. However, in the long run, as long as the policy rule is implemented and an equilibrium exists, the increase in the price level should be the same whatever expectations assumptions are made.

9.3 Learning about exchange rate realignments and oil price shocks

In this section we compare the results from a range of shocks conducted under three alternative expectations formation processes described in the previous section.

9.3.1 Realignments

We have analysed in turn the effects of depreciation of 10% in French, Italian and UK nominal Deutschmark spot exchange rates. Tables 9.6, 9.7 and 9.8 describe the results of the three realignments for the home country whose exchange rate has been depreciated where CED is the price level, REFEX the real exchange rate and GDP

Table 9.6 Percentage difference from base – France

	CED		REFEX		GDP	
	Year 1	Year 10	Year 1	Year 10	Year 1	Year 10
Full forward	0.465	7.639	−9.451	−1.551	0.428	0.065
IV	0.442	7.366	−9.474	−1.832	0.427	0.143
Filter	0.429	10.105	−9.488	0.964	0.424	−0.319

Table 9.7 Percentage difference from base – Italy

	CED		REFEX		GDP	
	Year 1	Year 10	Year 1	Year 10	Year 1	Year 10
Full forward	1.2970	7.384	−8.432	−3.037	0.574	0.156
IV	1.3301	6.091	−8.429	−3.052	0.574	0.157
Filter	1.2800	5.556	−8.449	−3.478	0.572	−0.370

Table 9.8 Percentage difference from base – UK

	CED		REFEX		GDP	
	Year 1	Year 10	Year 1	Year 10	Year 1	Year 10
Full forward	1.239	8.085	−8.688	−1.360	0.423	−0.193
IV	1.255	8.085	−8.673	−1.366	0.435	−0.189
Filter	1.244	8.339	−8.684	−1.089	0.437	−0.241

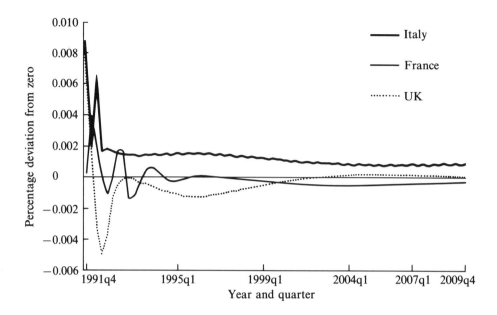

Figure 9.2 Expectations errors: three realignments

measures real output. During the initial stages of the simulation we would expect the errors to be large, but to decrease over time. Figure 9.2 plots the expectation errors on the Kalman filter over an 18-year simulation horizon for the three exchange rate simulations. In each case, all three filters are running but we only plot the error between the expected and model outturn for the country that has realigned. In all three of the exchange rate simulations, the expectations errors on the filter of the country whose exchange rate is not being depreciated are exceptionally small. The initial impact of the realignments is to make the variance of the expectations errors large for approximately ten periods but thereafter the size and variability of the error terms are considerably reduced and are asymptoting to zero. The movement of the learning parameters during the course of the simulation is also of interest. Figure 9.3 plots three of the coefficients from the UK filter for the case of the UK realignment as an example. The inflation coefficient shows significant volatility in the initial stages of the simulation, but thereafter the change slowly stabilises with the parameter asymptoting to a constant value. The same is true for the other two parameters, where the initial volatility is less for the term on capacity utilisation and non-existent for the constant. The movements in these parameters are representative of the general behaviour of the learning co-efficients. In general, the parameters appear to be stabilising slowly and hence we can claim the model is reaching a new rational expectations equilibrium with model consistent expectations.

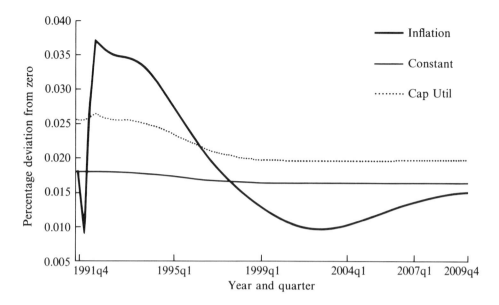

Figure 9.3 UK expectations parameters: UK realignment

The structures of the results are very similar whichever expectations generating mechanism we use, as can be seen from Tables 9.6 to 9.8. This is particularly true for the short-term outcome. This in part reflects the fact that we have 'turned off' the other forward-looking variables in the model. Exchange rates, long-term interest rates and equity prices are not allowed to jump and, hence this version of the model has a very small forward root. However, differences are larger when we compare the medium-/long-run results. For example, in the case of the French devaluation the filter-based expectations results show a change of 10% in the real effective exchange rate after 10 years compared with approximately 7.5% for the full rational solution and fixed parameter filter. Learning therefore speeds the movement back to real exchange rate equilibrium, given the 10% depreciation. In the case of Italy and the United Kingdom, the differences between the three solutions are less marked. However, in all cases the real exchange rate returns to the base, as can be seen in Figure 9.4 which plots the deviations from base of the real exchange rate for France with forward-looking wages and with rational learning.

In the case of France, inflation is initially faster in model-consistent expectations, and wages rise more rapidly. The devaluation is not anticipated, and the price dynamics in our model of France shows a considerable degree of nominal inertia. The combination of these two factors produces a very small rise in prices in the first period, reflecting the very small forward root in the system, especially when no other variables

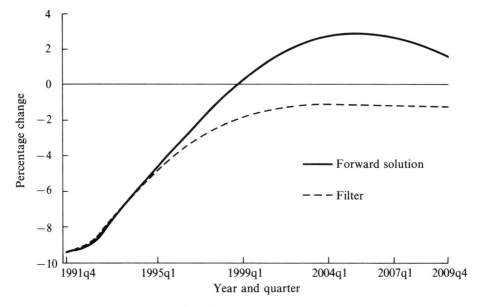

Figure 9.4 French real exchange rate: French devaluation

are allowed to be forward-looking. Reactions are considerably more rapid when other forward-looking variables are allowed to jump, as is demonstrated in Anderton *et al.* (1992b). However, after a couple of years the filter expectations cause the price level to rise more rapidly than in the forward model. As a result the price level and the real effective exchange rate both over-shoot. The terminal condition in the full forward model prevents this happening. The overshooting and overvaluation push French GDP below base (see Table 9.6, and Figures 9.4 and 9.5). With forward-looking wage, but no other forward-looking variables, the model needs 24 to 26 years to reach its full equilibrium.

The forward root in our Italian wage–price system is larger than that in France, largely because the price system displays considerably less nominal inertia. Hence, short-run Italian inflation rises more rapidly than in the French case (see CED first column in Table 9.7), both when the filter and the full forward-looking wage systems are operating. However, the long-run inflation effect is smaller in the Italian case than with France and the United Kingdom, with the combination of the filter and the equation for wages producing less wage inflation than when forward expectations are operating. This conclusion depends to a large extent on our result that there has been a change in the structure of the Italian labour market, as well as on the assumption that the operation of monetary policy in Europe will be successful and Italy will manage to stay in the ERM. The European Central Bank is presumed to be successfully operating monetary policy, targeting European-wide inflation and output. If Italy dropped out of

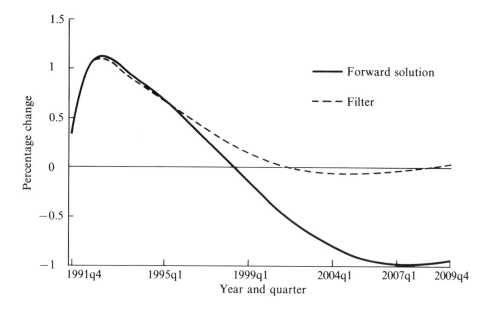

Figure 9.5 French output: French devaluation

the ERM, the inflationary consequences of a realignment could be much more significant.

Our UK model also has a larger forward root in the wage–price system than does France, and prices rise by 1% in the first quarter after the shock. The filter equation contains the exchange rate as one of its arguments, and if a realignment takes place then prices are expected to rise. The expectations generated by the filter and in full forward-looking mode in the first period are clearly similar, as the rise in wages is approximately the same (see Table 9.8). However, the filter embeds the United Kingdom's lack of success in its anti-inflation strategy, and expectations of inflation are higher using a backward filter than when model-consistent expectations are used. This suggests that the UK authorities' stance has lacked credibility. The real exchange rate and the nominal wage move quickly toward the same equilibrium (columns 1 to 4 in Table 9.8 show similar numbers for all three cases), suggesting that the filter, which should be a reduced form of the model, and the model, encapsulate the same information in similar ways.

9.3.2 Oil price shock

In this section we examine the effects of an exogenous common shock to GEM under the three expectations schemes. This takes the form of doubling the oil price and then returning to the base value after 5 years, while keeping exchange rates fixed (at their base values). A shock of this magnitude should change the distribution of world wealth and have long lasting effects on price levels and demand even in a backward-looking world. Figure 9.6 plots the expectations errors of the three learning filters over the period of the simulation. The initial period, as in the previous example, shows a high degree of volatility, as the change represents new information and thereafter the errors decrease. There is also a second period of volatility and large expectation errors occur when the oil price returns to its base value after 5 years. The error eventually goes to zero and, therefore, we can assume that the learning is converging towards an equilibrium.

The results reported in Tables 9.9, 9.10 and 9.11 would suggest that in both the short and the long run the equilibrium achieved under learning is very similar to that under rational expectations. For example, the short-run impact on the price level is very slow to come through and in the case of France the long-run effect is in fact smaller with forward-looking wages. After 5 years, output is below base by around 0.2–0.3% in France and Italy and there is an increase of the same order of magnitude in the United Kingdom because of the effects of higher oil prices and UK oil output. Analysis using learning and the avoidance of specifying terminal conditions could be thought of as being advantageous in this situation. If rational expectations were operating, then the movement up then down in the oil price would be anticipated and a smooth white noise profile of expectations errors would result. Hence, Figure 9.6 highlights an important

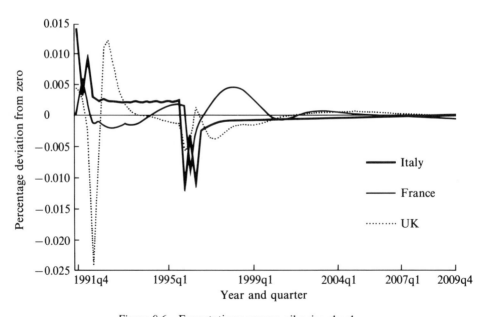

Figure 9.6 Expectations errors: oil price shock

Table 9.9   Percentage difference from base – France

	CED		REFEX		GDP	
	Year 1	Year 5	Year 1	Year 5	Year 1	Year 5
Full forward	0.692	0.432	−0.951	−4.918	−0.459	−0.199
IV	0.654	0.406	−0.992	−4.946	−0.463	−0.189
Filter	0.642	0.583	−1.000	−4.666	−0.464	−0.210

Table 9.10   Percentage difference from base – Italy

	CED		REFEX		GDP	
	Year 1	Year 5	Year 1	Year 5	Year 1	Year 5
Full forward	2.109	6.753	0.861	2.844	−0.175	−0.282
IV	2.112	6.772	0.872	2.873	−0.176	−0.296
Filter	2.080	6.197	0.840	2.238	−0.177	−0.140

Table 9.11   Percentage difference from base – UK

	CED		REFEX		GDP	
	Year 1	Year 5	Year 1	Year 5	Year 1	Year 5
Full forward	1.081	7.202	−0.370	3.232	−0.111	0.157
IV	1.080	7.129	−0.366	3.156	−0.111	0.163
Filter	1.091	7.158	−0.350	3.214	−0.070	0.172

difference between rational expectations solutions. Learning would, therefore, seem more reasonable as oil shocks or any other exogenous shocks are generally not seen to be anticipated by markets.

9.4   Conclusions

This chapter is the first attempt to implement learning filters on a model of the world economy, and also the first attempt to implement more than one learning filter. The model used is generally stable in rational expectations runs, and, as Anderton *et al.*

(1992a) show, the results are very similar when full rational expectations are replaced by fixed parameter expectations generating mechanisms. The properties of least squares estimation imply that the fixed parameter filters cannot be biased over the past, but they can be systematically wrong because they can display serially correlated errors, and, hence, may not produce rational forecasts. The same should not be true of predictions based on Kalman filters. The least squares updating formulae remove systematic bias. The hyperparameters give some indication of signal to noise in recent events, given an unchanged structure, and, hence, they embed the credibility (or lack of it) of the authorities' anti-inflationary stance. In two of our experiments, the filter-based learning models caused prices to rise more rapidly than they do under model-consistent, or strongly rational, expectations. This suggests that policy analysis with models that can only use model-consistent expectations can be seriously misleading. Such models are usually operated under the assumption that the authorities stance is fully credible. The filter-based analysis suggests that this is not always the case, and we should clearly bear this in mind when analysing intentional shocks to the price level.

Notes

1. We tried one-quarter-ahead and one-year-ahead expected inflation, and in all cases the one-quarter-ahead indicator performed better.
2. We have followed Hall and Henry (1987) and used a smoothed moving average for productivity in order to avoid the noise contained in the ratio of one period output to employment.
3. This is the procedure advocated by Pagan (1984). See Cuthbertson *et al.* (1992) for a discussion of the estimation of RE models.
4. We have also instrumented all other contemporaneous endogenous variables, and the exogeneity of the instrument set has been tested.
5. Further results for the European economies are reported in Anderton and Barrell (1992) where we have undertaken tests on ten countries. Wedge effects appear to be present in only two, Italy and Ireland, and only with a narrower definition of indirect taxes in Italy than that used here.
6. If we estimate $y = a + bx$ by IV we cannot use the standard Chow test for within-sample parameter stability. However, if we define the variable δx, where δx is zero before some date and takes the same value as x thereafter, and estimate:

$$y = a + bx + b^*\delta x$$

   and undertake a Wald variable deletion test on b^*, we have a valid IV stability test (see Godfrey 1988, pp. 200–3).
7. We have discussed the dismantling of the Scala Mobile at length elsewhere (see Barrell, 1990).

References

Afriat, S. (1967) 'The construction of a utility function from expenditure data', *International Economic Review*, 8, 67–77.

Akaike, H. (1974) 'A new look at the Statistical Model Identification', *IEEE Transactions on Automatic Control*, AC-19, 716–23.

Alogoskoufis, G. and Smith, R. (1991) 'Error correction models', *Journal of Economic Surveys*, 5(1), 95–128.

Andersen, T.M. (1991) 'Comment on Kydland and Prescott (1991)', *Scandinavian Journal of Economics*, 93(2), 179–84.

Anderson, P.A. (1979) 'Rational expectations forecasts from non rational models', *Journal of Monetary Economics*, 5, 67–80.

Anderton, R. and Barrell, R. (1992) *The ERM and Structural Change in European Labour Markets, A study of 10 Countries*, mimeo paper given at the Royal Economic Society Conference, March 1992.

Anderton, R., Barrell, R. and In't Veld, J.W. (1992a) 'Forward looking wages and the analysis of monetary union', in R. Barrell and J. Whitley (eds.), *Macro-economic Policy Coordination in Europe, the EMS and EMU*, Sage, London.

Anderton, R., Barrell, R., In't Veld, J.W. and Pittis, N. (1992b) 'Forward looking wages and policy analysis', in National Institute Global Econometric Model, *National Institute Review*, August.

Armington, P.S. (1969) 'A theory of demand for products distinguished by place of production', *International Monetary Fund Staff Papers*, 16, 159–78.

Artus, J.R. and McGuirk, A.K. (1981) 'A revised version of the Multilateral Exchange Rate Model', *IMF Staff Papers*, 28, 275–309.

Attfield, C.L.F., Demery, D. and Duck, N.W. (1985), *Rational Expectations in Macroeconomics*, Basil Blackwell, Oxford.

Ball, R.J. and Burns, T. (1978) 'Stabilisation policy in Britain 1964–81', in M. Posner (ed.), *Demand Management*, Heinemann/NIESR, London.

Barrell, R. (1990), 'Has the EMS changed wage and price behaviour in Europe?', *National Institute Economic Review*, 134, November, 26–40.

Barrell, R., Caporale, G.M., Garratt, A. and Hall, S.G. (1992) *Learning About Monetary Union: An analysis of boundedly rational learning in European labour markets*, Paper presented at the ESRC Macromodelling Conference, June, Warwick.

Barrell, R., Christodoulakis, N., Garratt, A., Ireland, J., Kemball-Cook, D., Levine, D. and Westaway, P. (1993) 'Policy analysis and model reduction techniques using GEM', in R.C. Bryant, P. Hooper and C.L. Man (eds.), *Evaluating Policy Regimes: New research in empirical macroeconomics*, The Brookings Institution, Washington.

Barrell, R. and Gurney, A. (1989) 'Changes to the world model', *National Institute Economic Review*, 130, 43–5.

Barrell, R. and Gurney, A. (1991) *Fiscal and Monetary Policy Simulations with Forward-looking Exchange Rates using GEM*, National Institute Discussion Paper, No. 200, National Institute of Economic and Social Research, London.

Barro, R.J. (1976) 'Rational expectations and the role of monetary policy', *Journal of Monetary Economics*, 2, 1–33.

Barro, R.J. (1977) 'Unanticipated monetary growth and unemployment in the United States', *American Economic Review*, 67, 101–15.

Barten, A.P. (1971) 'An import allocation model for the Common Market', *Cahiers Economiques de Bruxelles*, 50, 153–64.

Bayoumi, T. and Eichengreen, B. (1991) 'Shocking aspects of European monetary unification', IMF mimeo, International Monetary Fund, Washington.

Beenstock, M. and Minford, P. (1976) 'A quarterly econometric model of world trade and prices, 1955–71', in M. Parkin and G. Zis (eds.), *Inflation in Open Economies*, Manchester University Press, Manchester.

Begg, D.K.H. (1982) *The Rational Expectations Revolution in Macroeconomics*, Phillip Allan, Oxford.

Begg, D., Fischer, J. and Dornbusch, R. (1991) *Economics*, McGraw-Hill, London.

Blackorby, C., Primont, D. and Russel, R. (1975) 'Budgeting, decentralization and aggregation', *Annals of Economic and Social Measurement*, 4, 23–44.

Blackorby, C., Primont, D. and Russel, R. (1978) *Duality, Separability and Functional Structure: Theory and economic applications*, North-Holland, New York.

Blanchard, O. (1976) *The Non-transition to Rational Expectations*, mimeo, MIT Department of Economics, Massachusetts Institute of Technology, Boston.

Blanchard, O. (1989) 'A traditional interpretation of macroeconomic fluctuation', *American Economic Review*, 79(5), 1146–64.

Blanchard, O. and Kahn, C.M. (1980) 'Backward and forward solutions for economies with rational expectations', *Econometrica*, 48(5), 1305–11.

Blanchard, O. and Quah, D. (1989) 'The dynamic effects of aggregate demand and supply disturbances', *American Economic Review*, 79(4), 819–40.

Bodkin, R., Lawrence, G., Klein, R. and Marwah, K. (1991) *A History of Macroeconometric Model-building*, Edward Elgar, Aldershot.

Box, G.E.P. and Jenkins, G.M. (1976) *Time Series Analysis: Forecasting and Control*, Holden Day, San Francisco.

Brandsma, A.S. and Hughes Hallett, A.J. (1984) 'Economic conflict and the solution of dynamic games', *European Economic Review*, 26, 13–32.

Branson, W.H. (1972) 'The trade effects of the 1971 currency realignments', *Brookings Papers on Economic Activity*, 1, 15–69.

Bray, M.M. (1982) 'Learning, estimation, and the stability of rational expectations', *Journal of Economic Theory*, 26, 318–39.

Bray, M.M. (1983) 'Convergence to rational expectations equilibrium', in R. Frydman and E.S. Phelps (eds.), *Industrial Forecasting and Aggregate Outcomes*, Cambridge University Press, Cambridge.

Bray, M.M. and Kreps, C. (1984) *Rational Learning and Rational Expectation*, mimeo, Cambridge University.

Bray, M.M. and Kreps, D. (1987) 'Rational learning and rational expectations', in G.R. Fiewel (ed.), *Arrow and the Ascent of Modern Economic Theory*, MacMillan, London (pp. 597–625).

Bray, M.M. and Savin, N.E. (1986) 'Rational expectations equilibria, learning and model specification', *Econometrica*, 54, 1129–60.

Brenton, P.A. (1989) 'The allocation approach to trade modelling: Some tests of separability between imports and domestic production', *Weltwirtschaftliches Archiv*, 125, 230–51.

Britton, A. and Pain, N. (1992) 'The recent experience of economic forecasting in Britain', Discussion Paper No. 20, National Institute of Economic and Social Research, London.

Brock, W.A. (1986) *Distinguishing Random and Deterministic Systems: An expanded version*, Department of Economics, University of Wisconsin, Madison.

Brock, W.A., Dechert, W.A. and Scheinkman, J.A. (1987) *A Test for Independence Based on the Correlation Dimension*, Department of Economics, University of Wisconsin, Madison.

Brown, R.G. (1963) *Smoothing, Forecasting and Prediction*, Prentice-Hall, Englewood Cliffs, New Jersey.

Budd, A., Christodoulakis, N., Holly, S. and Levine, P. (1989) 'Stabilisation policy in Britain', in A. Britton (ed.), *Policy Making with Macroeconomic Models*, Gower, Aldershot.

Burns, A.F. and Mitchell, W.C. (1946) *Measuring Business Cycles*, National Bureau of Economic Research, New York.

Burrell, A. and Hall, S. (1993) 'A comparison of short-term macroeconomic forecasts', CEF mimeo, June.

Cagan, P. (1956) 'The monetary dynamics of hyperinflation', in M. Friedman (ed.), *Studies in the Quantity Theory of Money*, Chicago University Press, Chicago.

Canova, F. (1992) *Vector Autoregressive Models: Specification estimation inference and forecasting*, mimeo, European University Institute, Florence.

Cecchetti, S. and Karras, G. (1991) *Sources of Output Fluctuation During the Inter-war Period: Further evidence on the causes of the great depression*, mimeo, Ohio State University, Ohio.

Chow, G. (1992) *Statistical Estimation and Testing of a Real Business Cycle Model*, Econometric Research Program, Research Memorandum No. 365, Princeton University, New Jersey.

Clemen, R. (1989) 'Combining forecasts: A review and annotated bibliography', *Journal of Forecasting*, 15, 45–60.

Commission of the European Communities (1990) 'One market, one money: an evaluation of the potential benefits and costs of forming an economic and monetary union', *European Economy*, 44, October.

Confederation of British Industry (1992) 'Making it in Britain', *CBI Report*, London.

Cooley, T.C. and Leroy, S. (1985) 'Atheoretical macroeconometrics: a critique', *Journal of Monetary Economics*, 16, 283–308.

Cowen, T. and Lee, D. (1992) 'The usefulness of inefficient procurement', *Defence Economics*, 3, 219–27.

Crafts, N. (1991) *Productivity Growth Reconsidered*, CEPR Discussion Paper, Centre for Economic Policy Research, London.

Currie, D.A. (1985) 'Macroeconomic policy design and control theory – a failed partnership?', *Economic Journal*, 95(378), 285–306.

Currie, D.A. and Hall, S.G. (1989) 'A stock-flow model of the determination of the UK effective exchange rate', in R. Macdonald and M.P. Taylor (eds.), *Exchange Rates and Open Economy Macroeconomics*, Basil Blackwell, Oxford.

Currie, D. and Hall, S. (1994) 'Expectations, learning and empirical macroeconomic models', this book, ch. 6.

Currie, D.A., Holly, S. and Scott, A. (1989) *Savings, Demography and Interest Rates*, CEF Discussion Paper, No. 01-1989, Centre for Economic Forecasting, London Business School, London.

Currie, D.A., Holtham, G. and Hughes Hallett, A.J. (1989) 'The theory and practise of international policy coordination: Does coordination pay?', in R. Bryant, D. Currie, J. Frenkel, P. Masson and R. Portes (eds.), *Macroeconomic Policy in an Interdependent World*, IMF, Washington.

Currie, D.A. and Levine, P. (1987) 'Credibility and time consistency in a stochastic world', *Journal of Economics*, 47, 225–52.

Currie, D.A., Levine, P. and Pearlman, J. (1992) 'European monetary union or Hard-EMS?', *European Economic Review*, 36, 1185–204.

Currie, D.A., Levine, P. and Vidalis, N. (1987) 'International cooperation and reputation in an empirical two-bloc model', in R. Bryant and R. Portes (eds.), *Global Macroeconomics: Policy Conflict and Cooperation*, Macmillan, London.

Cuthbertson, K., Hall, S. and Taylor, M. (1992) *Applied Econometric Techniques*, Harvester Wheatsheaf, Hemel Hempstead.

Day, R. and Shafer, W. (1985) 'Keynesian chaos', *Journal of Macroeconomics*, 7, 277–95.

Deaton, A.S. and Muellbauer, J. (1980) 'An almost ideal demand system', *American Economic Review*, 70, 312–26.

DeCanio, S.J. (1979) 'Rational expectations and learning from experience', *Quarterly Journal of Economics*, 92, 47–57.

Dinenis, E., Holly, S., Levine, P. and Smith, P. (1989) 'The London Business School econometric model: Some recent developments', *Economic Modelling*, 4, 115–36.

Driffill, J. and Miller, M. (1992) *Learning about a Shift in Exchange Rate Regime*, paper presented to the annual conference of the Royal Economic Society, April, London.

Eisner, R. (1965) 'Realizations of investment anticipations', in J.S. Duesenberry *et al.* (eds.), *The Brookings Quarterly Econometric Model of the United States*, Rand McNally and Co./North-Holland, Chicago.

Engle, R.F. and Granger, C.W.J. (1987) 'Co-integration and error correction: representation, estimation and testing', *Econometrica*, 35, 251–76.

Engle, R.F. and Granger, C.W.J. (eds.) (1991) *Long-run Economic Relationships*, Oxford University Press, Oxford.

Engle, R.F. and Yoo, S. (1991) 'Cointegrated economic time series: An overview with new results', in R.F. Engle and C.W.J. Granger (eds.), *Long Run Economic Relationships: Readings in cointegration*, Oxford University Press, Oxford.

Evans, G. (1983) 'The stability of rational expectations in macroeconomic models', in R. Frydman and E. S. Phelps (eds.), *Individual Forecasting and Aggregate Outcomes: Rational Expectations Examined*, Cambridge University Press, New York.

Evans, G. (1987) *The Fragility of Sunspots and Bubbles*, mimeo, Stanford University.

Evans, G.W. (1986a) 'Expectational stability and the multiple equilibria problem in linear rational expectations models', *Quarterly Journal of Economics* 1217–33.

Evans, G.W. (1986b) 'Selection criteria for models with non-uniqueness', *Journal of Monetary Economics*, 18, 147–57.

Evans, G.W. and Ramey, G. (1992) 'Expectation calculation and macroeconomic dynamics', *American Economic Review*, 82(1), 207–24.

Fair, R.C. (1979) 'An analysis of a macro-econometric model with rational expectations in the bond and stock markets', *American Economic Review*, 69, 539–52.

Fair, R.C. (1984) *Specification, Estimation and Analysis of Macroeconometric Models*, Harvard University Press, Harvard.

Fair, R.C. and Shiller, R.J. (1990) 'Comparing information in forecasts from econometric models', *American Economic Review*, 79, 375–89.

Fair, R.C. and Taylor, J.B. (1983) 'Solution and maximum likelihood estimation of dynamic nonlinear rational expectations models', *Econometrica*, 51, 1169–86.

Feige, E.L. and Pearce, D.K. (1976) 'Economically rational expectations: are innovations in the rate of inflation independent of innovations in measures of monetary and fiscal policy?', *Journal of Political Economy*, 84, 499–522.

Fisher, P.G. (1990) *Simulation and Control Techniques for Nonlinear Rational Expectations*, ESRC Macroeconomic Modelling Bureau, Warwick University.

Fisher, P.G., Holly, S. and Hughes Hallett, A.J. (1985) 'Efficient solution techniques for dynamic nonlinear rational expectations models', *Journal of Economic Dynamics and Control*, 10, 139–45.

Fisher, P.G. and Hughes Hallett, A.J. (1988) 'An efficient strategy for solving linear and non-linear rational expectations models', *Journal of Economic Dynamics and Control*, 12, 635–57.

Fisher, P.G. and Wallis, K.F. (1990) 'The historical tracking performance of UK macroeconometric models 1978–85', *Economic Modelling*, 7, 179–97.

Fisher, P.G., Tanner, S.K., Turner, D.S. and Wallis, K.F. (1991) 'Econometric evaluation of the exchange rate in models of the UK economy', *Economic Journal*, 100(403), 1230–44.

Fisher, P.G., Tanner, S.K., Turner, D.S., Wallis, K.F. and Whitley, J.D. (1988) 'Comparative properties of models of the UK economy', *National Institute Economic Review*, 125, 69–88.

Fisher, P.G., Tanner, S.K., Turner, D.S., Wallis, K.F. and Whitley, J.D. (1989) 'Comparative properties of models of the UK economy', *National Economic Review*, 129, 69–88.

Fisher, P.G., Turner, D.S. and Wallis, K.F. (1992) 'Forward unit-root exchange rate determination and the properties of large scale macroeconometric models', in C.P. Hargreaves (ed.), *Macroeconomic Modelling of the Long Run*, Edward Elgar, Aldershot.

Flemming, J.S. (1976) *Inflation*, Oxford University Press, Oxford.

Frank, M. and Stengos, T. (1988) 'Chaotic dynamics in economic time series', *Journal of Economic Surveys*, 2(2), 103–31.

Friedman, M. (1968) 'The role of monetary policy', *American Economic Review*, 53, 381–4.

Friedman, B.M. (1975) *Rational Expectations are Really Adaptive After All*, Discussion Paper No. 430, Howard Institute of Economic Research, Boston.

Friedman, M. and Schwartz, A.J. (1991) 'Alternative approaches to analysing economic data', *American Economic Review*, 81, 39–49.

Frydman, R. (1982) 'Towards an understanding of market processes: individual expectations, learning, and convergence to rational expectations equilibrium', *American Economic Review*, 72, 652–68.

Ghosh, S., Gilbert, C.L. and Hughes Hallett, A.J. (1987) *Stabilising Speculative Commodity Markets*, Oxford University Press, Oxford.

Gilbert, C.L. (1986) 'Professor Hendry's econometric methodology', *Oxford Bulletin of Economics and Statistics*, 48, 283–307.

Godfrey, L.G. (1988) *Misspecification Tests in Econometrics*, Cambridge University Press, Cambridge.

Granger, C. and Newbold, P. (1986) *Forecasting Economic Time Series*, Academic Press, New York.

Greenhalgh, C., Taylor, P. and Wilson, R. (1990) *Innovation and Export Volumes and Prices: A disaggregated study*, CEPR Discussion Paper No. 4, Centre for Economic Policy Research, London.

Grunberg, E. and Modigliani, F. (1954) 'The predictability of social events', *Journal of Political Economy*, 62, 465–78.

Gurney, A. (1990) 'Fiscal policy simulations using forward-looking exchange rates in GEM', *National Institute Economic Review*, 131, 47–50.

Gurney, A., Henry, S.G.B. and Pesaran, B. (1989) 'The exchange rate and external trade', in A. Britton (ed.), *Policy Making with Macroeconomic Models*, Gower, Aldershot.

Hall, S.G. (1984) *An Investigation of Time Inconsistency and Optimal Policy Formula-*

tion in the Presence of Rational Expectations Using the National Institutes Model 7, NIESR Discussion Paper No. 71, NIESR, London.

Hall, S.G. (1985) 'On the solution of large economic models with rational expectations', *Bulletin of Economic Research*, 37, 157–61.

Hall, S.G. (1986) 'An investigation of time inconsistency and optimal policy formulation in the presence of rational expectations', *Journal of Economic Dynamics and Control*, 10, 323–6.

Hall, S.G. (1987a) 'Analyzing economic behaviour 1975–1985 with a model incorporating consistent expectations', *National Institute Economic Review*, 114, 58–68.

Hall, S.G. (1987b) 'A forward looking model of the exchange rate', *Journal of Applied Econometrics*, 2, 47–60.

Hall, S.G. (1987c) 'An empirical model of the exchange rate incorporating rational expectations', in K.A. Chrystal and R. Sedgwick (eds.), *Exchange Rates and the Open Economy*, St Martin Press, New York.

Hall, S.G. (1988) 'Rationality and Siegels paradox, the importance of coherency in expectations', *Applied Economics*, 20(11), 1533–40.

Hall, S.G. (1992) 'Modelling the sterling effective exchange rate using expectations and learning', *The Manchester School*, LXI, 3, 270–86.

Hall, S.G. and Garratt, A. (1992a) 'Expectations and learning in economic models', *Economic Outlook*, 16(5), 52–3.

Hall, S.G. and Garratt, A. (1992b) *Model Consistent Learning and Regime Switching*, CEF Discussion Paper No. 02-92, London Business School, London.

Hall, S.G. and Henry, S.G.B. (1985) 'Rational expectations in an econometric model, NIESR Model 8', *National Institute Economic Review*, 114, 58–68.

Hall, S.G. and Henry, S.G.B. (1986) 'A dynamic econometric model of the UK with rational expectations', *Journal of Economic Dynamics and Control*, 10, 219–33.

Hall, S. and Henry, S.G.B. (1987) 'Wage models', *National Institute Economic Review*, 119, 35–44.

Hall, S.G. and Henry, S.G.B. (1988) *Macroeconomic Modelling*, North-Holland, Amsterdam.

Hannan, E.J. and Quinn, B.G. (1979) 'The determinants of the order of an autoregression', *Journal of the Royal Statistical Society*, B41, 190–5.

Hanoch, G. (1971) 'CRESH production functions', *Econometrica*, 39, 695–712.

Hansen, L.P. and Sargent, T.J. (1991) *Rational Expectations Econometrics*, Westview Press, Boulder, Colorado.

Hansen, L.P. and Singleton, K.J. (1982) 'Generalised instrumental variable estimation of nonlinear rational expectations models', *Econometrica*, 50(5), 1269–86.

Hansen, L.P. and Singleton, K.J. (1983) 'Stochastic consumption, risk aversion and the temporal behaviour of asset returns', *Journal of Political Economy*, 91(2), 249–65.

Harrison, P.S. and Stephens, C.F. (1971) 'A Baynesian approach to short-term forecasting', *Operational Research Quarterly*, 22, 341–62.

Harrison, P.S. and Stephens, C.F. (1976) 'Bayenesian forecasting', *Journal of the Royal Statistic Society*, Series B, 38, 205–479.

Harvey, A.C. (1981) *Time Series Models*, Philip Allan, Oxford.

Harvey, A.C. (1987) 'Applications of the Kalman filter in econometrics', in T.F. Bewley (ed.), *Advances in Econometrics: Fifth World Congress*, vol. 1, Econometric Society Monograph No. 13, Cambridge University Press, Cambridge.

Harvey, A.C. (1989) *Forecasting, Structural Time Series Models and the Kalman Filter*, Cambridge University Press, Cambridge.

Haynes, S.E. and Stone, J.A. (1983) 'Specification of supply behaviour in international trade', *Review of Economics and Statistics*, 65, 626–32.

Helliwell, J.F. and Padmore, T. (1985) 'Empirical studies of macroeconomic interdependence', in R.W. Jones and P.B. Kenen (eds), *Handbook of International Economics*, vol. II, Elsevier, Amsterdam.

Hendry, D.F. (1987) 'Econometrics methodology: a personal perspective', in T.F. Bewley (ed.), *Advances in Econometrics Fifth World Congress*, vol. II, Cambridge University Press, Cambridge.

Hendry, D.F. (1988) 'The encompassing implications of feedback V. Feed forward mechanisms in econometrics', *Oxford Economic Papers*, 40, 132–49.

Hendry, D.F. and Ericsson, N.R. (1991) 'An econometric analysis of UK money demand', *American Economic Review*, 81, 8–38.

Herd, R. (1987) 'Import and export price equations for manufactures', *OECD Working Paper*, No. 43.

Hickman, B.G. (1973) 'A general linear tier model of world trade', in R.J. Ball (ed.), *The International Linkage of National Economic Models*, North-Holland, Amsterdam (pp. 21–43).

Hickman, B.G. and Lau, L.J. (1973) 'Elasticities of substitution and export demands in a world trade model', *European Economic Review*, 4, 347–80.

Hoderick, R.J. (1987) *The Empirical Evidence on the Efficiency of Forward and Futures Foreign Exchange Markets*, Harwood, New York.

Holden, K., Peel, D.A. and Thompson, J.L. (1985) *Expectations Theory and Evidence*, Macmillan, London.

Holly, S. (1991) 'Economic models and economic forecasting: Ptolemaic or Copernican?' *Economic Outlook*, 15(9), 32–8.

Holly, S. and Corker, R. (1984) 'Optimal feedback and feedforward stabilisation of exchange rates, money, prices and output under rational expectations', in A.J. Hughes Hallett (ed.), *Applied Decision Analysis and Economic Behaviour*, Martinus Nijhoff Publishers, Dordrecht.

Holly, S. and Hughes Hallett, A.J. (1989) *Control, Expectations and Uncertainty*, Cambridge University Press, Cambridge.

Holly, S. and Wade, K. (1989) *UK Exports of Manufacturers: The role of supply side factors*, CEF Discussion Paper, No. 14-89, London Business School, London.

Holly, S. and Zarrop, M.B. (1979) 'Calculating optimal economic policies when expectations are rational', *European Economic Review*, 20, 23–40.

Holly, S. and Zarrop, M.B. (1983) 'On optimality and time inconsistency when expectations are rational', *European Economic Review*, 20, 23–40.

Holt, C.C. (1957) 'Forecasting seasonals and trends by exponentially weighted moving averages', *ONR Research Memorandum 52*, Carnegie Institute of Technology, Pittsburgh, PA.

Holtham, G. and Hughes Hallett, A.J. (1992) 'Policy cooperation under uncertainty – the case for some disagreement', *American Economic Review*, 82, 1043–51.

Hornik, K., Stinchcombe, M. and White, H. (1989) 'Universal approximation of an unknown mapping and its derivatives using multilayer feedforward networks', mimeo, Department of Economics, University of California, San Diego.

Hughes Hallett, A.J. (1986a) 'Autonomy and the choice of policy in asymmetrically dependent economies', *Oxford Economic Papers*, 38, 516–44.

Hughes Hallett, A.J. (1986b) 'International policy design and the sustainability of policy bargains', *Journal of Economic Dynamics and Control*, 10, 467–94.

Hughes Hallett, A.J. (1987) 'Forecasting and policy evaluation in economics with rational expectations: the discrete time case', *Bulletin of Economic Research*, 39, 40–70.

Hughes Hallett, A.J. (1993) 'Changes of regime and the risk of stabilising speculative markets', *Scottish Journal of Political Economy*, 40, 1.

Hylleberg, S. and Paldam, M. (1991) 'New approaches to empirical macroeconomics', *Scandinavian Journal of Economics*, 93(2), 121–8.

Isard, P. (1973) 'How far can we push the law of one price?' *American Economic Review*, 67, 942–8.

Italianer, A. (1986) *Theory and Practice of International Trade Linkage Models*, Martinus Nijhoff Science Publishers, Dordrecht/Boston.

Italianer, A. (1987) 'Estimation and simulation of international trade linkages in the Quest model', *European Economy*, 31, 92–108.

Jarque, C.M. and Bera, A.K. (1980) 'Efficient tests for normality, homoscelasticity and serial independence of regression residuals', *Economics Letters*, 6, 255–9.

Johansen, S. (1988) 'Statistical analysis of cointegration vectors', *Journal of Economic Dynamics and Control*, 12, 231–54.

Junankar, S. (1988) 'The CBI's industrial trend survey: 30 years of interpretation and analysis', *Economic Situation Report*, July.

Katona, G. (1951) *Psychological Analysis of Economic Behaviour*, McGraw-Hill, New York.

Katona, G. (1958) 'Business expectations in the framework of psychological economics (towards a theory of expectations)', in M.J. Bowman (ed.), *Expectations, Uncertainty and Business Behaviour*, Social Science Research Council, New York.

Keating, G. (1985) *The Production and Use of Economic Forecasts*, Methuen, London.

Keating, G. (1986) 'The effect of answering practices on the relationship between CBI survey data and official data', *Applied Econometrics*, 1(4), 132–45.

Kemball-Cook, D. (1992) *Macroeconomic Policy Design under Uncertainty*, unpublished PhD Thesis, University of London.

King, R.G., Plosser, C.I., Stock, J.H. and Watson, M.W. (1991) 'Stochastic trends and economic fluctuations', *American Economic Review*, 81, 814–40.

Klein, L.R. (1987) 'The ET Interview: Prof L.R. Klein interviewed by Roberto S. Mariano', *Econometric Theory*, 3, 409–60.

Klein, L.R. and van Peeterssen, A. (1973) 'Forecasting world trade within project LINK', in R.J. Ball (ed.), *The International Linkage of National Economic Models*, North-Holland, Amsterdam.

Klein, P. and Moore, G. (1981) 'Industrial surveys in the UK: Parts I and II', *Applied Economics*, 13, 75–89.

Kmenta, J. and Ramsey, J.B. (eds.) (1981) *Large-Scale Econometric Models*, North-Holland, Amsterdam.

Kravis, I.B. and Lipsey, R.E. (1971) 'Price competitiveness in world trade', *Studies in International Economic Relations*, No. 6. National Bureau of Economic Research, New York.

Kydland, F.E. and Prescott, E.C. (1977) 'Rules rather than discretion: The inconsistency of optimal plans', *Journal of Political Economy*, 85, 473–91.

Kydland, F. and Prescott, E.C. (1982) 'Time to build and aggregate fluctuations', *Econometrica*, 50, 1345–70.

Kydland, F.E. and Prescott, E.C. (1991) 'The econometrics of the general equilibrium approach to business cycles', *Scandinavian Journal of Economics*, 93(2), 161–78.

Lahti, A. and Viren, M. (1989) *The Finnish Rational Expectations QMED Model: Estimation, Dynamic Properties and Policy Results*, Bank of Finland Discussion Paper 23/89, Bank of Finland, Helsinki.

Lau, L.J. (1986) 'Functional forms in econometric model building', in Z.Guiliches and M.D. Intriligator (eds), *Handbook of Econometrics*, vol. III, Elsevier, Amsterdam.

Lawson, N. (1992) *The View from Number Eleven*, Bantam Press, London.

Layard, R., Nickell, S. and Jackman, R. (1991) *Unemployment, Macroeconomic Performance and the Labour Market*, Oxford University Press, Oxford.

Lee, K., Pesaran, M.H. and Pierce, R.P. (1990) 'Testing aggregation bias in linear models', *Economic Journal*, 63, 402–9.

Leitch, G. and Tanner, J.E. (1991) 'Economic forecast evaluation: Profits versus the conventional error measures', *American Economic Review*, 81(3), 580–90.

Levine, P. and Currie, D.A. (1987) 'The design of feedback rules in linear stochastic rational expectations models', *Journal of Economic Dynamics and Control*, 11, 1–28.

Lipton, D., Poterba, J., Sachs, J. and Summers, L. (1982) 'Multiple shooting in rational expectations models', *Econometrica*, 50, 1329–33.

Litterman, R. (1980) *Techniques for Forecasting with Vector Autoregressions*, PhD Thesis, University of Minnesota.

Litterman, R. (1986) 'Forecasting with Bayesian vector autoregressions – five years of experience', *Journal of Business and Economics Statistics*, 4(1), 25–38.

Lomax, R. (1983) 'Cyclical indicators: Some developments and an assessment of performance', *Economic Trends*, November, 148–53.

Lucas, R.E. Jr (1972a) 'Econometric testing of the natural rate hypothesis', in O. Eckstein (ed.), *Econometrics of Price Determination*, Federal Reserve System, Board of Governors, Washington, DC.

Lucas, R.E. Jr (1972b) 'Expectations and the neutrality of money', *Journal of Economic Theory*, 4, 103–24.

Lucas, R.E. Jr (1973) 'Some international evidence on output inflation trade-offs', *American Economic Review*, 65, 326–34.

Lucas, R.E. Jr (1975) 'An equilibrium model of the business cycle', *Journal of Political Economy*, 83, 1113–44.

Lucas, R.E. Jr (1976) 'Econometric policy evaluation: a critique', in *The Phillips Curve and Labour Markets*, vol. 1, Carnegie-Rochester Conference Series on Public Policy, North-Holland, Amsterdam (pp. 19–46).

Lucas, R.E. Jr (1977) 'Understanding business cycles', in K. Brunner and A.H. Meltzer (eds.), *Stabilization of the Domestic and International Economy*, Carnegie-Rochester Conference Series on Public Policy, North-Holland, Amsterdam (pp. 215–39).

Lucas, R.E. Jr and Rapping, L. (1969) 'Real wages, employment and inflation', *Journal of Political Economy*, 77, 721–54.

Lucas, R.E. Jr and Sargent, T.J. (eds.) (1981) *Rational Expectations and Econometric Practice*, Allen & Unwin, London.

Lutkepohl, H. (1991) *Introduction to Multiple Time Series Model*, Axel Springer Verlag, New York.

Mankiw, N.G.(1988) 'Recent developments in macroeconomics: A very quick refresher course', *Journal of Money Credit and Banking*, 20(3), 436–49.

Marcet, A. and Sargent, T.J. (1988) 'The fate of systems with adaptive expectations', *American Economic Review*, 78, 168–71.

Marcet, A. and Sargent, T.J. (1989a) 'Convergence of least-squares learning in environment with hidden state variables and private information', *Journal of Political Economy*, 97(6), 1306–22.

Marcet, A. and Sargent, T.J. (1989b), 'Least squares learning and the dynamics of hyperinflation', in W.A. Barnett, J. Geweke and K. Shell (eds.), *Economic Complexity: Chaos, Sunspots, Bubbles, and Nonlinearity*, Cambridge University Press, Cambridge (pp. 119–40).

Marcet, A. and Sargent, T.J. (1989c), 'Convergence of least-squares, learning mechanisms in self referential, linear stochastic models', *Journal of Economic Theory*, 48, 337–68.

Mariano, R.S. (1987) 'The ET Interview: Professor L R Klein', *Econometric Theory*, 3, 409–60.

Masson, P.R., Symanski, S., Haas, R. and Dooley, M. (1988) *Multimod: A Multi Region Econometric Model*, Working Paper No. 88/23, IMF, Washington, DC.

Matthews, K.G.P. and Minford, A.P.L. (1987) 'Mrs Thatcher's economic policies 1979–1987', *Economic Policy*, 5, 57–101.

McCallum, B. (1976) 'Rational expectations and the natural rate hypothesis: Some consistent estimates', *Econometrica*, 46, 43–52.

McCarthy, M.D. (1972) 'The Wharton quarterly economic forecasting model mark III', Philadelphia Research Institute, University of Pennsylvania.

McKibbin, W.J. and Sachs, J. (1991) *Global Linkages: Macroeconomic interdependence and cooperation in the world economy*, The Brooking Institute, Washington, DC.

McNees, S. (1992) 'The uses and abuses of "consensus" forecasts', *Journal of Forecasting*, 11, 70–84.

Minford, A.P.L., Marawaha, S., Matthews, K. and Sprague, A. (1984) 'The Liverpool macroeconomic model of the United Kingdom', *Economic Modelling*, 1, 24–62.

Minford A.P.L., Matthews, K.G.P. and Marawaha, S.S. (1979) 'Terminal conditions as a means of ensuring unique solutions for rational expectations models with forward expectations', *Economic Letters*, 4, 117–20.

Minford, A.P.L., Matthews, K.G.P. and Marawaha, S.S. (1980) *Terminal Conditions, Uniqueness and the Solution of Rational Expectations Models*, mimeo, University of Liverpool.

Mitchell, W.C. and Burns, A.F. (1938) *Statistical Indicators of Cyclical Revivals*, National Bureau of Economic Research, New York.

Montfort, A. and Rabemananjara, R. (1990) 'From a VAR to a structural model, with an application to the wage–price spiral', *Journal of Applied Econometrics*, 5, 203–28.

Morgan, M.S. (1990) *The History of Econometric Ideas*, Cambridge University Press, Cambridge.

Moriguchi, C. (1979) 'Forecasting and simulation analysis of the world economy', *American Economic Review*, 63, 402–9.

Murphy, C.W. (1989) *The Macroeconomics of a Macroeconomic Model*, mimeo, Australian National University.

Muth, J.F. (1961) 'Rational expectations and the theory of price movements', *Econometrica*, 29(6), 315–35.

Nerlove, M. (1958) 'Adaptive expectations and cobweb phenomena', *Quarterly Journal of Economics*, 72, 227–40.

NIESR (1992) *NIGEM Model Manual*, National Institute of Economic and Social Research, London.

Owen, C. and Wren-Lewis, S. (1993) *Variety, Quality and UK Manufacturing Exports*, International Centre for Macroeconomic Modelling Discussion Paper, University of Strathclyde, Glasgow.

Pagan, A. (1984) 'Econometric issues in the analysis of regressions with generated regressors', *International Economic Review*, 25(1), 221–47.

Parzen, E. (1976) 'Multiple time series: Determining the order of approximating autoregressive schemes', in P.K. Krishnaiah (ed.), *Multivariate Analysis IV*, Academic Press, New York.

Pearlman, J., Currie, D.A. and Levine, P. (1986) 'Rational expectations with partial information', *Economic Modelling*, 3, 90–105.

Pesaran, B. and Pesaran, M. (1992) *Microfit 3.0*, Oxford University Press, Oxford.

Pesaran, M.H. (1985) 'Formation of inflation expectations in British manufacturing industries', *Economic Journal*, 95, 948–75.

Pesaran, M.H. (1987) *The Limits of Rational Expectations*, Basil Blackwell, Oxford.

Pesaran, M.H. and Potter, S.M. (eds.) (1993) *Non-linear Dynamics, Chaos and Econometrics*, John Wiley & Sons, Chichester.

Pesaran, M.H. and Smith, R.P. (1985) 'Evaluation of macroeconometric models', *Economic Modelling*, April, 125–34.

Pesaran, M.H. and Smith, R. (1992) *Theory and Evidence in Economics, and The Interaction Between Theory and Observations in Economics*, University of Cambridge Discussion Paper, Cambridge.

Porter, M.E. (1985) *Competitive Advantage: Creating and sustaining superior performance*. Collier-Macmillan, London.

Radner, R. (1982) 'Equilibrium under uncertainty', in K.J. Arrow and M.D. Intriligator (eds), *Handbook of Mathematical Economics*, vol. 2, North-Holland, Amsterdam.

Ramsey, J.B. (1969) 'Tests for specification errors in classical linear least squares regression analysis', *Journal of the Royal Statistical Society*, Series B, 31, 350–71.

Robertson, D. and Wickens, M.R. (1992) 'Stochastic trends representation, cointegration and economic activity', mimeo, London Business School.

Samuelson, L. (1973) 'A new model of world trade', *OECD Economic Outlook, Occasional Studies*, December, 1–15.

Samuelson, L. and Kurihara, L. (1980) 'OECD trade linkage methods', *Economic Bulletin*, vol. 18, Economic Research Institute, Economic Planning Agency, Tokyo.

Sargent, T.J. (1973) 'Rational expectations, the real rate of interest and the natural rate of unemployment', *Brookings Papers on Economic Activity*, 2, 429–72.

Sargent, T.J. (1976) 'A classical macroeconomic model of the United States', *Journal of Political Economy*, 84, 207–37.

Sargent, T.J. (1987) *Dynamic Macroeconomic Theory*, Harvard University Press, Massachusetts.

Sargent, T.J. (1991) 'Equilibrium with signal extraction from endogenous variables', *Journal of Economic Dynamics and Control*, 15, 245–73.

Sargent, T.J. and Wallace, N. (1973) 'Rational expectations and the dynamics of hyperinflation', *International Economic Review*, 14, 328–50.

Sargent, T.J. and Wallace, N. (1975) 'Rational expectations, the optimal monetary instrument and the optimal money supply rule', *Journal of Political Economy*, 83, 241–54.

Sargent, T.J. and Wallace, N. (1976) 'Rational expectations and the theory of economic policy', *Journal of Monetary Economics*, 2, 169–83.

Savage, D. (1975) 'Interpreting the investment intentions data', *National Institute Economic Review*, 73, August, 43–9.

Scheinkman, J.A. (1990) 'Nonlinearities in economic dynamics', *The Economic Journal*, 100 (conference proceedings), 33–48.

Scheinkman, J.A. and LeBarron, B. (1986) *Nonlinear Dynamics and Stock Returns*, mimeo, University of Chicago.

Scott, M.F.G. (1989) *A New View of Economic Growth*, Clarendon Press, Oxford.

Shiller, R.J. (1978) 'Rational expectations and the dynamic structure of macroeconomic models in a critical review', *Journal of Monetary Economics*, 4, 421–36.

Sims, C. (1980) 'Macroeconomics and reality', *Econometrica*, 48, 1–48.

Smith, R. (1984) 'The evaluation and comparison of large macroeconomic models', in P. Malgrange and P.-A. Muet (eds.), *Contemporary Macroeconomic Modelling*, Basil Blackwell, Oxford.

Smith, R. (1990) 'The Warwick ESRC Macroeconomic Modelling Bureau: An assessment', *International Journal of Forecasting*, 6, 301–9.

Smith, R. (1992) *The Macromodelling Industry: Structure, conduct and performance*, paper presented to ESRC Conference on the Future of Macroeconomic Modelling in the UK, November, London.

Spanos, A. (1986) *Statistical Foundations of Econometric Modelling*, Cambridge University Press, Cambridge.

Stock, J.H. and Watson, M.W. (1988a) '*A New Approach to the Leading Economic Indicators*', manuscript, Kennedy School of Government, Harvard University.

Stock, J. and Watson, M.W. (1988b) 'Testing for common trends', *Journal of the American Statistical Association*, 83, 1097–107.

Stock, J.H. and Watson, M.W. (1989a) 'New indexes of leading and coincident economic indicators', *NBER Macroeconomics Annual*, 4, 351–94.

Stock, J.H. and Watson, M.W. (1989b) *A Simple MLE of Cointegrating Vectors in Higher Order Integrated Systems*, NBER Technical Working Paper No. 83, National Bureau of Economic Research, Washington, DC.

Stock, J.H. and Watson, M.W. (1991) 'A probability model of coincident economic indicators', in K. Lahiri and G.H. Moore (eds.), *Leading Economic Indicators: New approaches and forecasting records*, Cambridge University Press, New York (pp. 63–85).

Stone, J.R.N. (1954) 'Linear expenditure systems and demand analysis', *Economic Journal*, 64, 511–27.

Summers, L.H. (1991) 'The scientific illusion in empirical macroeconomics', *Scandinavian Journal of Economics*, 93, 129–48.

Taylor, J.B. (1979) 'Estimation and control of macroeconomic models with rational expectations', *Econometrica*, 47, 1267–86.

Tinbergen, J. (1939) *Statistical Testing of Business Cycle Theories*, vols I and II, League of Nations, Geneva.

Tirole, J. (1986) 'Procurement and Renegotiation', *Journal of Political Economy*, 94(2), 235–59.

Tobin, J. (1959) 'On the predictive value of consumers intentions', *Review of Economics and Statistics*, XLI (1) 1–11.

Townsend, R.M. (1978) 'Market anticipation, rational expectation and Bayesian analysis', *International Economic Review*, 19, 481–94.

Townsend, R.M. (1982) 'Equilibrium theory with learning and disparate expectations: Some issues and methods', in R. Frydman and E.S. Phelds (eds.), *Individual Forecasting and Aggregate Outcomes: Rational expectations examined*, Cambridge University Press, Cambridge.

Townsend, R.M. (1983) 'Forecasting the forecasts of others', *Journal of Political Economy*, 91(4), 546–88.

Treasury and Civil Service Committee (1991) *Memoranda on Official Economic*

Forecasting, House of Commons, Treasury and Civil Service Committee, 532-i, HMSO, London.

Van der Ploeg, F. (1986) 'Rational expectations, risk and chaos in financial markets', *Economy Journal (Supplement)*, 96, 151–62.

Varian, H.R. (1982) 'Non-parametric tests of consumer behaviour', *Review of Economic Studies*, 50, 99–110.

Varian, H.R. (1983) 'The non-parametric approach to demand analysis', *Econometrica*, 50, 945–73.

Vines, D., Maciejowski, J. and Meade, J. (1983) *Demand Management*, Allen & Unwin, London.

Wallis, K.F. (ed.) (1984–87) *Models of the UK Economy*, vols. 1–4, Oxford University Press, Oxford.

Wallis, K.F. (1992) 'Comparing macroeconometric models: A review article', *Economica*, 60, 225–37.

Wallis, K.F. and Whitley, J.D. (1991) 'Sources of error in forecasts and expectations: UK economic models, 1984–8', *Journal of Forecasting*, 10, 231–53.

Walsh, J. (1991) 'The CBI Industrial Trends Survey – A guide to policy makers', *Economic Situation Report*, March, 41–50.

Walters, A.A. (1971) 'Consistent expectations, distributed lags and the quantity theory', *Economic Journal*, 81, 273–81.

Weale, M. (1984) 'Quantity and price effects in an analysis of world trade based on an accounting matrix', *The Review of Income and Wealth*, 30, 85–117.

Westaway, P. (1989a) *Does Time Inconsistency Really Matter*, IFAC Symposium on Dynamic Modelling and Control of National Economies, Preprints, International Federation of Automatic Control, London.

Westaway, P. (1989b) *Partial Credibility: A solution technique for econometric models*, IFAC Symposium on Dynamic Modelling and Control of National Economies, Preprints, International Federation of Automatic Control, London.

Westaway, P. and Whittaker, R. (1986) *Consistent Expectations in the Treasury Model*, Government Economic Services Working Paper No. 87, HM Treasury, London.

White, H. (1989a) 'Learning in artificial neural networks: A statistical perspective', *Neural Computation*, 1, 425–64.

White, H. (1989b) 'Some asymptotic results for learning in single hidden layer feedforward network models', *Journal of the American Statistical Association*, 84, 1008–13.

Whitley, J.D. (1992) 'Comparative simulation analysis of the European multicountry models', *Journal of Forecasting*, 11, 423–56.

Whitley, J., Bray, J., Hall, S., Meen, G. and Westaway, P. (1992) *UK Policies, Non-price Competitiveness and Convergence to an EMU*, ESRC Macroeconomic Modelling Bureau Discussion Paper No. 28, Warwick University.

Whittle, P. (1982) *Optimization Over Time: Dynamic programming and stochastic control*, vol. I, John Wiley, Chichester.

Wickens, M.R. (1982) 'The efficient estimation of econometric models with rational expectations', *Review of Economic Studies*, 49, 55–68.

Wickens, M. (1993) *Interpreting Cointegrating Vectors and Common Stochastic Trends*, Centre for Economic Forecasting Discussion Paper No. 14-93, London Business School.

Winters, L.A. (1984) 'Separability and the specification of world trade', *Journal of International Economics*, 17, 239–63.

Winters, P.R. (1960) 'Forecasting sales by exponentially weighted moving averages', *Management Science*, 6, 324–42.

Wold, H.O.A. (1938) *A Study in the Analysis of Stationary Time Series*, Alquist and Wiksell, Upsala.

Woodford, M. (1990) 'Learning to believe in sunspots', *Econometrica*, 58, 277–308.

Wren-Lewis, S. (1985a) 'An econometric model of U.K. manufacturing employment using survey data on expected output', *Journal of Applied Economics*, 15, 107–20.

Wren-Lewis, S. (1985b) 'The quantification of survey data on expectations', *National Institute Economic Review*, 113, 45–52.

Yoo, S. (1986) *Multi-cointegrated Time Series and Generalised Error-correction Models*, working paper, Economics Department, University of California, San Diego.

Zarnowitz, V. (1991) 'Has macro-forecasting failed?', Discussion Paper No. 76, National Bureau of Economic Research, Washington, DC.

Index